Endings & Beginnings

Endings & Beginnings

A Story of Healing

Redi Tlhabi

First published by Jacana Media (Pty) Ltd in 2012
Second impression 2012
Third impression 2013
Fourth impression 2013

10 Orange Street
Sunnyside
Auckland Park 2092
South Africa
+2711 628 3200
www.jacana.co.za

ISBN 978-1-4314-0461-2

Cover design by publicide
Set in Sabon 11/16pt
Printed by Ultra Litho (Pty) Ltd Johannesburg
Job no. 002065

See a complete list of Jacana titles at www.jacana.co.za

For Mabegzo, for letting me in

Love & gratitude

MABEGZO'S FAMILY – for opening themselves up and trusting me with the darkest chapter in their lives.

Imelda – to remain as beautiful and tenacious as you are, in spite of the horror of your childhood, takes a special person.

My late father and mom – what a cherished child I was. Thank you.

Jacana Media, Thabiso Mahlape in particular, for believing in the book, even when I didn't.

Gwen Hewett for expert editing of Mabegzo's story.

My husband Brian, whose eyes light up every time I have a new dream. Thank goodness I CAN believe that someone loves me this much.

Preface

I CANNOT REMEMBER A TIME when I was not thinking about Mabegzo, the subject of my book. Long after he had died, I wondered if his life could have been different had he been brought up differently. With every news item about a young man who has raped, murdered or robbed someone, I have found myself asking, is this another Mabegzo? Where do these criminals come from? Who raised them and was there ever a time in their lives when they had hopes and dreams and their laughter filled the air? This is not only a story about a young man who has shaped my life. It is not a celebration of a flawed human being, but a reflection of the contradictions of his being.

In sharing Mabegzo with the world, I hope this book will

offer some insights on the effects of trauma and how it often morphs the child into a hardened adult. My fervent belief that social conditions create the monsters who terrorise our lives and make us prisoners in our own country has made me curious about their background. My relationship with Mabegzo exposed me to a different side to him and over the years, I have often wondered why that positive side was not more dominant.

I have spent months visiting his family, friends and neighbours and, in my conversations, unravelled layers of a complicated life and secrets that tore families apart. The events related in the book are, according to my knowledge and memory, an accurate reflection. I have tested what I know and remember against what has been written and published. The content is therefore informed by memory and conversations. I have taken the liberty to change some of the names – not all – in order to protect the identities of those about whom I am writing.

Writing about Mabegzo has been a gift to me. A gift of healing, introspection and maturity.

Introduction

I'M STANDING AT THE STREET corner and, for the second time in my short life, looking down on a dead body. I mustn't go crazy this time. There's blood coming out of his mouth, just like with Papa two years ago. But unlike Papa, his eye isn't hanging out of its socket. It still looks weird though, like he's winking at me. Papa also winked at me.

A gentle spring rain is washing the blood from Mabegzo's face. His family aren't here yet. I'm the only one here who cares about him, and I'm powerless to fend off the human vultures circling his body, eager to kill him again and again. Silently I whisper the Catholic prayer for the dead. '*Moya wa hae, le bohle ba falletseng, e phomole ka kgotso ka mohau wa Modimo.* May his soul and all of the departed rest in peace, in God's mercy. Let it be.' I say it three times, just as our priest does, hoping he won't be in pain for long.

Since my father died two years ago, I've often wondered whether my prayers helped him survive in purgatory, and if he's still there. The nuns who taught Sunday school made purgatory sound horrific, a place where people cry and scream in preparation for heaven. But if anyone could survive it, Papa could. He was big and strong and never cried, so I knew that this place of suffering wouldn't break my father. I knew it.

But Mabegzo? I'm not sure he'll be okay. So, standing at the corner – our corner – I pray and pray and pray. He was very sad lately, and cried a lot when we spoke. Since he killed his friends two months ago, he came to me and cried a lot. And now he's dead like them. I need to pray faster and harder to help him.

More people are gathering around his body. There's a lot of singing and dancing. Some are even ululating. If Mabegzo were alive he would beat them all up and demand, '*Le shebile eng*? What are you staring at? *Voetsek*!'

The onlookers are feasting their eyes just like they did with my father – poking him a bit, swinging his legs, wanting to see if he's really dead. But with Papa there was sorrow and shock, and neighbours and friends tried to keep order and control the crowd. They covered his face with newspapers out of respect. But still there were people who turned my father's death into a circus, lifting the newspaper and exclaiming, '*Tjo, tjo, tjo! Bamulimazilie.* They've really mutilated him.'

He was an ugly corpse, my father, because of that eye. But Mabegzo, his face is still fine. I'm glad about that.

A mother drags her son to the scene and forces him to take a long, hard look at Mabegzo. 'Look at this dog,' she admonishes. 'Look. This is how you'll end up if you don't clean up your act! I'll have to pick you up off the street, too. *Botsotsi ba shwa ba sa le banyane.* Criminals die young.'

Stupid woman. My father wasn't a tsotsi. Someone just stabbed him, pushed the knife straight into his heart and then dug it into his eye, gouging it out and leaving it hanging on his cheek. And Mabegzo? Well, he may have been a criminal, but that's not all he was. And I know. Better than all of them.

An elderly woman starts to pray, but it's not a prayer of sorrow or gratitude for the life that was. She's thanking God for hearing her prayers to remove this menace from society.

A stray dog is now licking the blood from Mabegzo's face. It horrifies me that no one intervenes.

'*Ja, khota le nja.*' It should be funny that a grown man is cheering on the dog, begging it to lick the 'dog' lying dead on the street. But it's not funny. It's the ultimate insult to a young man who never harmed me when he could have. I want to tell them all how loving and kind he was, how he could switch on the lights of my heart with a smile and a wink. He had so many opportunities to hurt and defile me, but he never did.

But who here cares? There are no ears for my story right now. The world has snuffed him out and for them it's time to celebrate. So I lock the words deep inside the dispirited crevices of my soul, and continue to pray silently.

An old woman comes forward, bends over his body and gently strokes his forehead. Then she steps back sadly. She must be his grandmother. '*Haai,*' says a woman, 'this granny is strong to stand here and see her child like this.'

A police van pulls up. Very soon it will disappear around the corner with Mabegzo in it. Finally, the tsotsi who has eluded the police for so long will be in police custody. Just a few weeks ago he told me he'd never be caught dead in a police van; that only cowards get caught or killed by the police. His arch-nemeses, the men in uniform, are now hard at work cordoning off the area and asking questions – very few – about him. They, too, are keen to know who the heroes are who slaughtered the 'dog'. There will be no investigation into this murder, unless it's to reward those responsible.

Finally, they're ready to load him into the back of the blue and yellow police car, to remove him at last from the streets he thought he owned. An officer kicks his lifeless body and the crowd erupts in jubilation and applause. I look to his grandmother to intervene and defend him. But she stands by in silence as the police assault a lifeless man before throwing him clumsily into the back of the van. Even in death they're determined to punish him. I look away. I mustn't go crazy again.

When Papa lay dead in the street with his eye hanging out, everyone wanted to see him. He was popular and charismatic, so his death caused unease, shock and deep sadness. But some were only there to satisfy their morbid fascination with the dead – the more brutal the murder, the better. The newspaper that was put over his face was lifted again and again as people took turns to look at his grotesque face. My proud father was turned into a spectacle for the entertainment of lesser human beings.

Conversations about his mutilated face have never stopped. On the streets of Orlando East my poor father suddenly had no other identity but that final gory visage. My identity too has been forever tainted by this image. Despite decades in his company, frequenting his shebeen when he was still a bootlegger, my neighbours had nothing to say about him, us, me, except, 'Her father lay on the streets like a stray dog,' or 'That's his daughter; *eish*, they messed up his face.' It seems people only started noticing me when my father died. On the twenty-sixth of July 1987, I stopped being Redihentse, or Momo as everyone called me; I became the child whose father was gutted like a fish.

Some of the stories are ridiculous. Like Mfeka's grandmother, who told me that my father's killers would never be found because by removing his eye the killers made sure Papa could never see and follow them. She told me to take a message to my mom that unless we performed a ritual at the scene where his body was found, we would never know who'd murdered him. She said we should put a photo of my dad in the exact position in which he had been found, draw a circle around his eye and use some muti to invoke his spirit to guide us.

'But you must all be careful to instruct his spirit to return to its place of rest. Otherwise he'll be up all night, roaming the streets of Orlando East, haunting the living.' She also declared that my father couldn't rest in peace because he was pacing up and down, searching for his eye. Well, if he was up roaming the streets anyway, why bother? Those stories always made me tired.

Stories of Papa's death followed me everywhere I went. Casual acquaintances who barely knew him claimed he'd had a premonition; that out of the blue he'd spoken about death and how he missed his late mother. Even Bra Godfrey – one of our many village drunks – had his story. 'Hey, just the day before he died, you know, I bought him two beers, and we sat talking. Bra Peter said he wanted to go home, he was tired. Now I know what he meant.'

These stories were full of flaws. Godfrey never had money to buy himself a beer, never mind two for my father. And Papa avoided him like the plague because he smelt so bad. 'His body odour could kill a baby,' Papa used to say.

But many others claimed that on the Saturday before his death, they witnessed my dad crack a morbid joke as a woman dished up for him after a funeral near our house. Mourners always get fed when they return from the graveside, and hundreds had formed an orderly queue moving slowly to the front where the mothers were serving food. As the woman dished out my father's meat, in his typical loud and mischievous way, he joked, '*Haai, wena, mphe nama. Le ba ka ho tla ba le lefu and ke tlo go tima nama.* Dish me some more meat, or when the funeral comes to my house, I won't give you any.'

At my dad's funeral this woman was so traumatised that she refused to eat the meat, because she felt my dad had not only predicted his own departure, but warned that she shouldn't have any meat. I may have been a child, but I don't believe in such silly superstitions. Even Papa used to enjoy making fun of people's strange beliefs and practices.

While the police were putting Papa's body in a bag, someone started singing a hymn. They put him in slowly, taking their time, prolonging the fire in my heart. All heads were bowed in respect and the collective grief was palpable. One of Papa's cousins started to chant, invoking my father's clan names and urging him to go well. '*Tsamaya ka kagiso Motlhaping o tlhapang ka mashi.* Go in peace progeny of the Tlhaping, you who wash with milk,' she pleaded with the ancestors. And then, finally, the six policemen lifted up the heavy bag and placed it carefully into their blue and yellow van.

But not today. This time they throw Mabegzo into the van like a load of rubbish. '*Voetsek nja*,' one says. '*Ba ho thotse nou; masepa a fedile* today,' says another. 'They've got you now; your shit ends today.'

I mustn't go crazy now, like I did with Papa. Back then my

nine-year-old legs had a mind of their own. I didn't even feel them as they ran behind the van. They moved by themselves. Someone far behind was shouting my name, but a louder voice in my head was telling me to stay with my father. They couldn't do this! I had to save Papa. On TV when the green light straightened and the machine beeped, doctors and nurses always came and pumped the chest so the person woke up. I had to do this for Papa. As the van disappeared around the corner, I ran faster, screaming, blinded by tears. I tripped and got up and started running again, but strong arms grabbed me from behind and lifted me up.

'No, no, let's go. It's finished now. It's over.'

Helplessly, I watched the van disappear out of sight. Maybe Papa did want to be dead.

PART 1

Chapter 1

Orlando East, where I grew up, was the oldest and most densely populated part of Soweto. The Urban Areas Act prohibited black people from owning or occupying property in cities or towns. So all across South Africa, black residents were forcibly removed and scattered across remote, outlying areas, often far from any mode of transport or economic centre. Soweto's first township, Orlando, was founded in 1931 when a group of evictees were settled on a piece of farmland. The settlement was named after the first township administrator, Edwin Orlando Leake.

I learnt about the history of our neighbourhood as a little girl by badgering Papa with questions. It began when a friend of mine, Thobile, announced that we were all going to die.

'But why?' I asked her.

'It says so at the bottom of our road,' she said. 'Sofasonke Street, see?' *Sofasonke* indeed means 'we shall all die', although in this context it meant 'we all die together'. I went home with a deep sense of foreboding, and pictured my family and our neighbours all dying at once. Who would be left to take care of our houses, our pets and our dolls?

'What's wrong?' my parents asked that evening, noticing that I was troubled.

'You didn't tell me we're going to die.'

'Where did you hear that?'

'Thobile told me. It's written at the corner of our street.'

My parents laughed, but seeing me on the verge of tears, my father took time to explain the origin of our street name.

Sofasonke was the motto of a civic party that was started by a local hero, James 'Magebula' Mpanza. Born in rural Zululand – now KwaZulu-Natal – in 1889, he had moved to Johannesburg like most of his contemporaries in search of work. But in his twenties Mpanza was sentenced to death at the Pretoria Central Prison for the murder of an Indian merchant. Sympathisers claimed that the merchant was abusing black women, but others believed Mpanza was just a thug.

In prison, Mpanza became an active Christian. He began preaching to his fellow inmates and wrote a small book called *The Christian Pathways*. This evidently helped in his quest for clemency, and he was finally pardoned after nine years in jail. He then settled in eastern Johannesburg, where he began agitating about the appalling shortage of housing for black people, writing numerous letters to the authorities and warning of social unrest.

In 1944, fed up with the lack of response, Mpanza led a group of homeless people to invade some unoccupied land, where they erected a squatter camp near what is now the Orlando Stadium, and named it Masakeng after the thick material for carrying coal from which they built their shacks. Mpanza became the camp's unofficial mayor and made a colourful character riding around the camp on horseback while most people walked or cycled.

When heavily armed police arrived to evict the squatters, Mpanza and his wife were thrown into prison, where their baby died and Mpanza suffered a heart attack. He recovered and was later let out of prison.

But the government had seen the might of the people and the following year a new site was provided to house the homeless. Ernest Oppenheimer visited Masakeng and arranged a loan of six million rand to build Soweto's legendary matchbox houses. This was a breakthrough, but conditions were hardly luxurious. Ablution facilities and sanitation were inadequate, and residents endured the much abhorred bucket system until toilets were finally built in the mid-fifties. My mother remembers the buckets in the back yard with deep repugnance. 'You got used to it,' she said. 'But the stench enveloped the township.'

The buckets were collected in the late evening, and parents would immediately order their children indoors. Nobody wanted to be in the way of those buckets of human excrement.

Mpanza continued to agitate for improved conditions. When the authorities tried to deport him to KwaZulu-Natal using a bogus legal process, he won an appeal and remained in Soweto, still riding his horse and going about his crusade. Later, a civic movement called the Sofasonke Party was started, its name evoking the tenacity of a united people determined to fight to the death. Mpanza lived until 1970, and was loved and revered by everyone.

13

'Did you know him, Papa?'

'He used to visit here.'

'In our house?' I asked in awe.

'Right where you're sitting.'

I was overjoyed that this great man had actually known and visited my dad.

'And which is the best soccer team in the world?' asked my dad.

'Orlando Pirates.'

'And what is our chant when we face other teams?'

I made the Orlando Pirates sign with my small arms and shouted, '*Ezimnyama nge nkani, ezi ka Magebula!*' meaning 'Magebula's black ones', as black was the team colour.

Soweto was a wonderfully eclectic mix of languages, cultures and traditions. Since the discovery of gold back in 1886, Johannesburg was always a magnet for men desperate for work. They streamed in from the rural areas and neighbouring states like Lesotho and Swaziland to provide cheap labour for the mining industry. Leaving young wives and children behind, they risked life and limb in search of the gold whose profits they would never taste while the white man ruled. As the city grew more prosperous, many rural women also arrived to serve as domestic workers.

Although the apartheid government tried hard to segregate black people according to ethnicity, their plan failed dismally. The different groups attended the same churches, migrated freely within the confines of the township and intermarried. My own parents were a reflection of this: Papa was a Motswana and my mother an umXhosa. Some areas of the township were so fully integrated that you couldn't work out which group was in the majority. Most of its citizens spoke more languages than their own, and the

easiest way to tell if someone was new to Soweto was if
they couldn't converse in more than one tongue. But there
were a few who felt superior and wouldn't bother to speak
another's language. Since the military reign of King Shaka in
the 1800s, some Zulus still considered their tribe superior. A
popular joke had a Zulu character responding to anything
and everything with a boast about his fighting skills. 'My
neighbour's child is clever.' 'But I can beat him in a fight.'
'My brother found a job.' 'But I can beat him in a fight.' 'My
friend is getting married.' 'But I can beat him in a fight.'

My upbringing in Orlando East was very loving, but
firm discipline was a big part of it. Disobedience was always
punished with a hiding. Afterwards I usually felt wounded,
not just from the physical pain but from the adults' lack of
trust that I would do the right thing if I knew what it was.
If an adult told me to do something, I did it, and if they told
me not to, I didn't. So I never felt I deserved the hidings I got.

Religion was also a mainstay of life in Soweto, and
weekends were filled with weddings, funerals and church
services. Many believed in ancestor worship, but Christianity
was paramount, and even those who didn't go to church still
believed in God and Jesus. On Sunday mornings the streets
were a parade of colourful church uniforms. The baZion
wore green and yellow, the Methodists red and black, the
Anglicans black and white and the apostolic churches blue
and white, with a big white cross embroidered on their backs.
The Catholics had three uniforms: purple and black for the
St Anne's grannies; blue, black and red for the middle-aged
Sacred Hearts; and blue and white for the Children of Mary.

Especially formidable in our community was the Zionist
church, and the khaki overalls and white shoes of its male
members were ubiquitous in the township. This church was
known for its ancestral beliefs and for evoking the spirits of

the departed to guide services and impart wisdom. Zionists were rumoured to believe in muti, witchcraft and spiritual powers, and there were stories of making people disappear, solving mysterious murders and detecting evil intentions at a glance. But they often had no church to worship in and would simply rotate their services among members' homes.

I was raised in the Catholic faith of my mother. My father wasn't a regular at his Methodist church, but he always woke us for church, made sure our clothes were nicely ironed and our shoes polished, and gave us money for offerings. I loved church because I loved dressing up. But as an altar girl, although I loved my solemn role in the mass, I was sad to hide my nice clothes beneath our unflattering red and white uniform. Papa used to brush my hair every morning, and on Sundays he took extra care to put in multi-coloured ribbons. He'd kiss my lips and remind me to pay attention in church. And I had to, because afterwards Papa would ask my older brother and me what we'd learnt at church. If we didn't know, we got our ears pinched or were denied a treat – it was a serious matter.

When we returned from church Papa would make us all breakfast, and then he'd call us to relate the day's lesson. I'd pray that my brother wouldn't pick the same lesson I'd picked, or it would seem as if I hadn't been listening while Father Lodi was giving his homily.

Easter weekend was the most sacred period in the Catholic calendar, and the Good Friday service was long and solemn, with different people preaching as we built up to the final crucifixion of our Lord, Jesus Christ. Especially haunting were the Stations of the Cross, which highlighted Jesus's suffering on his final journey. I was most moved when Jesus cried out from the cross 'I am thirsty'. Our choir conductor always recited this with great drama and pathos, shouting so loudly that the walls of our church seemed to shake. '*Ndinxaniwe, ndinxaniwe, ndinxaniwe.* I am thirsty.' He sounded so desperate that I wanted to get up and fetch him some water.

One Good Friday, a big Xhosa man with a booming voice recited the part when Jesus, about to die, addresses his mother Mary and his disciple John. Jesus says, 'Woman, this is your son,' and to his disciple, 'This is your mother' (John 19: 26 – 27). But instead of saying *mama* and *baba* for mother and father, he used the formal terms, which my friends and I had only heard used in cursing. All the youngsters erupted in shrieks of astonishment and laughter. Deeply shocked, I looked to my mother – always the epitome of morality and decorum among the adult choir – and found her also laughing, along with most of the adults. So when Papa enquired about church that day, my brother giggled but I was distraught.

'Papa, a naughty father called Jaxa was swearing in church!'

'*Hawu,* Zanazana?' Papa said, using his special name for me.

'Yes, and people were laughing.' On cue, my mother laughed again.

'What was the naughty father saying?'

I looked at my mother, wondering whether to risk a hiding, but Papa wanted to know. So, imitating Jaxa's gestures, I said, '*Nanku unyoko, nanku uyihlo*! Here is your mother, here is your father'. When my parents roared with laughter, my brother, a great mimic, began acting out the scene. Their reaction was very confusing, but it was a joy to see them so entertained.

While Sundays were filled with church services, Saturdays were taken up with the weddings and funerals of relatives, colleagues, fellow church members and neighbours. Children would only attend a funeral if it was a very close family member. But on one occasion the funeral was for a friend of mine, Zanele, who'd lived on Sofasonke Street.

At first Zanele and I hadn't hit it off. I didn't mind her, but her adoration made me uncomfortable – I hadn't earned it, I felt, and I wanted a more equal relationship. So I often hid from her and asked my dad to say I wasn't home. To my frustration, Papa would say, 'She's home, but she said I should tell you she isn't.' I'd then be forced to come out and play with her. My father would make us food and give us some dough to 'bake cakes' for our 'babies'. Once, while I was hiding from her, my father took me aside.

'Why don't you want to play with Zanele?'

'She follows me everywhere, Papa. It annoys me.'

'That's because she loves you. Sometimes, my baby, it's good to love someone just because they love you.'

After that I loved her. But she left Soweto in 1986 to live with her mother's family. I never saw her again until her father's mother, who lived a few houses away, came to tell my dad that she'd gone to bed with a headache and died in her sleep. Her funeral would be in Soweto that weekend.

That Friday afternoon all her friends were invited to view her body and say goodbye. Had my parents been home, I knew I wouldn't have been allowed, so I went quickly before they got back. But as soon as the coffin was opened I panicked, and would have left if the doorway hadn't been blocked. First her father looked in, and then her mother, who wailed and began kissing her over and over. Finally someone pulled her away, saying, 'It's enough now, it's done.' As if it could ever be enough.

Then we children were called over. My throat was sore and heavy as if I'd swallowed a bag of oranges. People were singing hymns, everyone was crying, and some even collapsed in theatrical displays of grief. Everyone who returned from Zanele's coffin was wailing, so I thought she must be in pain. But when I looked inside, it seemed as if she was sleeping. I kissed her mouth as her mother had done, and when she didn't respond I left her. On my way home I hummed the hymn I'd just heard. *'Nje nge mbali e qhakaza namhla, ngakusasa isifile nya.* Like a flower that blooms today, and tomorrow is all withered, don't cry my brethren, we are parted for a little while. In heaven we will see each other again, when all our sorrows have passed.' It sounded good, but the oranges in my throat were still choking me.

Weddings were my favourite Saturday activity, and around the festive season there could be as many as three weddings at once in our street alone. We would then move from one to the next, dancing and singing as we went. Everyone was invited to a wedding, and those who weren't often came when they saw the celebrations and commotion in the streets. For that was where weddings happened – in the streets where everyone could watch and join in. A typical wedding invitation went like this:

'Hey, you look smart, where are you off to?'

'A wedding.'

'Whose wedding?'

'Nomsa.'

'How are you related?'

'*Haai*, I'm not sure.'

'Where is it?'

'Somewhere in Orlando East.'

'Oh, I know Orlando East, I'll come with you.' In Orlando East they'd soon get lost and ask a passer-by where the wedding was.

'*Haai sisi*, which one?'

'Nomsa's.'

'What's her family name?'

'Cele.'

'What does she look like?'

'Dark, with big eyes and short hair.'

The passer-by would look uncertain and then ask, 'Who are her friends?'

'I'm not sure.'

Another moment of thought would be followed with, 'Try that way,' while pointing randomly.

My mother loved to sing at weddings, and I learnt all the wedding songs from her. One of my favourites was *Iqhude we ma, la khala ka bili ka thathu. Se ku sile amanzi awekho.* The cock crowed, twice, thrice. Morning has broken and there is no water. Why it was a wedding song I have no idea, but it was certainly popular. Women would ululate and jump around, giving the newlyweds advice in the middle of the singing. Often the entourages of the bride and the groom would both start a song simultaneously and then compete to drown out the other. The loudest group would prevail and everyone would take up their song. The most popular wedding song for grooms had the crowd answering each line with *siyavuma*; we say yes:

Umakoti ngo wethu. The bride is ours. *Siyavuma.*

Ungo wethu ngempela. She's really ours. *Siyavuma.*

Uzosiwashela a siphekele. She'll wash and cook for us. *Siyavuma.*

Asimufuni emaparthini. We don't want her at parties. *Siyavuma.*

Asimufuni emadodeni. We don't want her around men. *Siyavuma.*

Simufuna emabodweni. We want her around pots. *Siyavuma.*

I loved playing outside with my friends but I was always happiest at home with my parents. I adored Papa and was proud of his constant presence in our lives. Few friends had a father like ours. Most fathers either regularly beat their wives or passed out drunk in the streets. Many of our friends didn't know their fathers and envied the way Papa played with us and made us yummy food to share with them. I was also proud of my mother, who was pretty and clever and worked as a nurse at Baragwanath Hospital. But I missed her a lot because she worked long hours. I felt sorry for her when she was on night duty and missed our evening games of snakes and ladders. When she returned home in the mornings Papa would make her a cup of tea, and when my brother and I clambered all over her, Papa would insist that we leave her alone because she was tired.

When our mother did night duty we had to be quiet during the day while she slept. But our house was so tiny you could hear a penny drop, and I found it a huge effort not to chat to my father. The two of us often sat out under the peach tree, talking softly and trying hard not to laugh, which was impossible with my father's wicked sense of humour.

Although Papa was a great storyteller, he never revealed much about his life as a bootlegger. Long after his death I still heard anecdotes from those who'd frequented his shebeen in the sixties and early seventies. Papa's silence about it was not from shame because he always glowed when people reminisced with him about it. Yet whenever we asked, he said only that it was a place for adults and we should go to school so we never had to own one. I only learnt how popular his shebeen had been when I built my own career in media. When I interviewed politicians, musicians, journalists or soccer players from that era, many would say, 'Direko? Any relation of Peter "Five Piece" Direko?' When I said he was my father, I got hugs and high fives along with joyful recollections of times spent at his joint. Others who had been in exile when Papa died would sometimes ask how he was or send greetings.

Papa's shebeen thrived at a time when blacks weren't allowed to own bottle stores or any entity that sold alcohol. At first, black people weren't even allowed to buy alcohol, and hard liquor was still prohibited until 1962, when the apartheid regime, unable to sell its alcoholic products abroad, decided to increase the local market to keep the state-supported liquor industry afloat. And even then the government continued its paternalism towards black people, who were only allowed to buy and drink alcohol from a government supplier, and could not get a licence to run such a business themselves.

But traditional beer was an intrinsic part of black culture and religion. No ancestral ritual, traditional wedding or funeral took place without the women brewing *umqombothi*. Unable to stop this practice, the government decided to control it. In 1938, the year my father was born, the Johannesburg municipality started brewing traditional beer and establishing controlled beer halls. These were now the only establishments where black people were allowed to buy alcohol. My grandfather told me that the white-owned breweries had stolen the recipe for traditional beer from blacks. And because black people were no longer allowed to brew their own, they bought copious amounts, with extortionate returns for the government.

But the prohibition on home brewing was unenforceable. Nobody was prepared to travel long distances to buy from the white man. And with the pass system, blacks were constantly being rounded up and arrested for being in the wrong place at the wrong time, so it was almost impossible to enjoy a drink in peace without the police stepping in. Large numbers of men and women were unemployed, and even those in employment battled to make ends meet. Being prisoners in their own country added to the sense of isolation and dejection, and many sought comfort and respite in alcohol. One popular concoction was named Kill Me Quick, renowned for its power to knock a man out quickly and completely.

Due to the high levels of unemployment and the meagre salaries of those employed, women turned to home brewing to augment the family income. For some families, selling alcohol became the core economic activity. The government tried endlessly to shut these places down by arresting the owners and patrons, but there were too many keys to the door. Many went on operating despite the ever-present risk of arrest.

When Papa opened his shebeen in the sixties, he was unmarried and living with his grandparents in Sofasonke Street where they had raised him. He had dropped out of high school to become the breadwinner when they got too old to work, and he continued to support them until they died in their late eighties. When he lost his city job and struggled to find other work, starting a shebeen had seemed the best option. He soon had a large clientele among the black middle class, who visited his three-roomed house daily, often drowning their sorrows until late at night.

Papa's mother was unmarried when she had him in 1938, and she already had a two-year-old daughter. The family patriarch, Outata, banished her to live with relatives in Evaton, fifty kilometres from Soweto. But it helped that Papa was a boy, and soon he was welcomed into the family. Within months of his birth, his mother was back at 1401 Sofasonke Street, where my father remained for the rest of his life. When his mother later married and moved to another part of Soweto, he stayed with his grandparents but kept a close relationship with her.

There was little my father couldn't turn his hand to. He sewed, cooked, fixed shoes and taps, paved the yard and singlehandedly built the wall that still stands around the Sofasonke Street property. I cannot remember a moment when he was idle, and even when he was a child, visitors to his home had marvelled at this boy who worked like a woman. 'Your house is so clean,' they would say to his grandparents, 'it's as if you have daughters and granddaughters living here.'

Papa's shebeen came to an end when he married my mother in 1973. She was doing her nursing training at the Natalspruit Hospital on the East Rand, and she felt strongly that it wasn't right for a nurse's home to be a shebeen. The shebeen also attracted some unsavoury characters, including criminals and many who just misbehaved when drunk. By the time my brother was born in 1976, number 1401 was just a home, and we lived there until 1990. Papa then worked at different places in the city, including the stock exchange and Bowring Barclays insurance brokers.

Soon my mother grew tired of working for a pittance at Baragwanath and being unable to spend holidays with the family. But to make it in corporate South Africa she needed further education. So the year before Papa died, she registered for a degree by correspondence through the University of South Africa. To study she needed flexible working hours, and we were very excited when she landed a job as a health consultant for the Carlton Paper company. The job came with a company car, and required her to present workshops on hygiene and sexual health at schools, community centres and private companies. But I was mortified when she came to talk to the older students at my school about sexual reproduction, and relieved to see her leave at the end of second break.

Growing up in Soweto I had no sense of deprivation. We always ate well and got presents and new clothes at Christmas. Birthdays were also celebrated with cake and party packs for our friends. We had everything we needed for school and compared to many children in Orlando East, our lives were good. Although some Soweto families had bigger houses with more rooms, most were just like ours. It was only when we went to a Christmas staff party at the home of Papa's white boss in 1986 that I got a new perspective. I'd never been to the suburbs before and was aghast at this magnificent home the size of my primary school set among sprawling gardens with a swimming pool and a tennis court. I knew no white people apart from the nuns at school, but here we were the only black family. I understood a little English, but not enough to construct even a single sentence, and I was petrified we'd make fools of ourselves. But they were all very nice and Papa and Mama seemed comfortable chatting with the adults.

The white children in the pool stopped playing at the sight of us. It didn't cross my mind that they'd never seen black children and were as surprised as we were, but they recovered and invited us to join them. I'd never been in a swimming pool and was too shy to take off my clothes, but my brother was more adventurous and didn't mind that he had no swimming trunks like the white children.

Soon afterwards my parents entertained an American woman who had come to give a talk at my mom's workplace and wanted to visit Soweto. When we hosted her at our home, she was warm and hugged us, and then asked where we lived. When my mom told her this was it, she was baffled. 'But where do you all sleep?' she asked. On hearing that my brother and I slept on the couch, she was visibly shocked. As we left to drive her to the airport, we passed a wedding with singing and dancing in the streets, and I was bemused when she stopped to take photographs of total strangers.

Although our home was no longer a shebeen, our neighbourhood had its fair share of resident alcoholics. One of our local drunks, Toto, lived right next door. The mascot of Sofasonke Street, Toto vacillated between ecstasy and combat; when he wasn't either singing, dancing or jumping around for no reason, he could usually be found taking part in a drunken brawl. On the rare occasions when he was sober, he was moody, prickly and uncommunicative. But he loved my father. Papa took good care of our little garden, but because Toto was a gardener and always broke, Papa paid him to work in it. Toto would blow all his pay on beer, and then come to taunt my father, 'Have you ever been as happy as I am? Ha, *thina si dla izimali zethu*. I'm enjoying my money.' An hour or two later he'd be out of cash and back demanding more. When my father denied him the extra cash, Toto would threaten to find all the grass he'd cut from our lawn and replant it. Papa would laugh.

One evening when my parents were all dressed up for a function at my dad's work, Toto really got my dad laughing. He became so utterly enthralled with my mother's appearance that he followed her everywhere, refusing to let her out of his sight. When my father insisted that they had to leave, Toto said, 'Oh, afraid of me, are you? Well, you should be. I can steal her from you with ease.'

Other neighbours who provided regular entertainment on Sofasonke Street were Thiza and his girlfriend Pinkie. Most Sundays after lunch, Thiza would chase Pinkie and give her a vicious beating. The adults in the neighbourhood speculated endlessly about the causes of this recurring drama, although it seemed to me that a powerful man and a screaming woman hardly constituted a fair fight. On one occasion it was claimed that Thiza had given Pinkie money to buy meat for lunch, but she'd disappeared until late afternoon and returned without the money or the meat. Another time it was said that when he was trying to 'do it' to her he had discovered that she'd been with another man.

'How did he discover that?'

'He felt it when he was doing it.'

The adults around us had these conversations openly, and expected us children not to hear. I knew instinctively that I'd get a hiding if I repeated any of this to my parents. Thiza's method of executing 'discipline' was also considered a joke. He would pummel her eye until it was half closed, and then start on the other. My friends and I once actually witnessed him sitting on her chest pounding her eye, one blow after the next. When she screamed, 'Thiza, I'm dying!' he responded, 'Die, you dog!' The next morning, as usual, we saw him escorting Pinkie to the clinic because she couldn't see properly.

This routine caused a lot of merriment among the neighbours. As children even we laughed about it, enacting what we'd seen and trying to outdo each other. But one day I saw the look on their son's face as Thiza beat his mother. His name was Innocent and there he stood, losing his innocence as he watched his mother being beaten to a pulp. I never found it funny again.

One Sunday afternoon my father was sitting with his friends when Thiza attacked Pinkie again. Together they dragged him off her and carried him to our yard. My father ordered me indoors, so I didn't see what happened, but we heard Thiza scream and howl, and saw him emerge bloodied and limping. We never saw him hit Pinkie again.

Soweto was certainly a perplexing place. The palpable jubilation and energy on the streets was no veneer; it was genuine. There were choir competitions, games in the streets and dancing at weddings, all of which offered some respite from the quagmire of suffering and oppression of the black nation. Besides the shebeens, small businesses like funeral parlours, general dealers, dry cleaners and butcheries provided much-needed services in the community. People made the best of an enervating situation and got on with life, work, childrearing and church. There were also rich families, educated ones, celebrities and entertainers living side by side with the desperately poor. But poverty and unemployment lurked everywhere, always threatening to bring weary men and women to their knees. And the deprivation and violence brutalised many, crushing dreams and swallowing innocence.

Chapter 2

THE SOWETO IN WHICH I grew up in the eighties was very different from that of my father's day. Political violence was now the norm; young men and women disappeared, swallowed up by the never-ending struggle. It was also a time of confrontation between students and the apartheid police. School would be interrupted and the 'comrades' – some of whom were just thugs – would take advantage of the political turmoil, barge into our classrooms and order us home. 'There will be no schooling until we've won this war,' they would declare.

'Is there a war, Papa?' I asked him.

'Yes, South Africa is a battleground.'

'Who's fighting?'

'We are.'

'Who are we fighting?'

'The white people.'

'Why are we fighting them?'

'To make everything right.'

My head spun, not only in confusion but also in anxiety. What about the two white nuns, Sister Rita and Sister Susan, who taught at our school, spoke isiZulu and Sesotho and were so kind and warm? What would happen to them if we were fighting them? And the white family we'd visited a few months before? How could we be at war with them?

I got used to the big army tanks that patrolled our streets. I didn't know they were there to watch over the undisciplined blacks and enforce the government's state of emergency, which curtailed black people's freedom and restricted their movements. Adults spoke so much about the state of emergency that I thought this was what a tank was called. Every time I heard their roar, I'd rush to the gate.

'Where are you going?'

'To watch the state of emergency.'

I wasn't the only one; all children were fascinated by the menacing soldiers with their big guns who spat on the ground as they rolled past.

'Papa, why are the soldiers always angry?'

'Because when you do bad things, you can't smile. They're here to destroy us.'

My favourite time of the year was Christmas and New Year, because we got presents and new clothes, and there was always so much to eat. Most children, except for the very poorest, wore new clothes on Christmas Day and New Year's Day. My brother and I were lucky to get several new outfits, even one for Boxing Day. Wearing a new dress or new shoes made me delirious with happiness, and I loved putting ribbons in my hair and packing my little handbag with pink tissues and plastic sunglasses. I always saved my best dress for New Year's Day. But in 1985 my parents refused to let us wear our new clothes, saying that we'd get into trouble for it. I was heartbroken.

'Why? They're our clothes!' I actually shed tears because dressing up was my favourite pastime. It felt like the world was ending when I had to leave my new clothes in their packaging because my mom and dad said so. 'I want to wear my clothes!'

'No! The comrades will kill us.'

I didn't understand then that a consumer boycott had been declared in which township folks were refusing to buy from white businesses. Those who bought groceries, clothes or other items were often attacked by 'comrades' who waited at bus stops and taxi ranks for any traitors who had dared to shop in town. I never saw it happen, but stories abounded. One woman was made to drink the fish oil she'd bought, while they rubbed the cake flour into her hair.

What I did see on my way home from school, though, was a necklacing. Children were told to go home, but it was too late. We'd seen a little, and seen too much. They'd beaten the man to a pulp. While he bled and begged for mercy, they stoned him, placed a rubber tyre around his neck and poured paraffin over him before setting him alight. Nobody quite knew what he'd done; the story kept changing, depending on who was telling it. This practice blighted the township agitation for a democratic South Africa. Many families suffered the agony of watching their innocent offspring necklaced because someone somewhere had seen them speaking to an enemy of the people. And so an already brutalised people turned on each other, speaking the only language they knew: more brutality.

The funerals that drew the most attention when I was growing up were those of the comrades – teenagers and young adults caught up in the cycle of political violence and killed by adversaries or, of course, the police.

But criminals also thrived and made their presence felt. There were the thugs and notorious gangsters who committed murders during their turf wars, displaying their acts of bravado to see who could instil the most fear and commit the most heinous crime. Using the lowest forms of cunning and dexterity, they tricked those in hot pursuit and lived to see another day. For them, life was not about contemplating and planning for their future. They asked little of life beyond surviving another day. But as they watched friends and enemies die in violent confrontations, they realised that they too were living on borrowed time, which made them even more reckless.

I was expressly forbidden to be on the streets when a criminal was being buried. But I wasn't worried about missing the entertainment and spectacle, because soon enough there'd be another. My parents weren't always around and I didn't always play close enough to home for them to call me inside. To mark the send-off of the dead young man, the entire neighbourhood would be treated to a spectacle of fast cars spinning violently with their passengers hanging out of the windows, to the deafening sounds of gunfire as the colleagues of the dead criminal demonstrated their fearsome skills. The crowds would clap and cheer, urging on the showmen and their girlfriends. This sordid tribute would take place in broad daylight, and the entire street would come to a standstill, onlookers lining up as if they were watching a grand prix.

Eventually, the police learnt to use these occasions to identify and arrest elusive suspects. A police van would sometimes even wait patiently at the graveside for the coffin to descend, and as the priest offered the last prayer, they'd pounce on the rogues who'd been showing off. So criminals learnt to lie low or even avoid the funerals of fellow gangsters.

During the mid- to late-eighties, one of the most notorious gangs in Orlando was the Makabasa, a group of youths among whom owning and driving a Colt was the ultimate status symbol. The community generally viewed the Makabasa as benign because, apart from their rivalry with other gangs, they actually protected rather than terrorised the local residents. They committed their crimes in the city, and were rumoured to stage the most daring bank robberies. They stole cars and often drove around in Colts of different colours, which they'd spin on the streets after a successful day's work. When they failed in their robberies, they'd return to the township in a convoy of up to eight or nine cars, hooting to let the public know that it had been a bad day. It was quite a sight to behold a procession of Colts of different colours driving slowly and sombrely like a rainbow on wheels. Our parents tried to keep all this malaise away from us, but it was impossible. You couldn't grow up in Soweto and remain impervious to such goings on for long.

Surprisingly, it was from my parents that I learnt about the Makabasa. One day, a robbery in the city made the TV news while we were having supper – Papa on his big cane chair, Mama on the old sofa and my brother and I on the carpet. My father refused to watch the public broadcaster, the SABC, which he called Botha's propaganda. I felt rather sorry for PW Botha, because I knew my father would discipline him severely if he ever bumped into him. Instead we watched Bop TV, which, although also sponsored by the apartheid government, was at least run from the homeland of Bophuthatswana and broadcast in our home language,

Setswana. The newsreader announced that two members of a notorious Soweto gang had been killed in a robbery, and others had been arrested.

'I'm sure it's the Makabasa,' said Papa.

'No Papa!' I objected. 'They're nice people.'

'How do you know?' my father demanded.

'They gave me and Thobile each one rand after they sent us to the shops.'

I got an instant hiding, but my parents didn't tell me why. I had to read between the lines and figure out what part of what I'd said or done was wrong. It was confusing because we were always taught to respect adults and run errands for them without complaining. Was it that I had accepted money from them? I hadn't asked for it, after all.

Although many parents, church and community leaders warned impressionable youngsters that the adulation of these criminals was foolhardy, the Makabasa were legendary. They were admired not because the community had no values, but because they were daring young men in a township where men were emasculated by apartheid, and they ventured out to do unspeakable things that the more subdued wouldn't dream of doing, even though they too were battling to put food on the table. That was the marvel of Soweto; the family next door could be drunkards or criminals, yet next to them a hardworking nurse, teacher, reverend or doctor would be successfully raising his or her children in a morally upright manner.

Still, there was no denying the legend of the Makabasa. My mom's cousin Thami was one of them, and was also quite a hit with the ladies, I learnt from the adults around me. But the truism that those who live by the sword die by the sword meant that the Makabasa, like so many gangs, were being rounded up by the police, one by one. And they certainly weren't being read their rights or even given a chance to hand themselves over. The police would barge into their homes in the still of the night, leaving a trail of bullets and bodies. The public didn't stop to mourn but got on with their lives. There was too much death in our midst, and no time to be paralysed by it.

My parents were very strict and, even when the wrongdoer was a relative, they were steadfast in their resolve not to be seen in bad company. I knew we were related to Thami, but he never set foot in our home, and my brother and I weren't allowed any interaction with him. So I didn't know him personally, although I used to see him in the streets in his orange Colt. When he'd stop and offer me a lift home, I wouldn't answer, but run home fast, remembering my earlier hiding. On New Year's Eve in 1988 – my father had died by then – Thami's shack was raided by the police in the early hours. According to the story, he was in bed with his girlfriend when they pelted him with sixteen bullets, and two officers then raped his girlfriend right beside his dead body, although this may have been pure embellishment on the part of the storytellers. Nonetheless, the police made quite sure he was dead.

It was a given that the death of a criminal at the hands of the police would be followed by the death of a police officer. Any police officer would do, but someone had to pay. And so the cycle continued as surely as day followed night. Police would round them up, shoot and kill, and a day later we'd hear of a police death.

Apart from the Makabasa, there were other gangs and gangsters that were admired by some and despised by others. One was Tora, famous for escaping police raids, but later arrested for domestic violence after hitting his girlfriend, the mother of his child. While the police were holding him on the domestic violence charge, they persuaded his girlfriend to disclose details of his robberies and police killings, duping her into thinking that this would shorten his sentence.

Angry as she was about the beating, she certainly didn't want Tora to rot in jail. If he couldn't 'work', she and her child would starve; so all she had intended was to stop him beating her. At the trial she was called to the witness stand to confirm Tora's involvement in various crimes, and when her testimony resulted in a long jail sentence, she attacked the police officers as Tora was led away.

'*Ke batla monna wa ka!* I want my man!' she shouted. When they tried to restrain her, she yelled, 'That's why my man kills you dogs! When he gets out of there, he'll blow your brains out!'

But Tora never made it out of prison alive. It was claimed that other gang members killed him after the police promised to reduce their sentences. But he may also have been killed by the police or by rival gangs that he'd spent his time fighting.

When Tora died, those familiar with gangster politics anticipated that Mabegzo, Tora's protégé, would take the reins. And Mabegzo was reported to be even more brutal and peerless a criminal than his mentor had been.

'*Mabegzo wa wina.* Mabegzo will win,' was the word on the streets.

I had heard plenty about Mabegzo already. He was a legendary, almost mythical figure who could walk right through roadblocks and taunt the police who were 'too scared' to arrest him. This was nonsense, of course. The South African police were feared and detested in the townships, and well known for their supreme cruelty and racism. Black officers were regarded as spies and sell-outs who did the bidding of their white masters. Policemen beating up peaceful anti-apartheid protesters, kicking and punching vanquished parents in front of their children, and arresting helpless mothers and underage children were an everyday part of township life. The police were despised as public enemies, and soliciting their help or sharing information with them was viewed as treachery. Nobody associated the police with protection or law and order. Too many people had been maimed or raped by the police, and too many simply disappeared after the police picked them up. Often, police officers went to the wrong address but were too proud to admit it. They'd then search the house of a very confused and frightened family, overturning furniture and throwing the family's meagre belongings on the floor. Their visits always left a trail of destruction and a lot of bitterness. So the community preferred to apply its own forms of law enforcement, and errant young men were often rounded up and beaten by the elders. In the eyes of most people, not even the most vicious criminals deserved punishment at the hands of the police.

It was in this context, where cruel racist laws were constantly being enacted to subjugate people, that a sadistic killer could come to be viewed as a hero, a messianic figure even. Anyone who was wanted by the police was a hero, for he had dared to defy the law.

Mabegzo's feared and revered name rolled off the tongues of many who had never even seen him. Groups would gather at street corners to give 'eye-witness' accounts of his misdemeanours, even if they hadn't been there. A particularly bizarre story of how he'd set a man on fire and later called emergency services to rescue the victim was recounted over and over, often with a macabre combination of fascination and hero worship. Such stories often ended with the words *Mabegzo ke boss*; Mabegzo's the boss. Although most adults despised Mabegzo, the township youths narrated tales of his revenge on others with admiration and subtle justification, as if his victims had earned their fate. In one story, Mabegzo and his mates had killed two policemen, pushed them out of their car, and then done wheel spins in the police car to amuse the crowd while the policemen lay dead in the road. In another story, when a criminal named Zibi raped the sister of Mabegzo's friend, Mabegzo and his friend barged into Zibi's home late at night while his family were asleep, and forced Zibi at gunpoint to have sex with his own mother and sister.

Perhaps the story people relished most was that of a fatal robbery at the Mzamo Moleko bottle store in Diepkloof, three kilometres from our area. Legend had it that Mabegzo had walked into the store one New Year's Eve and politely asked them to hand over some alcohol for his gang's celebration. When the shopkeeper laughed at him, Mabegzo threatened to shoot him. Thinking it was a joke, the man laughed even harder. Mabegzo shot him at point blank range and calmly started loading crates of alcohol, inviting the shocked onlookers to join their New Year's Eve party.

In spite of myself, a story that impressed even me was his appearance at Orlando East Magistrate's Court, in which the police apparently forced him to testify against his archrival in another gang. The two gangsters didn't see eye to eye, and although they hadn't had a physical fight, there was a cold war between them over criminal politics. The prosecution promised Mabegzo indemnity for his own misdeeds in return for revealing those of his enemy in a robbery case, and waited for Mabegzo to crucify him. Even the accused expected Mabegzo to sing like a canary. But when he was asked to put his hand on the Bible and swear to tell the truth, Mabegzo answered, 'Stop asking me shit, man; just convict us all.' The story spread like wildfire and was told with deep admiration. Here was a criminal with class and loyalty to his profession.

Undoubtedly, Mabegzo had a formidable presence in the township, and the wisest thing was to avoid any encounter with him at all costs. I had heard more than enough to be frightened of him. When girls misbehaved or played in the streets past their curfew, mothers would demand, 'Do you want Mabegzo to take you? He will if he sees you in the streets. He rapes girls.'

Like all girls who lived with the ominous threat of Mabegzo's presence, I felt like I knew him, even though I hadn't met him. Filled with tales of his evil deeds, I took for granted that I'd know him without a doubt as soon as I saw him. He would be an ugly beast, and I'd be able to identify him from a mile away and run for cover.

Violation of women and girls was commonplace in the late eighties and early nineties. Yet as horrendous as it was, the community seemed to treat rape as if it were just some minor inconvenience. It wasn't uncommon for a young woman to be walking down the street and for someone, even another woman, to point at her and snigger, '*Phela*, this one got raped by so-and-so'. So-and-so would be a well-known thug still roaming the streets without a care in the world.

Our neighbour, Tokai, was in her early forties and was another of our village drunks. I once witnessed a group of young boys luring her to a house not far from my home. She was so drunk she could never have found her way home, and the boys assured onlookers that they were helping her home. Yet I clearly saw them take her in a different direction. The next morning I heard that Tokai had been found naked on a street corner and some little boys had had sex with her – not *raped* her, simply had sex with her! That it was treated as a joke left me deeply disturbed. People would say matter-of-factly that Tokai should stop drinking, but no one ever suggested that she deserved justice or that the boys should be punished. The implication was that drunken women deserved abuse, yet all around us drunken men who were abusive to their families were always helped home when they were too drunk to manage – and no one ever considered harming them.

The 'in' thing among young thugs then was jackrolling. A group of guys would stumble upon a woman and kidnap her in broad daylight. She would then be repeatedly raped for as long as her captors felt like it, and only when they were good and ready would they let her go. More 'charitable' rapists might then give her a lift back or walk her home. From then on, this girl was marked in the community.

I'd known it to happen to girls and young women around me, and I lived with the suffocating fear that one day it would be my turn. I was big for my age, and while my classmates were still sitting with their legs apart, I couldn't afford to be so childlike and carefree. With breasts and hips budding by the age of ten, I often attracted the attention of much older boys and young men. When I ignored them, the word rape fell from their lips with ease while their friends and onlookers just laughed. And even when they weren't threatening rape, their lewd, explicit language about what they wanted to do to my innocent body sent chills down my spine. So I lived with the fear of rape every day of my life, a fear that has never dissipated. Even the families who protected their rapist sons often denied any support and protection to the girls in their families.

The sense that girls were always responsible for male attention was reinforced by the teachers at my school. One Monday morning after assembly, which took place outside in the courtyard, the girls were told to remain behind while the boys went off to their classes. I assumed we were going to get hidings for not wearing our red berets, as had happened once before, but there was no sjambok in the headmistress's hand this time.

Instead she said loudly, '*Mantombaza, yekelani ukulala nabafana!* Girls, stop sleeping with the boys!'

This was primary school, not high school, and we were mere children. Couldn't they just leave us alone? Why did adults always make such humiliating assumptions about us girls? Boys were spared these stupid lectures, but as girls it felt like we were constantly being insulted with slurs about how immoral and naughty we were.

'*Abafana ba zo dlala ngani uma ni phapha*. Boys will play you if you're so *tjatjarag*,' she went on. 'So today, we're going to check all of you to see what you've been up to with the boys!'

The teachers then began to walk around each row of girls, squeezing our breasts in the belief that sexual activity somehow changed a girl's breasts. We were then told to take off our panties for the teachers to examine us to see whether we had slept with a boy or not. While all this went on, we could see the boys peeping at us through the windows, having a good laugh. It made no sense that they'd been sent to the privacy of the classrooms while we were left standing out in the open having our genitals examined. Some girls were crying, but most of us were just trembling violently from the horror and violation of it all.

When my turn came, Mistress Angela walked up to me, winked and moved on. I noticed that she wasn't really checking anyone, but pretending to. Nobody tried to comfort the girls who were crying, or who were bitterly ashamed because their sanitary towels were exposed for all to see. I lacked the vocabulary then to define the range of emotions

I felt at that moment, but it was mostly a searing rage. I remained mute, but I was overwhelmed by the unfairness and injustice of this entire exercise. To be a girl meant to be powerless.

Then the principal spoke again. 'There is a pregnant child in this school. She will not be back next term, because she's a naughty child! The same will apply to anyone else who falls pregnant.' A terrified silence descended on us. Then she ordered us back to our classrooms, where the boys were still hooting with laughter.

Once an older boy pulled my hair, the elders chastised him and he ran off, but they said, '*Haai*, no wonder these big boys are drawn to you. You don't look or behave like a child.' So the attention of men always made me feel guilty. I thought I was doing something wrong, inadvertently sending a message that I was available. Older men were fathers, they were there to love and protect children like my father had always done. If they didn't, it was somehow my fault.

The year after Papa died, my mother got in builders to put up back rooms in our yard; it would bring in extra income and also make her feel safer. The presence of other males on the property would make us less of a soft target. My mother was kind to the builders and expected us to make them lunch as soon as we got home from school. I was always home before my cousin and brother, so I would make the builders their lunch and retrieve their empty plates from under our peach tree when they left. But one day as they knocked off work, the friendly Swazi builder brought the dishes inside and closed the door with his foot. I opened it again and stood aside to let him out. But he kicked it closed again, grabbed me by my hair and planted an unwelcome kiss on my lips. His tongue forced my lips open and I froze. I had never had that kind of kiss before. It was brutal, and I could taste the cement dust as he crushed my wrists in one huge rough hand and squeezed my tender, developing breasts.

'We're friends, right?' he said. Then he pulled up my school dress and ran his hands across my panties. Suddenly I knew I was in big trouble. But in my terror I simply froze, and it never occurred to me to scream.

Luckily, at that moment, our local drunk, Toto, yelled from outside, singing and demanding food as he always did. The man released me and fled. Toto was far too drunk to read anything into this, and I was too deeply confused to do anything about the incident. But from that day on, I delayed coming home, and spent my time playing with friends or visiting the local library until I was sure there'd be someone else at our house.

Whenever the men worked on weekends, I stayed close to my older cousin Thembi, who had come to live with us. The lecherous man was still working there, and each week he came inside to give my mom a progress report. Whenever he met my eyes, he'd wink at me. One Saturday evening my mom went to the bedroom to fetch him some money, leaving me alone with him in our tiny lounge. I was uncomfortable but not afraid, because my mother was right there. But as he winked at me, ran his predatory tongue across his lips and then massaged his crotch, I suddenly vomited all over the carpet. My mom gave him the money and then asked him to leave, apologising for not offering him anything to eat, because 'my child needs me'. She cleaned it all up without complaining, and I started to sob. Mama just assumed I was crying because I was sick. And in a way I was; I was sick in my soul, my body merely a conduit for the toxicity.

When teenage girls fell pregnant, they were often sent off to distant relatives, as with my paternal grandmother, so that their expanding stomachs wouldn't bring shame on the family. Nothing much seemed to happen to the boys who impregnated them; they generally carried on with their lives and sired more children. When a pregnancy was discovered, relatives of the girl would gather some elders and take her to the boy's family to report *molato*. These meetings would start with the girl's family introducing themselves and reporting their reason for being there. A child's paternity was important, because identity was defined by the clan name derived from the ancestors in the male line. This was of great significance for birth and marriage, particularly for males. While women took on their husband's clan, it was crucial that a boy knew his father's name and clan – even if he was born out of wedlock and hadn't known his father – just so that he knew his lineage. Once his paternal lineage was determined and appropriated, the boy had an identity. Some sought no further relationship with their fathers once they knew their lineage and had been introduced to their ancestors.

For some reason, these meetings had to take place at the crack of dawn; that was how it was done. The boy would then be called and asked the question. The girl would sit there, biting her nails, nervously waiting to be acknowledged. These encounters were often dramatic, because to be denied by the boy was a death knell for the girl and her child. Typically, his parents and family would then take his side and chase the girl's family away.

I had witnessed such messy scenes playing themselves out on the streets. Thoko, the highly intelligent sister of my friend Thabang, had fallen pregnant from Chippa, a no-good, dagga-smoking bully on our streets. The boy's family was known to be difficult, so my father, who had a good relationship with them, was asked to accompany Thoko's deputation. He later reported that he'd never realised just how crude and nasty Chippa's family was until that day. He was particularly shocked that both the boy's mother and another female relative had become combative, while the matriarch, then in her early eighties, swore like a trooper and even challenged the girl's grandmother to a physical fight. Not one of them ever bothered to ask Chippa if he knew the girl. '*A le mobe so, ngwanaka ne ka se ke,*' his grandmother yelled. 'Your child is so ugly my grandchild would never sleep with her.'

Thoko and her family were never able to avoid Chippa because they lived in the same street. But Thoko picked up the pieces of her life and even obtained a bursary to study overseas, while her mother and grandmother helped raise her daughter Thuso, who was also very intelligent. Thabang and I sometimes bumped into Chippa while walking Thuso to and from nursery school. He grew more loathsome as the years went by, and always denied any relationship with Thoko. On seeing us, he'd shout, '*Mara*, why *le re ke ncosi ya ka ena?* Why do you say this is my child?' But we were too small to argue with him.

Years later the dictum that you reap what you sow came true for Chippa's family: his malicious grandmother lived long enough to bury her son and all the grandchildren she'd raised. Chippa spent much time in prison before he died, leaving his mother and grandmother all alone. Eventually the two old women made overtures to Thuso, the grandchild they had earlier denied. But after fourteen years, it was too late.

Chapter 3

AFTER MY FATHER'S DEATH, the world felt a bit colder, darker and more dangerous, and I stayed off the streets as much as I could. But the walk home from school, St John Berchmans Primary, was always pleasant; long enough to give me time to chat and play with my friends, but not enough to be tiring. Some children had to walk much further to school, and I was thankful not to be one of them.

As girls we always walked home in groups, not that it protected us from the predators and bullies who hung around the shops and street corners looking for mischief. Every girl I knew had a boy who was harassing and threatening her. The boys called it 'propositioning', but it was sheer torment. My tormentor was a boy called Siphiwe.

I'd never confided in my mom as a child, nor had we ever discussed boys, sex or rape. Although my mom had never actually said that it was always the girl's behaviour that 'caused' boys to pick on her, I had learnt this indirectly from the comments and attitudes of those around me, and had fully accepted this burden by the age of eleven. Girls who were harassed by boys carried a stigma.

My mom and I shared the bed after my father died. Usually she slept through the night while I lay awake, thinking. But sometimes, she also couldn't sleep. In the early hours of the morning when the world was dead quiet, I'd hear her get out of the bed and kneel down. I'd pretend to be asleep, but when I was sure her eyes were closed in prayer, I'd peep at her. She'd be in another world. This was when the fire in her heart came pouring out. I felt like an intruder witnessing a moment of raw pain yet indescribable beauty. Speaking in her mother tongue, isiXhosa, she would literally throw herself at the feet of God and plead for healing. She would remind God about us, her children, begging him to help her be a good mother and do her best for us. Her voice would get louder and louder with raw, unsanitised emotion and pain. I tried not to stir. Even as a child I knew that these were intensely private moments, and I am yet to hear anyone pray so movingly. Time would stand still as she bared her heart and asked for forgiveness for my father, for all that he had done in life that hadn't pleased God.

'*Uyazazi iintlungu zomphefumlo wam.* You know the pain in my soul, and I give it all to you,' she would conclude. '*Ndilungise bawo.* Heal me, Father.'

I felt so sorry for my mother at these times that I resolved to be a good child, work hard and make a success of my life, so that she had one less thing to worry about. I also made it my mission every Sunday at church to pray for her without fail.

But since my father's death my mother had also become stricter and a bit more withdrawn and austere. She was determined to keep order in our home to protect us, but to me she just seemed prickly. Yet we lacked for nothing and she took good care of us, so in return I was determined to give something back – and all I could offer was good behaviour. I certainly didn't want to worry her, so I tried not to add to her pressures by sharing my problems.

My first encounter with Siphiwe took place during a lunch-break at school, when he was nineteen and I was eleven. Although my mom always packed me lunch, others bought their lunch from the shops behind our school, and I would accompany them. As we turned the corner that day, we passed a group of boys smoking and hanging out together. One walked up to me and told me I was pretty, and I smiled back.

From that day on, he bullied me incessantly. He'd grab my wrist and twist it, and I'd smell the sweat and dagga on him.

'Say it,' he'd tell me. 'Say, "I am Siphiwe's wife"!' He'd slap me if I didn't. Then he'd grab my budding breasts and give them a painful squeeze.

Every time Siphiwe appeared in front of me I began to shake like a leaf. He was ugly and menacing, and I would break out in a sweat that trickled down my back and legs. I was beyond afraid; every time I encountered Siphiwe I thought my last day had come. He made a point of reminding me that I'd smiled at him, which was confirmation that I wanted the same thing he wanted. 'O *mphile* promise. You made me a promise,' he'd say. Finally he would release me, and I'd walk away on trembling legs. I knew that it was only a matter of time before he violated me. His intentions were written all over his face. And I was bitter with myself for that first innocent smile.

One day I had just escaped Siphiwe's sweaty hands and

reached the corner with my friends when another young guy walked right up to me. Something in the atmosphere changed; it was as if the air was suddenly charged. People around me began scattering, while others stopped to watch, looking worried yet curious.

Still gripped with fear and wondering how I was going to survive Siphiwe, I took a long moment to come out of my trance and register that this young man and I were the centre of attention. Everyone was looking at us and waiting.

'*Jo, nna*! Oh my!' an elderly woman shouted, but I didn't have time to figure out what she meant or why my friends had run off and left me.

'Hello, nice,' the young guy in front of me said.

'Hello.'

'*Lebitso la hao ke mang?* What's your name?'

'Redihentse.'

'*Mang?* What?'

My unusual Setswana name wasn't easy for people to grasp, so I reverted to my nickname.

'*Ke Momo.*'

'*O ya kae?* Where are you going?'

'Home.'

'*O dula kae?* Where do you live?'

'*Ka kwa.* That side.' I pointed.

'*Ko number mang?*'

'1401 Sofasonke Street.'

I was confused but calm, definitely not disturbed by him. There must have been a reasonable explanation why this decent stranger was asking me questions. Street bullies were never polite like this young man, and he smiled all the time he was talking to me. I liked him already.

Then he touched my cheek very, very gently, and kissed my lips softly.

'*Wa nchaza*. You please me.'

Apart from my brutal encounter with the builder, I had never kissed a boy. My father was the last male I'd ever kissed, and he'd been dead more than a year and a half. I was embarrassed now, because the whole neighbourhood would know that I'd been kissed by a boy. My biggest worry was that my mom might find out. I knew I'd get a hiding and people would question her parenting skills.

I heard voices in my head: my mom saying, '*Tshwanetse o itshware hantle,* always behave yourself'; my Sunday-school teacher saying, 'Be a lady' and 'Stay away from boys'; and my English teacher, Mistress Magdalene, saying, 'When a boy comes close to you, say get thee away from me, Satan'.

In a voice quieter than a whisper, I said, 'Get thee, get…'

'*O reng*? What did you say?'

I couldn't carry on. My throat was dry and the words wouldn't come out. '*Niks*. Nothing.'

He walked away as quietly as he'd appeared. And again I noticed the odd behaviour of those around me. Time had stood still for everyone, me included, although for entirely different reasons. Though I didn't realise it then, the shuffling around me represented a collective sigh of relief.

'You're still walking and not running?' one man demanded of me. 'That means you want it.'

Want what? I wondered. Before I even reached my own street, hordes of neighbours – men, women, grandpas, grandmas, young boys and girls, children, all recognisable faces – came walking or running towards me. I was swept up in different arms, held in the air, tickled, kissed and embraced. I wondered what I'd done to deserve this sudden display of affection. Even Toto swept me up in his arms, his odour indescribably foul. Then one of my elderly neighbours started praying, right on the street corner, thanking the Lord for my safe return, even though I was still a good way from home. Return from where? And she began praising the Lord's name because I'd been rescued from the clutches of Satan. Satan? Where was he?

Now Toto started wailing. '*Futhi ubaba wakhe ushonile nkosi yami, siyabonga*. Thank you, God, for her father is dead.' *Eish*, that label again.

As we walked home amid all this jubilation, Nonhle's mother ordered us straight home. 'I don't want to see you outside your yard! These streets aren't for young girls.'

'*Phela, bashemane ba reipa*, these days! Boys rape!' added Mme Oliphant.

I couldn't make sense of all this until finally someone said, 'Be careful. Mabegzo won't let you go next time.'

Mabegzo? That clean, gentle, drop-dead charming gentleman was *Mabegzo*? No!

As this realisation sank in, it began to dawn on me that I now faced an even bigger problem than Siphiwe. Siphiwe was small fry compared to what I'd have to endure from now on. And then the fear set in. He had clearly marked me. That entire exercise of greeting and kissing was to prepare me for the onslaught to come. Siphiwe had also smiled the first time and paid me a compliment to get me to drop my guard.

I knew of girls who'd stopped going to school because some boy was harassing them and threatening them with beatings and rape. When you had no one to defend you, you were totally at their mercy. It was bad enough walking the streets knowing that Siphiwe could appear at any time, and now would I have to dodge an even worse criminal, Mabegzo?

I was devastated. All I wanted now was to be dead. I resolved to die before school the next day. The decision gave me comfort because now I wouldn't have to suffer this endless, insidious torture.

But something still puzzled me. The guys who preyed on us usually smelt of cigarettes and dagga, and had bloodshot eyes with that hard, cruel glint. Some were *vuilpops*, dirty types who rarely washed. But Mabegzo was probably the most handsome man I'd ever laid eyes on, his shirt was neatly tucked into his pants and he didn't have the swaggering tsotsi walk. Most delinquents had a *bampa* or 'bouncy' walk. They'd lift their right heel so it looked like they were standing on their toes, and merely drag the left foot forward while leaning their upper body to the left. When you saw one of those you knew he was a criminal, a bully or a wannabe cool cat. But not Mabegzo.

When night came, we said our prayers as we did every night before going to bed; it was a house rule. We first prayed together as a family, and afterwards we could continue on our own. After the Hail Marys and the Our Father, my brother went to sleep and my mother went to the kitchen to prepare our lunch boxes – a lunch I wouldn't live to eat.

I started killing myself. 'Dear God. Thank you for today, thank you for my family and friends and thank you for the food and clothes you give me. Please help me and kill me tonight, so that I'm dead in the morning and I won't have to see Siphiwe and Mabegzo ever again. Amen.'

I was pleased with myself, but sad that I wouldn't see my mother again.

But I did see her when she woke me for school the next morning. I was stunned to still be alive, and I felt angry that God hadn't given me what I'd asked for. I'd asked so nicely. What was I going to do now?

For a while I didn't see Mabegzo in the streets, although I was still constantly aware of him. I would run my fingers over my lips, reliving that strange encounter. I didn't know why I did that, but by kissing me, it was as if he'd implanted his presence on me. It wasn't an unpleasant feeling, just surreal. I liked it.

My awareness of Mabegzo was heightened by the never-ending retelling of my encounter with him. All my schoolmates were talking about it.

'What was it like to speak to this hard-core guy?' they wanted to know. 'What did he say?' 'Did he threaten you?' 'Did you cry?' 'Is he ugly?' 'Is he missing an eye?' 'Is your father going to kill him?' On and on it went.

I didn't see Mabegzo again until about four weeks later. By then I'd stopped asking God to kill me; he wasn't listening. Suddenly, Mabegzo was right there in front of me. I froze. Somehow I'd known he would reappear. He was standing on the corner of Kuzwayo Street, not far from my school, waiting for someone. Not me, please Lord, not me, I prayed.

I thought about turning and running, but he'd already seen me. He called out my name. As before, passers-by stopped in their tracks to watch. Others ran for dear life – mainly girls. I just stood there, facing him, and he walked towards me. He was gorgeous, and clean. He didn't greet me, but simply took my school bag and said, '*A re ye*. Let's go'.

The game was up. I didn't even cry. What good would it do? All these people were scared of him, and none who valued their lives would dare reprimand him. He was beyond that. This was a man who shot and stabbed people; a man who wasn't even afraid of the police. So who could challenge him?

We walked quietly, not saying a word, and because I kept my eyes downcast, I wasn't even aware of where we were going. After what seemed like an eternity, we reached my street. Outside our gate, he gave me my school bag and said, 'O *itshware hantle*. Be good.' And he simply walked away.

The next morning I was called into the office of the principal, Mistress Constance. She wanted to know what had happened to me the previous afternoon.

'Nothing,' I told her.

'Do you know that boy?'

'Yes, ma'am.' The words were out before I could even think. In those days, girls played with girls and boys played with boys. Any young girl who walked with a boy in broad daylight was out of order, and admitting to it was very risky.

Mistress Constance didn't say another word, but the next morning she announced at assembly that the boys were to watch over the girls, and she didn't want to see any girl walking alone. She also urged the boys to gang up against the naughty boys to protect the girls. 'While the rest of you hit the naughty boys with stones and fists, one of you must run back to the school or find the nearest home to report any wrongdoing.'

Pre-teen boys from a local primary school were supposed to throw stones at a hardened, gun-toting thug? Her words sounded absurd.

From then on, Mabegzo regularly waited for me at the same corner after school, took my schoolbag from me and walked me home. I was always very self-conscious, worrying that people were talking about us, and wondering what he wanted from me, why he was stalling and when he would finally strike.

'Are you ashamed of me, Lala?' he'd ask. Perhaps he hadn't heard my name correctly, but I wasn't about to correct him.

'No. I just don't want to get into trouble.'

'I can get you out of any trouble, anytime.' His confidence sent a shiver down my spine. '*O se ka wara ka dikolobe tse. Ga ba voetseke.* Don't worry about these pigs. They must *voetsek*,' he'd say. '*Nna, Lala,* I live for nobody. You can never make people happy. Try as you like, they're always out to get you.'

He told me he was used to people staring, pointing fingers and whispering behind his back. He'd grown up with it as a small child. Adults had always sniggered and whispered too loudly as if he couldn't hear. 'That's the one'. Or 'Shame *ke sono*. They pitied him'. One day, he said, he just decided to start swearing at anyone who did that, which got him into even more trouble for disrespecting adults.

'But why? Why did they pick on you out of all the children?'

'I was born with bad luck.'

'How do you know that?'

'My real name says so.'

'What is your name?'

'If I tell you, you'll laugh.'

'I won't. I promise.'

'It's *Mahlomola*. Sorrow.'

After many walks with Mabegzo, I couldn't stand the tension of wondering when he would do it to me. So I said, 'There are boys who did bad things to my neighbour, Tokai.' I was actually hoping this would get him to speed things up for me.

'What did they do?'

'They raped her.' I shivered and I must have reflected the fear I was feeling, because he soothed me so gently.

'Don't worry. Don't be afraid. Do you know these boys?' I nodded. 'What are their names and where do they live?' His questions and interest confused me. Why did he seem so concerned for me? I grew a little more relaxed on our walks home, but I still didn't trust him, especially because of the disapproving stares that followed us.

A few weeks after Mabegzo had begun walking me home, I was on an errand to the shops when a group of three boys encircled me. One pulled my hair while the other twisted my wrist and said he wouldn't let go until I agreed to be his girlfriend. I knew exactly what he meant by that. Without stopping to think I said I couldn't; I belonged to someone else.

'*Ubani*? Who?'

'Mabegzo.'

His grip slackened immediately, and he stared at me with his mouth open.

'She's bluffing!' said the third guy, standing on one side.

One by one, they questioned me about Mabegzo. Where did he live? What did he look like? I answered all their questions confidently, and even gave his real name.

'*Magents, masingaenzi amasimba, yi meidi ka Mabegzo, so waar.* Guys, let's not cause shit, she's Mabegzo's girl for sure.' As they left me they begged me not to tell Mabegzo about this encounter.

I had escaped, but it brought me no relief. Mabegzo was clearly regarded as the big cheese, before whom even these other hardened criminals crumbled in fear and worship. By running off like scared chickens, they had just confirmed Mabegzo's cruelty. From then on I used Mabegzo's reputation to ward off other dangerous boys, but I was still afraid, certain that it was only a matter of time before he showed his true colours and raped or killed me.

Three or four days a week I would find Mabegzo waiting for me at the corner after school. Each time he took my school bag and walked me home. Gradually I grew more at ease with him. He asked endlessly about my late father, and I would grow animated as I described Papa and related stories about him. It meant so much to be able to talk about my lost Papa with someone, and Mabegzo could never hear enough. He was fascinated when I told him how Papa had covered our school books, packed our lunchboxes and cooked for us when my mom was asleep after night duty.

'Did your father really love you that much?' he would ask. Yes, I would say, he did, and more.

'*Eish*,' he would say. '*Ba go cowarthile*. By killing him, they really deprived you.'

'And you?' I once asked. 'What's your father like?'

He said his father had died before he was born.

'Do you also miss your father?'

'*Ja*. I'll see you tomorrow.' He always became evasive when I asked about his family.

The only time we spoke about me rather than my father was because I was crying from stomach cramps. It was the second day of my first period, and I hadn't told my mother. I didn't yet understand what was happening. The sudden flow of blood had badly frightened me. I thought I was bleeding because I'd done something wrong.

'Has someone hurt you?'

'No. I'm bleeding.'

'Where?'

I cried even harder.

'Oh, okay, okay. *Ke dintho tsa dimeidi. Eintlik, o na le dijara tse kae vele, wena*? It's a woman's thing. How old are you?'

'Eleven,' I said, struggling to speak.

'*Tjo, tjo, tjo. U ncosi*. You're a baby. And you are bleeding already?'

I sobbed even more.

'Okay, okay, Lala, *o se ke wa lla*, don't cry. Don't worry about it.'

He really wasn't helping. How could I not worry about it? It was a catastrophe, and I didn't know what had brought it on.

'My stomach is also sore.'

'*Haai bo! O mit*? Are you pregnant?'

'Is that why I'm bleeding?'

'No, no, no.'

'*Sheba*. Look. From now on you must never, never let any boy touch you or you'll get pregnant.'

I sobbed even harder, thinking that he'd already held my hand and also kissed me on that first day. Did that have something to do with my bleeding? I didn't know what had caused this crisis. Had I done something wrong? What?

Mabegzo grabbed me by the shoulders and shook me. 'Do you understand what I'm saying? Don't let any boy take your clothes off. Don't lie with any boy now that you're bleeding. Otherwise you'll have a baby.'

'I don't want a baby, I don't want it.'

'Good girl. Now you must be careful of boys.'

I had heard that girls bled when they did naughty things with boys. I knew what the naughty thing was, but I hadn't been naked with Mabegzo, and he didn't lie on top of me. So why was I bleeding?

'You must go talk to your mother.'

'About what?'

'About the bleeding. She'll know what to do.'

I wasn't sure about that. My mother hardly spoke these days, and I didn't want to worry her. I wasn't sure if she'd give me a hiding for this whole mess. I knew I'd brought it upon myself, even though I wasn't sure how.

'Do you have tissues?'

'No.'

'Come.' He led me to the Spar shop behind our school and told me to wait outside. Then he came out with a package wrapped in paper inside a plastic bag. We reached my street and he handed me the package. When I locked myself in the bedroom and opened the package, I got such a shock I threw it on the floor and screamed. As a little girl I'd heard that women used these when they'd done naughty things with men. If my mom saw it she'd think I was sleeping with boys. I had to find a way to get rid of it somewhere in the streets.

After a couple of days of trying to hide my bleeding, my cousin Thembi informed my mother. My mother was upset and strongly reprimanded me for not coming to her about it. Then she lectured me about what it meant. As a nurse, she knew all the correct words to describe this milestone, but I was a confused little girl and I needed something warmer and more nurturing. During this awkward lecture, she warned me that sleeping with boys was wrong and caused pregnancy. I certainly had no wish to sleep with a boy, but with Siphiwe still threatening rape I resigned myself to the probability.

One Sunday morning a month later, my second period started as I was leaving for church. The sky was dark and the wind was howling. I should have known it wouldn't be a good day. My stomach was cramping badly, and I didn't yet know that this was normal during a period. Still, there were no exemptions from church. The bleeding made me feel very alone, as none of my friends had started, so this natural process didn't feel normal at all; it isolated me and made me feel my childhood had been snatched away. At eleven, I still wanted to play. And my mother's lecture had instilled even more fear.

On my way home after church that morning, I

encountered Siphiwe again. I didn't notice him at first among the large group of youths playing dice in the street until he abandoned the game and came towards me. This time he had a determined look in his eye. It was about our tenth encounter, but on this gloomy Sunday morning he decided he'd been patient long enough. He'd been nice to me, he said, but now I must go with him. It was time to honour my debt.

I couldn't look at him – not only because I was afraid, but also because of the scabs he always had on his lips. They revolted me.

'Today we're going, you hear me?' He waited. 'I said, today you're coming with me to be my wife!' When I didn't answer, he slapped my face. 'Say "Yes, Siphiwe!"'

I nodded.

'Good. You've given me permission.'

His friends had stopped playing to watch us. '*Yekela umntwana*. Leave the child,' I heard one say.

He grabbed my hand and started pulling me. How was it possible for my life to belong to the thugs who roamed the streets? Coming from a strict but loving home, how had I ended up with no choice but to yield to this scumbag? Remembering suddenly that I had my period, without pausing, I told him so.

He hesitated briefly. 'Show me.'

Now I didn't know what to do. I was shaking so much I couldn't have done anything anyway. Suddenly he yanked my pants down, right there on the street in front of his friends. I heard laughter around me as I stood there exposed, with the winter sun peeking out shyly. Siphiwe pulled the front of my panties down until he saw my sanitary pad. Then he told me to cover myself.

'*Eish!*' he announced loudly to his friends. '*Uyavuza*!

She's leaking!'

They laughed. But my pain was too intense to be able to cry.

'I'm not done with you!' he said, his face contorting as he demonstrated with his fingers. 'Next time I'm going to take you and fuck you!'

With his friends laughing at my humiliation and others just standing there watching, I walked home, shoulders slumped, my heart weeping blood. I imagined his phallus invading me, violating me, destroying me. That morning I knew my luck had finally run out. I should have been crying on that walk home, covering my face from the shame of Siphiwe's deed and threat. But I was too lost, too afraid to even care what people were saying. I felt so many things during that short walk. At first it was just raw fear, but soon it turned to rage.

For the first time since my father's death, I yelled at him, silently but loud enough for him to hear. It was *his* fault that this was happening! He'd never prepared me for this. He'd never told me that boys did this to girls. He'd taught me nothing but love, and I'd thought that was all there was out there. But there was all this, and I didn't know how to deal with it. And now he was dead. How convenient! He should have been here to fight Siphiwe for me.

When I arrived home, my mother was in the kitchen peeling potatoes for our Sunday meal. She was cross that I'd stayed out so long after church was out. I interrupted her – a mortal sin in our home – but I didn't care.

'There's a boy who's treating me badly. He said next time he's going to take me.'

'Do you know where he lives?'

'Yes.'

She switched off the stove, took off her apron and grabbed

her car keys. 'Let's go,' was all she said.

We arrived at the house that I thought was Siphiwe's. It wasn't, but they knew Siphiwe; he was buddies with their youngest son. The mother of the house told us we were very lucky we'd come to the wrong house.

'There's no order at Siphiwe's house,' she said. 'His mother drinks, his uncles drink and nobody disciplines the children. In fact, they would have attacked you.'

Her eldest son, Vusi, told us not to worry, he'd fetch Siphiwe and bring him to my mom.

I sat there quietly while the adults lamented the wild behaviour of young boys and men. Then Vusi and Siphiwe walked in. I couldn't believe my eyes. My tormentor was nervously biting his nails. He looked frightened.

My mother looked him in the eye. 'What do you want from my child?'

He didn't answer.

'I'm talking to you. Answer me.'

'*Be ngi dlala naye.* I was just playing with her.'

'Is that how you play with girls? By threatening them? You're too old to even talk to my daughter. If you say one more word to her, I will destroy you.' My mother was very calm and measured, but occasionally, much to everyone's surprise, she could adopt a frightening, steely resolve. Everything about her voice and demeanour left us in no doubt that she meant what she said. 'Do you hear me?'

'*Yebo.* Yes.'

Just for good measure, Vusi added, 'You'll get hurt if you don't stop it.'

Siphiwe never came near me again. The next time we met in the streets I looked pointedly at him, my confidence back. He couldn't look me in the eye.

Two weeks later, as Mabegzo walked me home, carrying

my bag as always, we passed Siphiwe walking in the opposite direction. They greeted each other with familiarity and camaraderie. It hurt me deeply to discover that Mabegzo knew such a lowlife. He had no business greeting this unsavoury character, and I told him as much.

He listened quietly while I related all the abuse and bullying Siphiwe had subjected me to. When I told him about his threats to rape me, and pulling my pants down in public, he stopped and stared at me. His face reflected shock and disappointment. I was always on the lookout for signs that Mabegzo was a decent person, and that everything people said about him was fiction, so it pleased me that he seemed so appalled at such cruelty.

'Why didn't you tell me, Lala?' he asked.

'What for?'

'I could have helped you.'

'It doesn't matter now. My mom sorted him out.'

'It does matter.'

The following Monday, our headmistress announced during assembly that we were each to bring ten cents the next day to donate to the family of one of our pupils, whose elder brother had died. After school, the choir and all class captains had to visit the bereaved family for prayers. As a choir member and class captain, I was among the entourage.

Only when we arrived at Siphiwe's rundown home did I realise that the deceased was Siphiwe. I broke out in a sweat, remembering that I'd told Mabegzo about him just the other day. And now he was dead. I was asked to lead the group in prayer, and as I did, questions were whirling through my mind. I was in great discomfort standing in the dark bedroom before Siphiwe's relatives, offering condolences for someone I had loathed. But I took no pleasure in his death, and I had certainly never wanted him to die. Ever since he'd withered under my mother's glare he had stopped being a threat to me – he just became a nobody, a coward who got his kicks from terrorising others. But I kept thinking of Mabegzo's words. 'It does matter.' Could he…? Of course not.

After prayers, I went around to Vusi's house, which I had once mistaken for Siphiwe's house. I wanted to know how Siphiwe had died. I remembered that Vusi had warned him about his behaviour.

Vusi was out on the pavement with a group of guys. Before I could even broach the subject, he said, '*Uzwile ngaleya nja*? Did you hear about that dog?'

'*Ja.*'

'*Bamqumile* – they slaughtered him on Saturday.' For a while they spoke among themselves, almost forgetting I was there. One animated guy claimed to have seen it all, and demonstrated how 'they' had fetched Siphiwe from his house around midday.

'No, no,' interjected another. 'It was around two pm.'

'And because Siphiwe knew them, he went with them…'

'I still don't understand why Siphiwe just went with them. They weren't his friends. Those guys are hard core.'

'No, my brother, when death comes knocking, *umuntu u ba dom*; you become stupid.'

They all pointed to different spots where Siphiwe was murdered, but it seemed he'd been stabbed in broad daylight not far from his home. His killers had apparently just walked away calmly. They were seen and known by some.

'Who did it?' I asked.

'No, *sisi, amagama a bantu a wa shiwo*. We don't name names.'

I walked away more unsettled than when I'd arrived. The sick feeling in the pit of my stomach wouldn't go away.

It was much later than usual when I finally headed home, and I was glad Mabegzo wasn't at the corner. I had too much to process. Although we often stopped chatting and walked together in comfortable silence, his personality was so magnetic that I couldn't have gathered my thoughts with him next to me that day.

But the next day I was happy to see Mabegzo waiting as usual. It was the proof I needed that he had nothing to hide, and it calmed my anxiety. If he had just committed murder, he'd be on the run now.

'You alright?' he asked.

'*Ja*, I'm alright. Why do you ask?'

'*Okare o bang; o se ka wara*. You seem afraid. Don't worry.'

'Worry about what?'

'Anything. Everything.'

I looked for any sign that he knew about Siphiwe's death. If he'd killed someone he would surely be jittery, but he didn't look in any way nervous or uncomfortable.

After Siphiwe's funeral, his little brother returned to school. I recognised him now from my visit to his home to offer condolences. I walked up to him on many occasions, tempted to ask who had killed his brother. He was only about nine, but children overheard a lot because adults always shared secrets too loudly. Yet I never managed to get the question out. Perhaps I was afraid of the answer. What would I do if the truth shattered my world? Deep down I suspected something because of the timing of Siphiwe's death. But I walked away from his brother each time without asking. I was caught up in a never-ending cycle of uncertainty with Mabegzo, trying to reconcile the conflicting signals to work out if he was good or bad. Who was he? And what was he doing in my life?

In one of our conversations, Mabegzo told me he was going to visit his traditional healer for cleansing.

'Why do you need cleansing?'

'To ward off the bad luck I was born with.'

I told him I thought this was nonsense; by now I'd grown confident enough to challenge him.

'You'll never understand,' he told me.

I invited him to church with me and told him all about confession and speaking to the priest, who was a representative of Jesus on earth, and would absolve him of his sins and bad luck.

'I have no sins.'

'Everyone has sins. Come to church with me.'

'You don't understand. I need to cleanse myself, and only my traditional healer can do it.'

'But if he's so good, why do you still have bad luck?'

He seemed to consider my question for a moment. 'You don't understand,' was all he said.

'*Ke eng, o bolaile motho gape*? What is it,' I asked. 'Did you kill someone? People say that's what you do.' I saw a flash of fire in his eye as he clenched his jaw. I pulled away from him.

'Why *o nketsa so*? Why are you doing this to me?' he asked, reaching for my hand again.

I pulled back again. 'You're scaring me,' I said.

'Am I hurting your feelings, Lala?'

'*Ja.*'

'You think I like doing that?'

'I don't know.'

'You should know, you should know. By now you should know.' He walked away.

Chapter 4

CHANGES WERE ON THE cards for our family as 1990 approached. My mother was making plans to move us to better schools in the suburbs. Private education was very expensive, but teachers had advised my mom to find me a better school. My teacher, Mistress Angela, had never said so, but I knew I was her favourite student. I did my work on time and got good marks, and she always held me up as an example to the others, which was a burden, as students didn't like those who were favoured by teachers. But when our reports were handed out, I loved the moment when the teacher called out my name and my position in class. I was usually first, and it made me happy.

Even though all Catholic schools were private, and ours

was one of the best schools in Soweto, it certainly didn't have the same resources as the multiracial private schools in the northern suburbs. Our school offered little help for those with learning difficulties, and there were some in our class who really struggled. One of them was Moses, the second-oldest person at our school. Popularly known as TaMoss, he was a pimply-faced bully who teased others mercilessly, and I didn't like him much. He had a deep voice and a penis that fascinated the eleven-year-old boys in our class. When the teacher was out, he'd call them all over and show it off to them, and they'd applaud and call him the boss. One boy stared adoringly at TaMoss's penis, exclaiming, '*Tjo, tjo, o champ, TaMoss!* You're the champion!' Moses loved it.

As class captain, I was expected to report anyone who was noisy or disruptive when the teacher was out of the classroom. While I loved the role of disciplinarian, I took no pleasure in ratting on my classmates. So I'd often write down their names just to keep them well-behaved, but when it came to handing over the list, I'd claim that no one had spoken while she was out. But on one occasion, Moses's penis caused such a commotion that I didn't even notice our teacher walking in.

'Sit down!' She turned to me. 'Why do you let them make such a racket? What's going on?' All eyes were on me, nervously waiting for me to say what had happened. 'Where are the names?' she demanded. 'Don't tell me no one was talking. I heard the noise from the staff room.'

I could see the younger boys were nervous, but you could never tell with Moses, who just stood there with downcast eyes. 'It's the boys,' I said calmly. 'They, they were laughing at Moses because he fell.'

Our teacher gave us a lecture about why it was wrong to laugh when someone got hurt. Then she turned on Moses.

'*Le wena o dom, ntate o mo kana, a ba tlo wa feela.* You're stupid, an old man like you just falling like that.'

While Moses's penis earned him respect, nobody dared tease him when he struggled to read out loud. Even though he couldn't get past the first word in a sentence, the teachers would pick him to read out loud. Whether it was Sesotho, English or Afrikaans, he just couldn't do it. But instead of helping him out or letting him stop, the teacher in charge would sit silently, waiting until he finished the prescribed paragraph. It was agonising and humiliating, because poor Moses couldn't read a single word properly. 'Mo... mo... mo... s... h...' He would struggle on for thirty minutes or so, and the entire lesson would be lost. He clearly had a serious problem – he couldn't even write his name properly – yet nobody ever bothered to get him the care he needed. Finally during one lesson the teacher declared that he was too much trouble, and ordered him to go to the Reform class. Moses slapped her and stormed out, and we never saw him again.

In addition to a change of school, my mother was planning a move to a better suburb on the East Rand. Although her main motivation was for us to grow up in a safer community with better role models, I suspect she also wanted to get away from our house. It had too many memories of Papa, of the four of us as a family. Every corner of our small house still carried Papa's presence; he had grown up here after all. And because he had died in mysterious circumstances we had many unanswered questions, and my mom didn't want to live her life looking at everyone with suspicion. We had also never had a break-in until Papa died, but in the year of his death we had several. Once my mother had built the back rooms and let them out to tenants, the break-ins seemed to stop, but we still felt more vulnerable and exposed than before. A clean start was the answer, she decided.

I was excited about our pending move. After living in a house with only one bedroom and no bathroom, I looked forward to each of us having our own bedroom. My mother would even have a private en suite, and our car would have a garage!

I wasn't worried about leaving my friends behind because I'd still see many of them at church. And I looked forward to making new ones. But Mabegzo? The thought of not seeing him again made me profoundly sad. Although I didn't quite understand what was happening between us, I knew it was special. He was nourishing my soul in a way no one else at that time seemed able to.

I told him our plans to move to a new school and a new suburb.

'So *wa ntatlha*. You're abandoning me,' he said, with such trepidation that I squeezed his hand. I felt at that moment that he needed me. He looked into my eyes and returned my squeeze. '*Mara wena, Lala*! Oh, you!' he said.

One day Mabegzo took me to visit a friend of his, Katlego. When we arrived at his house, Katlego came out onto the stoep.

'Here's Momo,' he said. 'Lala, this is Katlego. He's okay, but he has absolutely no football talent. We lost all our games because of him.' We all laughed, but Mabegzo wasn't done teasing. 'He was the butt of the boys' jokes, and no one wanted him on the team when we were playing against another street.'

'*Tjo, jaja e. O zama go chaza cheri ya hao ka nna!* C'mon, man. Stop trying to impress your cheri!'

'She's not my cheri!' Mabegzo countered sharply. 'She's not that kind of girl.'

Katlego looked confused, but decided to leave it.

Mabegzo turned to me again. 'One day, one of the boys

on the team punched Katlego for playing like a cow.'

'Yes, and Mabegzo got into such a rage that even I had to try to calm him down,' Katlego chuckled. 'All our games ended up as boxing matches because this one liked to fight.'

'Don't lie; you also liked to punch people. Sometimes I was just a spectator and I only jumped in when you were losing the fight.'

'Which I never did, of course!'

They laughed as they sat together reminiscing, and I could see their genuine love for each other. It confused me even further. Why did all the street gossip about Mabegzo never mention this side of him? Where did the stories about all his crimes come from? Were they just urban legends? Oblivious to my silent musings, they went on recalling their street fights, and how they would degenerate into chaos as each boy punched and kicked whoever was closest.

'In the mayhem, sometimes our punches landed in a team mate's face. Then he'd hit whoever he could, sometimes even the one he'd joined the fight to protect!'

'*Ja*, but I was always careful not to hit you, Katlego, and you also looked out for me. But when it came to everyone else, we just did what we could with our fists, knees and feet.'

We were laughing so hard that a woman shouted from inside the house, 'Hey! You're making a racket! Behave yourselves, this isn't a shebeen!'

We must have soon grown noisy again because suddenly Katlego's mom bolted out onto the stoep and flung a bucket of water over us. '*Voetsek*! Go away, I told you to stop making a noise!'

Katlego darted away, but I was too stunned to move. Mabegzo stood up, dripping wet and glared down at her, daring her to make the next move. 'If you weren't my buddy's mother, I'd show you a ghost,' he growled.

'You bastard!' Katlego's mom screamed, going totally berserk. 'I told you never to come back here, you cursed child! You're so selfish, you even got your mother raped so you could be born and cause shit on earth!'

Mabegzo slapped her hard across the face. But she was a big woman, and she wasn't prepared to take this. The two of them wrestled each other to the ground. Eventually she ended up on her back with Mabegzo sitting on her ample bosom, a tight grip around her neck. Her eyes were literally popping as she struggled to breathe.

'Stop, stop!' I cried. 'Stop it!'

But Mabegzo was beyond hearing. He was possessed, and spat at her as he tightened his grip.

Suddenly a brick landed on Mabegzo's head, and Katlego took the moment to punch Mabegzo in the face.

'*Ke mme wa ka enwa*! That's my mother!' he yelled. 'I won't allow this!'

Mabegzo froze, and Katlego and his mother attacked him together. Katlego was crying, I was crying, his mother was screaming obscenities and Mabegzo was on his knees, head in his hands, blood dripping from his head onto the floor.

'*Vayang*. Just go,' Katlego said quietly. 'You can rape and kill whoever you want, but not my mother.'

We left.

A heavy, uncomfortable silence sat between Mabegzo and me as we walked away. We didn't always talk when we walked together, but it had always seemed okay. Not this time. I'd learnt to read him by then, and I knew he was humiliated. He didn't have to say a word. His shoulders were slumped and his eyes had the most desolate, distant look. He must have been swallowing hard; I could see his Adam's apple going up and down. I reached out for his hand, but he pulled away.

He didn't wait for me at the corner for more than a week after that incident. It made me sad – and scared. I shouldn't have tried to hold his hand. He hated me now. He would never speak to me again. I thought about him a lot. I replayed the episode at Katlego's house, trying to figure out how I had offended Mabegzo. And Katlego's words rang in my ears. 'You can rape and kill whoever you want...' Katlego had known Mabegzo all his life. The chattering masses were easy to dismiss, but Katlego's words had shocked me. He must be a rapist. He must be a killer. Yet I loved him.

Suddenly, the days stretching in front of me felt dull and lonely. There was nothing left to look forward to. The walk home from school was a blur. I tried hard to concentrate on the conversations with my giggly friends, but I was always restless. My eyes kept wandering, searching for Mabegzo.

One day, there he was again, waiting and whistling. I ran towards him.

'*Haai, wena, tlogela go tsamaya le bo abuti.* Stop chasing after grown men,' someone admonished me. I was used to the disapproval of my schoolmates and others around us by now. Some threatened to tell my mom, and I knew that sooner or later someone would. That's how it was then.

'*O tswa kae?* Where have you been?' I asked him.

'Around.'

'Why haven't you been waiting for me?'

'I had some business to do.'

This time he walked me all the way to my house, talking about everything except what mattered. I had so many questions for him. I'd seen how he could turn from sweetness to violence in a split second. Although I felt very safe in his presence – perhaps the safest I'd felt in a long time – I didn't want to press his buttons and lose the affection he was showing me. Yet, I had to know.

When we reached the gate, I opened it and invited him inside, without pausing to consider the risks. I just wanted to be in his presence. He hesitated. 'Lala, your mother won't like me being here.'

'She's not here.'

'And your brother?

'Not here.'

'I don't want you to get into trouble. *Phela*, everyone hates me.'

'I don't.'

Our gate was very noisy and there was no way anyone could come in without my knowing. We hid behind the back rooms and sat on the grass. Mabegzo seemed very nervous, and suddenly I wasn't sure of myself. My heart felt funny and I was suddenly hot. We'd never actually been alone together. He stroked my cheek, and I stroked his. He was breathing very heavily and his eyes were closed. I studied his face as I stroked his hand. How could this hand have held guns and knives? It wasn't possible.

Letting out a heavy sigh, he declared, 'If you weren't my little sister, I'd marry you.'

'Why are people frightened of you?'

'*Ke* bad luck.'

'Where does your bad luck come from?'

Suddenly, for the first time, he launched into the story of his life. Life had singled him out for pain and suffering, he said, and he told me again how he envied my relationship with my late father.

'I wish he was also my father.'

'He is. If I'm your sister, then he's your father.'

Mabegzo said his life had been fine until the adults destroyed it. 'My grandmother always treated me like her son. But every time I called her Mama, my grandfather would shout, "She's not your mother!" So I asked, "*Mama ka ke mang?* Who's my mother, then?"' Nobody would answer. After a while, my grandmother would say, "You're God's child. God gave you to us." But when I was out playing in the streets, the other children said, "*Bo papa ba hao ba mo reipile and e be o a tswalwa.* Your fathers raped your mother and you were born."'

Mabegzo had always avoided telling me anything about his family before. Now he seemed in a rush to share his story, as if it was a cleansing, an unburdening of his soul.

He had always sensed a certain distance and disconnect from his family, he told me. Although they were mostly civil to him, they weren't loving or affectionate. Even his little cousins weren't keen to share their toys with him, and would walk off saying, 'My mommy said I mustn't play with you.' His grandmother was always trying to make things better for him, and he loved her for it, although even she couldn't save him from the world. But his grandfather never spoke to him directly.

'Not even to send you to the shops or ask you to make him tea?' I asked, incredulous.

'Never. He still doesn't talk to me or even say my name. I'm just "the boy". "Tell the boy to polish my shoes." "Tell the boy to post this letter for me."'

'Even when you're standing next to him?'

'Even when I'm standing next to him. Sometimes I'd come home from school and try to talk to him about what happened at school. He'd nod but never say a word to me.'

'He's a horrible man,' I said, still holding his hand in mine.

Mabegzo seemed unperturbed. 'I think he's strange, but I'm not offended, because he isn't mean or nasty to me. He's never shouted or punished me; he just doesn't speak to me. But my uncle Tshepo is nice.'

I was relieved to hear that someone else was nice to Mabegzo.

In the nine days that Mabegzo hadn't fetched me from school, he said, he'd visited his sangoma for cleansing after the fight with Katlego's mother. His sangoma had advised him to stay away from everyone until the darkness dissipated. He was badly hurt by the fallout with Katlego, but unrepentant about attacking his mother.

'I grew up with these fat women pointing their dirty hands at me, whispering, "That's the one," loud enough for me to hear.'

'*Ba phapha*. You mustn't mind them.'

'Even when I was minding my own business, they were always talking about me. When I was ten I got up the courage to ask my grandmother why all the mothers in the street and at church pointed at me. I'd overheard some of the things they said about me.

'"Tell the boy," my grandfather said. "Tell him now." But my grandmother would only say I was a child of God. "So if God is my mother, who is my father?" I asked her. "Your father is God. He's everyone's father." "So God got raped and I was born?" I didn't know what rape was then, only that it was something bad.'

He'd just said rape was bad! I was still constantly trying to make sense of all the contradictions he represented. How could he be a bully, a murderer and a rapist and yet find these acts abhorrent? I spent endless hours wrestling with such questions about this man that I loved, who was my brother in every possible way.

'When my grandmother's daughter Greta got married, I was eleven. Lots of relatives came from Lesotho and stayed at our home in Soweto, where a big celebration was held. One was called Imelda, a name I often heard when women were pointing at me. I knew she was a relative, and some people at the wedding pointed at me and said, "*Ke wa Imelda*. He's Imelda's." I decided she was my sister. My grandmother's sister from Lesotho, Mme Moipone, kept remarking on how good I'd been as a baby and that I never woke them at night. She asked when I would come to Lesotho to visit her again. But I didn't remember being in Lesotho.

'Mme Moipone used to smile at me and kiss me. It was nice. I wished she was my mother. She remarked on how I'd grown, and she said she hoped I'd be a good boy and well mannered, just like my mother. "Are you my mother?" I asked her. "Please be my mother." Some adults heard me and laughed. But my grandmother told me to stop asking so many questions, and Imelda left the room.'

Mabegzo started to cry as he poured his heart out. And I knew better than to tell him to stop. When Papa died, all everyone seemed to say to me was, 'Don't cry'. When I stopped crying my unshed tears must have gone to my heart, because it was always sore after that. So I let Mabegzo cry. I couldn't bear him to have a heart as sore as mine.

'The wedding was nice and I was dancing with everybody. People at the wedding were admiring Imelda's little girls, and someone said they looked like their brother. I was asked if I was happy to see my sisters. I asked Imelda if she was my sister and she just walked away. I'd upset her. Everyone was happy except Imelda. She sat alone and hardly spoke to anyone. The only time she seemed happy was when she was playing and talking to her little girls. So I went to say sorry to her for making her upset earlier. And she smiled at me.'

'If Imelda smiled at you,' I told him, 'it means she wasn't upset with you.'

'You know what she did next? She kissed me on the mouth! I wanted to ask her if she was my mother, but I was too afraid. I thought it would upset her – and my grandmother. I remember feeling everyone's eyes on me and Imelda. As if they wanted to see how we interacted.

'The weekend of the wedding was full of activity and jubilation. There were so many adults in the house and they kept saying strange things and asking me odd questions. "Are you happy to see your mother after such a long time?" "What did your mother bring you from Lesotho?" "You look so much like Imelda." What haunted me most were the words of an elderly neighbour. She was always kind to me so I knew she didn't mean any harm. She said, "I wonder what those dogs who raped your mother have to say now. Look at Imelda, she's still beautiful and she's found a good husband. You'll grow up and take care of your mother, won't you, big boy?"

'Then when I was fifteen Mme Moipone died. There was a debate about whether I should go to the funeral or not. In the end, they left me behind, even though I cried and begged. I watched my whole family leave for Lesotho early on a Tuesday for the funeral that Saturday. I was miserable. I asked Katlego to sleep over to keep me company, but his family refused. So I spent the night alone. The next day I was amazed when my uncle Tshepo walked in the door. "*Hawu*," I said. "You're back from the funeral so quickly?" But he said, "No, pack your bags. You're coming to Lesotho." I was elated. I forgot that I wasn't supposed to be happy about a funeral.

'At the funeral Imelda cried a lot, and I felt protective towards her. But after the burial, she was always surrounded by people, and I never had a moment alone with her. Even the Sunday after the funeral was busy. Us boys had to help carry the heavy pots so the mothers could wash them. There was lots of cleaning up to do, and we had to fetch wood for the fire and slaughter the remaining lamb for lunch.

'We also had to be up at the crack of dawn for a cleansing ritual. Mme Moipone had no children of her own, and so only her siblings could undergo the cleansing. When Imelda insisted on being cleansed, my grandmother got upset and refused to let her. But Imelda went hysterical. She kept saying, "*Mme Moipone e ne e le mme, e ne e le mme!* She was my mother, she was my mother." Imelda's husband tried to calm her, but something was raging inside her. My grandfather stayed out of it; he hardly spoke to her anyway. In the end, she got her way. An elderly uncle finally declared that Imelda could be cleansed because she'd lived with Mme Moipone as a daughter and taken care of her when she was ill. But my grandmother insisted it wasn't right. She was so offended that she decided to return to Soweto with the rest of the family that same afternoon.

'I had a lot of questions but I didn't want to set off another explosion. Imelda was prickly and fed up, and my grandmother wasn't talking to anyone, so I kept quiet. While we were chopping the wood, Imelda's husband asked me about school and about Soweto. I was awkward around him. I didn't know what to say. "Soweto sounds like a bad place," he said to me. "You must come and live here." I wasn't sure what he meant. "Live where?" I asked him. "Here in Lesotho," he said. I asked if he meant with Imelda, but before he got the chance to answer, someone reprimanded me. "Don't call adults by their first name!" And he never said any more to me.

'Then just before we left, Imelda came and kissed me on the lips. She told me, "I'll send for you." My grandmother won't be happy, I told her. "She's not your mother," she said.

79

"You don't have to make her happy. It's *me* who carried you in my stomach for nine months. It's *me* who gave birth to you, and it's *me* who fed you from my breast. She took you without asking me. She's not your mother, do you hear? Your mother is *me*, Imelda."

'That was the best moment of my life. *Ke ne ke thabile blind*, I was so happy on our way back to Soweto.'

He looked down. 'It didn't last. I waited, but she never sent for me.' Mabegzo started crying again. We were both crying now, and holding hands.

'After several months I asked my grandmother if I could go back to Lesotho. But she said, "If Imelda wants you, she knows where to find you. She must come and fetch you." I begged her for the money to go to Lesotho. She just said, "*Ngwanake*, I don't have any." Nobody had money, not my grandmother, my uncles, my aunt, no one. That's because bad luck follows me. So I couldn't go to Imelda. And she didn't come looking for me. I think she hates me.'

'She doesn't hate you.'

'Everyone hates me.'

'That's not true. Your gran loves you. Tshepo loves you. I love you.' But he wasn't listening.

'I'll only rest when I've killed those dogs who raped Imelda. Maybe she'll start to like me if I destroy the people who destroyed her.'

It wasn't possible to take his threat literally, because in that moment he seemed like just a little boy, wanting to protect his mother and punish those who had harmed her.

Chapter 5

ONE SATURDAY AFTERNOON, I was on my way home from the church youth meeting when I saw Mabegzo. He had his back to me and didn't see me approach. I saw him twist a girl's arm and then slap her across the face.

'*Mabegzo, o etsang!?* What are you doing!?'

He froze, and the girl took flight.

'*O etsa eng?*'

'I'm sorry.'

I stormed off and ignored him as he called out my name. He ran after me and tried to speak to me as I made my way home. He remained at my side even though I maintained a stony silence. We reached the corner of my street and he said goodbye, promising to wait for me at our corner on Monday.

'Don't wait for me. You're a rapist and you hit girls! I saw you.'

He did wait for me. And when he smiled, I was conflicted again. He seemed unsure of himself. Often he would walk confidently towards me as I approached the corner. This time, he remained rooted to the spot, hesitating, waiting for me to invite him back into my life. His pleading eyes found something deep inside my soul, and without pausing to think, I said, 'Why are you standing there? Let's go.'

As we walked, I said, 'Were you going to rape that girl?'

'She wanted me.'

'How could she want you? She was crying, stupid.'

Anger flashed in his eyes; the word stupid had stung. He'd heard it so many times before.

'If you call me stupid again I won't come and wait for you.'

'I don't care. These aren't your streets; I know how to get to my house.'

'Why o *nkaraba masepa* today?' Why are you giving me such shit today?

'It's you who's starting with me.'

'So you want me to go now?'

'If you're going to make girls cry, then yes. I don't want you anymore.'

'Okay, *askies* Lala, I won't do it again.'

'You promise?'

He made the sign of the cross and promised.

'Why don't you go to school?'

'I finished school long ago.'

'Why don't you go to church?'

'I don't like church.'

'Church is good. It's better than a sangoma.'

'Okay.'

'Come to church with me this Sunday.'

'You're crazy. Me? Church? *O se ka tlo bapala.* Stop fooling.'

'I want you to come to church with me. Maybe they'll teach us to pray like my mother. She prays so beautifully.' He seemed interested in my mother, so I carried on. 'My mother knows everything, but I think her heart is very sore. Like yours and mine.'

'My heart's never sore,' he said defensively. 'How does your mother pray?'

I tried to describe something of the intensity and beauty of her faith and passion as she begged God for help when she thought no one was listening.

I wanted Mabegzo to join me, so we could pray for my mom together. And it seemed that telling him about my mother's prayers had worked because the next Sunday he was waiting at the corner of the street that led to my church.

'*Ke neng ke eme.* I've been waiting since seven. I thought you'd never come.'

'But church starts at eight forty-five.'

'*Askies.* Let's go.'

Suddenly I was nervous. My mother attended the seven o'clock service, and I often passed her and other relatives on my way in to church. I'd forgotten who Mabegzo was. People in this area knew him. This was also Siphiwe's street, and I still wasn't sure if Mabegzo had been involved in his death. I could get into a whole lot of trouble. I was about to tell him not to come anymore, but here he was, chattering non-stop, a sign that he was happy. He'd waited for me for nearly two hours, and what if this was his opportunity to mend his ways? My heart was beating faster and faster as the enormity of Mabegzo's presence in my life hit me. We were a few hundred metres from the church and there were many people walking to the same destination; we would soon meet the others coming from the early service.

And then he did it again; he made everything alright, and I loved him for it.

'How many entrances does your church have?'

'Three.'

'Okay. Let's use different entrances so that people don't talk, and after church, don't come to me. I'll see you another time.'

'But how will I know if you liked the service?'

'*Haai*, you ask too many questions. People will see us. See you later.'

I was relieved, but also disappointed. I wanted to sit with him and watch him be renewed by the prayers and hymns, but being apart was the only way to do it. The service started as usual, but it was all a blur. I kept looking out for Mabegzo, trying to read his face. We weren't sitting far from each other, and I really wanted him to like it.

But it was such a stupid idea of mine. During the singing of the Apostle's Creed, three elders and a senior member of the youth choir walked up to him. I don't know what they said to him, but he got up and walked out. Mme Sejeke, a prominent member of the St Anne's Women's Movement, spat on the floor as he passed and hissed, '*Jou vuilpop!* You dirty thing!' So much for the forgiveness of sin in the Apostle's Creed, and the pledge of the St Anne's Movement to emulate Anne, the Virgin Mary's mother. At that moment Mme Sejeke, like all the rest, had no thoughts of forgiveness for Mabegzo. For him they saw no redemption.

When church ended that Sunday, the topic on everyone's lips was how a cold-hearted murderer had dared to enter the house of God. But wasn't that exactly what God wanted – for sinners to come to him? Not according to my fellow parishioners; God wanted all the sinners except those like Mabegzo.

In typical township fashion, the story of Mabegzo's visit grew increasingly colourful. Some said he'd escaped from the police who were chasing him that morning. '*O ne, a nagana gore. O tla ipata mo ntlong ya Modimo.* No way, over my dead body! He thought he could hide in the house of the Lord!' Others added that the devil had brought Mabegzo to church, but Jesus loved us so much that he gave angels and soldiers to the people of our congregation to fight this battle.

Mme Sejeke, who had called Mabegzo a *vuilpop*, would for years regale her audience with tales of her bravery; she had stared down a cold-blooded murderer and ordered him out of the church. '*Waitse, a ke tsebe hore sebete se se kalo ke ne ke se nka kae.* I don't know what gave me the guts to face him.'

'It was the Holy Spirit,' others would say. 'It was the cross you wear around your neck. *Ka sefapano re tla fenya.* With this cross, we're triumphant.'

She would nod piously and add, '*Ke ne ke utlwa mollo o tuka mo pelong ya ka.* I felt a fire in my heart and I knew the Lord was calling me to save his people.' During prayers, when the service was open for anyone to pray, Mme Sejeke would go to the altar and pray for evil spirits to leave the church. For years after Mabegzo had died, she would still end her prayer with 'and I thank you Lord for giving me the power to face your enemy and defeat him.'

I saw Mabegzo three days after that church incident. I was dreading it. I felt terrible for exposing him to so much hurt and ridicule. Now he'd never trust me again. He had been rejected so many times in his life, and I couldn't bear to expose him to more hurt than his heart could handle.

I was ashamed that the people of my church had behaved so appallingly towards him. So I was anxious and ready to apologise when I saw him.

'Hello, Lala.' He seemed cheerful.

'Hello.'

'*O hantle*? Are you okay?'

'*Ja, wena*?'

'*Ke* grand. Do you think Paul Ndlovu is a ghost or that he's not dead at all?'

'What?'

'Some people have just seen Paul Ndlovu wearing yellow jeans, and they started following him, but he disappeared.'

Stories about Paul Ndlovu's ghost refused to die. Ndlovu was one of the leading black musicians of his time, and he became even more special because he sang in Xitsonga, his native language. The chorus of his hit love-song to a woman called Tsakane went, '*Ndi to famba moyeni, Tsakane*. I'll walk on air.' When he died in a car accident shortly after releasing this song, many took these words as a prophecy that he'd walk the streets for eternity. Even radio talk-shows had long debates about these words and whether sightings of Paul were real or not.

As children, virtually every weekend we'd be in the middle of an exuberant game of hide-and-seek or *dibeke* when an agitated group with a huge following would appear, accompanying someone who claimed to have seen Paul Ndlovu. This caused much fanfare and excitement. Our game would stop and more people would join the mob, walking to goodness knows where, hoping to spot Paul again. Then it would quieten down for a few weeks until someone else claimed to have had this epiphany, and so the madness would begin again.

'Did you see him?'

'No, but I want to.'

'Why?'

'I want to know how he did it.'

'Did what?'

'Rose from the dead. That's power. To die and rise again, that's power.'

'Jesus died and rose again.'

'*Ja*, but he died again, because nobody has seen him since. But Paul is here.'

'Where?'

'*Mo kase*, here in Orlando. I want to touch him.'

I'd never seen Mabegzo so restless and excited. He really believed this Paul Ndlovu rubbish.

'Okay, so you don't want to walk with me today? You want to go to a ghost?'

'What if this is my only chance? What if I miss my chance to become strong like him?'

'You want to rise again when you die?'

'I never ever want to die.'

'Okay, go.'

'*O nkwatetse*? Are you cross with me?'

'*Vele*. Obviously.'

'Okay, I'll come and wait for you tomorrow. Today I want to see Paul.'

When Mabegzo arrived the next day, he immediately apologised for having abandoned me the previous day.

'So, did you find Paul?'

'No, but I will. I know I'll see him and talk to him.'

We hadn't walked far when he said he had to leave me to go and fetch his things.

'What things?'

'Nothing.'

'So why do you need to fetch them?'

He shrugged.

'Okay, then fetch your things. I'll come with you.'

'*Haai, wena!* You're crazy. My grandfather won't like that. He doesn't want to see me anymore.'

'Why not?'

'*Haai*, Lala, you ask too many questions. He just kicked me out.'

'What? Why would he kick you out?'

'He's crazy.'

I kept asking why his grandfather had kicked him out, but he would only repeat that he was crazy.

'So where do you live now?' He didn't answer.

'I'm talking to you!'

'I live here, in Orlando East.'

'But where?' He didn't answer.

'Have you eaten?'

'I'm fine.'

'Have you eaten?'

'Not today, no.'

He was reticent, and seemed ashamed of his circumstances. My brother wouldn't be home for another two hours at least, but my mom could drop in at any time. By now she was a medical rep for Adcock Ingram, a big pharmaceutical company, and she called on doctors and pharmacists in various townships in the province. If she was doing her rounds in Soweto today, she could easily pop home for tea. So inviting Mabegzo to my house for a meal was risky, but I felt I had to.

My other worry as we walked home was the embarrassing state of our kitchen chairs; they were torn and worn out. I also prayed that our dog, Topsy, hadn't messed on the carpet. He knew the rules, yet he would often just deposit the day's innings on the carpet. Even more annoying was that he couldn't stand the smell of his own poo, so he would quietly go outside for some fresh air, often with my shoe in his mouth.

'What's that?' Mabegzo asked when we were inside.

'A microwave.'

'What does it do?'

'It warms food.'

'*Tjo, tjo, tjo, le makgoa mos lona.* You live like white people here. You have a microwave and your dog lies on the couch. *Haai, le makgowa.* Your house is nice. Why are you moving?'

'It's not safe anymore, and we need a bigger house and better schools.' I simply repeated what I'd heard my mom say.

'But it'll be safe if we find out who killed your dad.'

'No, not really. It's not just that. Barely a week after we buried my dad, someone broke into our car outside. It never happened while my dad was alive. So it's time to go.'

'To go and forget me.'

'What do you want to eat?'

'Anything. Anything would make me happy.'

In the end I made him a feast of Russian sausage, a beef patty, two eggs, cheese, polony, baked beans and bread. He ate without saying a word, and when he was done I mixed some orange squash.

'What will you eat tomorrow?'

He shrugged. I packed some bread, cheese and polony for him to eat later. When I gave him the food, he got down on his knees and put his head on my feet. He stayed like that for a long time, and something told me not to interrupt him. '*Ke a go tlotla.* I worship you.' Keeping quiet seemed the only appropriate response to his act of supplication.

After that day, my mother questioned why my appetite

had suddenly grown. I wasn't a big eater, and I'd often get home with my lunch untouched. At suppertime, I was always happy with just a piece of meat. My lunch pack contained a slice of bread, fruit and juice, but from that day on I asked for four slices of bread.

'Four slices, *wena*?' My mom asked.

'*Ja, a ke sa kgora*. I don't get full on one anymore.'

She was happy that I was eating, and duly increased my provisions. I was thrilled, because it meant I could see Mabegzo more often. From then on he waited for me every day at the corner to get his meal. I consumed only my apple and my juice, while the four slices of bread, spread with cheese and polony, chicken mayonnaise or sometimes boiled eggs, went to Mabegzo. Chicken mayo was his favourite and I also saw the glee with which he tackled the hotdogs, a Friday treat. I got such a thrill from providing for him. These were some of the best times I spent with him. He needed me, and his presence beside me finally made sense – he was hungry and I had food for him.

One day as I gave him his food, he said, '*Ke a go ncanywa*,' township lingo for 'I love you'. I was about to respond when he said, '*Askies*, I'm sorry, I'm sorry.'

'How come you've never raped me?' The words were out before I could stop them.

'What are you talking about?'

'People say that one day you're going to rape me.'

'*Haai, sies man, batho ba bua masepa*. People talk shit. How could I rape such a little girl? You're a baby.'

One day soon afterwards the police came to our house looking for me. I'm pretty sure I was the only eleven-year-old they'd ever questioned, but it wasn't funny then. It was July, the second anniversary of my father's death. My mom was out of town at a conference, and my aunt was looking after us. I didn't think there was anything odd about the police knocking on our door. Our family was respected in the community, and apart from uncles who occasionally got up to no good, there was no drama in our family – or so I thought.

But the blue and yellow police car parked on our pavement drew a lot of attention, and in typical township style, people started milling about. The presence of the police in our community made them angry, and even though people didn't have the might to fight them, they wanted to keep an eye on them, to bear witness to their evil deeds. This was Soweto during the grip of apartheid, with police patrolling the streets, using state resources to sow fear and division and to settle political battles. But this time the police weren't looking for a political activist. Mabegzo had been up to no good again, and as usual he was wanted by the police. They were looking for him, and they had questions for me. My aunt insisted that I couldn't know such a horrible person; I was a child.

'A *child*? A child who plays with grown men? She's no child.'

My heart was thumping, every pore in my skin secreting litres of sweat. I'm going to jail, I thought. This is the end. I started silently apologising to my dad, telling him that, given a chance, I'd fix my life and do the right thing. But when I thought about my mother, I started crying. I was afraid of her. She was so strict and expected only the best from me. And with the deep pain in her eyes, I couldn't imagine what she'd go through if I went to jail for the rest of my life.

'You see?' the police officer said to my aunt. 'She's crying because she's hiding something.'

He turned to me. '*Khuluma!* Talk! Where is that devil,

Mabegzo? Where does he live? When last did you see him?'
He was hurling the questions at me like bricks.

Someone had clearly told the police that I knew a lot
about Mabegzo, and that we were always in each other's
company. Without even pausing to think, the lies just came
out of my mouth. In between loud sobs, I told them I knew
Mabegzo, but I hated him, and that every day he followed
me home and threatened to rape me. The pain in my heart
was intense. Here I was, betraying my brother, yet I couldn't
protect him or myself without lying. I claimed he was
bullying and harassing me and that I was afraid of him.

'So why didn't you tell anyone?' the police asked.

'He threatened to kill me if I did.'

'You can see she's frightened. She's just a child, a little girl.
How could she possibly know what a hardened criminal is
up to?' my aunt said.

The officers bought my story and one of them squeezed
my hand as I cried. 'Don't worry, we'll find him. You'll be
safe again.'

After they left I wailed. I should have been celebrating for
fooling them all. But something told me that the battle had
just begun. My tears wouldn't stop. So I was taken aback
when my aunt gave me a hiding.

'You think I don't know about you and this boy? What
are you up to? The police were right to question you because
you're a naughty little girl who brings big boys home. What
are you doing with him?' She wasn't giving me a chance to
answer, not that I had anything to say.

'If I hear that you've brought that filthy boy here again,
I'll give you a hiding, do you hear?'

Why did all adults do that? They were hitting you anyway,
yet they threatened you with a hiding. It made no sense. I
didn't cry from this hiding; I felt I deserved it for betraying

Mabegzo and lying about him. He would be very hurt if he knew I'd badmouthed him just like everyone else did. I had to find him and apologise. And I'd make it better by going to confess my sins to Father Lodi, our parish priest.

Now that the police had visited my house, I knew I couldn't carry on seeing Mabegzo.

But I needn't have worried. He stopped waiting for me, and I was gutted. He had disappeared. I searched for him, longed for him and wondered why he'd left me. Which was silly, because I wanted to see him only to tell him that hanging out with him would land me in jail. I thought about him all the time, wondering what he ate and where he slept, but as the weeks turned to months, I worried and feared for him. Had someone killed him and buried his body where it couldn't be found? Or had the police arrested him?

Two months later he reappeared at the corner. It was the first week of spring, but it was still windy, dusty and cold. I was shocked at how thin he was. He looked so forlorn that I simply didn't have the heart to turn him away.

'*Oh wena, ke neng; o tsamaile?* You've been gone so long; where were you?'

'I was lying low.'

I couldn't risk people seeing us and telling my aunt or the police. But our church was always empty on weekdays; if I was caught there, I could come up with an explanation. So I asked Mabegzo to use a different street and meet me at the church. We walked to the church using parallel routes and entered the empty hall.

We sat on the floor and I unpacked his lunch. I still carried lunch for him every day, and I would give it away when I got home. There were enough hungry people in our street, and I couldn't ask my mom not to pack me a big lunch anymore; it would seem odd. So for two months I had still carried his portion every day, hoping he'd turn up, as he finally had today.

'*O se ka phaka*, stop gobbling everything at once, you'll choke. Are you in trouble, Mabegzo?'

'Yes.'

'The police came to ask me about you.' He stopped chewing for a moment but didn't respond. 'Don't you want to know what I told them?'

'I want to know if they hurt you. Or if you got into trouble.'

'No, they didn't hurt me. But I lied and told them you were troubling me. I'm sorry.' And then he laughed, and everything was okay. For now. 'Why are you in trouble? What did you do? Did you rape someone?'

'No.'

'Have you ever raped someone?'

'I no longer do that. I promise. I no longer do it. I've stopped that.'

'You just stopped?'

'Yes, I just stopped. You said I mustn't come to you if I make girls cry. Remember?'

'You're not telling me lies?'

'I'd never lie to you. Never. Who else would do for me what you do?'

'Did you steal?'

'No.'

'Have you killed someone?'

'I'm sorry.'

'Have you killed someone?'

'I'm sorry.' He started to cry, but I wanted to know and so I kept asking. I was tired of second-guessing him and trying to read between the lines.

'I won't tell, I promise.'

'I'm sorry.' He was choking on his words by now and weeping. The food fell out of his mouth and the snot and tears were running down his face.

'Did you kill someone?'

'I made a mistake, I made a mistake.'

'*Did you kill someone!?*'

He nodded.

'Who?'

'Hector. And Nicchy,' he said, barely audible.

As he went on crying I thought about his admission. I may have been a child, but even I knew it wasn't possible to kill two people by mistake.

Mabegzo confessed that he and his gang members had had a fallout over missing loot. Eight of them, including Hector and Nicchy, were meant to share the proceeds of their daring bank robbery two months earlier, but the money had disappeared. Mango had given it to his mother for safekeeping and they were all happy with that. But Mango got arrested for something else. During his incarceration, three armed men had apparently come to his mother's house in the middle of the night, roughed her up and demanded the money. His mother identified Hector and Nicchy as the culprits, and the rest of the gang members believed her. It didn't cross their minds that Mango and his mom were lying and had kept the money for themselves.

'So you killed them?'

He nodded. Mabegzo claimed that he and the four remaining guys had called a meeting to discuss it. They were all feeling aggressive, but he never thought it would end in bloodshed. There was a lot of shouting and swearing and throwing things about, and a gun went off. He didn't know who fired first, but it wasn't him, he claimed.

'They're going to kill me, too.'

'Not if you pray. You must pray.'

He carried on as though I hadn't spoken. 'It shouldn't have happened.'

'But you've killed before, right?' He nodded. 'And no one killed you back, so they won't kill you this time.'

'Things have changed. It's easy to fight enemies when you're united, but once you start fighting among yourselves, it's the end. We're all going to die now, one by one.'

I was getting scared; this talk of guns and death was more than I could handle. I wasn't afraid of him, but I was unsettled by his ability to point a gun with such ease at someone who was once a friend. Yes, he regretted killing his mates and was crying about it, but he'd been able to do it. I could see he didn't want me to leave yet, but I was uncomfortable and wanted to go. He held my hand and looked deep into my eyes.

'Do you forgive me?'

'Are you going to die?'

'If they find me, I may die. Do you forgive me?'

'Yes, I forgive you.'

'For everything?'

'For everything.'

He started crying again. 'Are you afraid?' I asked him.

'No, no.'

I believed him. He wasn't afraid; he was cut up about killing his friends. His biggest fear was that he might die at the hands of the police. 'Only cowards get killed by the police,' he said.

After that day, I grew anxious about Mabegzo. He'd left me in no doubt that he was waiting for his death, and when he didn't appear at the corner the next day, I worried that he'd never be able to come again. But the day after that, there he was. Relief and joy took over, and I forgot all about being seen and getting into trouble. But he wouldn't stop this talk of dying. He spoke about how he wanted his death to take place, like he was ordering from a menu.

'I think I'm going to die at night. Did your father die at night?'

'Yes, in the early hours of the morning. Why do you want to die at night?'

'So people will know that my killers were cowards who couldn't face me in broad daylight.'

'Is that what you do? You kill during the day so that people know you're brave?'

'*Ja, vele*, obviously. How many people killed your father?'

'I'm not sure. But they think there was a huge struggle between him and several attackers.'

'That's what I want. If it's just one person, he won't succeed. There must be more.'

One day, on the twenty-fifth of October, just before school ended, the once-sunny sky had turned to darkness and a torrential rain began pelting down. I sat in class praying for the rain to let up and the clouds to clear before the bell rang. But it didn't let up. Our streets were untarred, so a heavy downpour transformed them into muddy pools, with cars, pets and feet all battling through the sludge.

While most children stayed and waited for the rain to subside, I and a handful of others decided to brave the deluge. Although our parents had bought us raincoats, wearing them drew such derision from our schoolmates for being softies that we always left them at home. I hated walking through a downpour, which made the three-kilometre walk seem like an eternity. But when I turned the corner at Kuzwayo Street, there he was, waiting as usual. He'd brought a bright green umbrella and some plastic bags to cover me.

'I thought you'd never come,' he said as he put the umbrella over me.

The umbrella wasn't big enough for us both, but he held it so that I didn't get a single drop on me, while he was exposed to the downpour. I was so touched by this kindness that tears began to roll down my cheeks. I knew he noticed, but he didn't say a word. I thought I saw a teary glint in his eyes, too. I wept all the way home, and not a word passed between us.

When we reached my gate he asked rhetorically, 'O *hantle akere*? You're okay, right?' I nodded and opened the gate. '*Mara wena*, Lala.' He stroked my cheek and was gone.

The next day as I walked home from school, he was waiting for me at our corner again. Except this time he was lying lifeless in the street.

It felt as if he had deliberately died at this time, so that I would find him on my way home. This was our time, our corner. And his killers must have known. I stood there looking down at him. He was still so handsome, a light drizzle falling on his bloodied face. I had known him for just eight months, but it felt like my whole life.

The jubilation around me was unbearable. But I just stood there, willing my heart to hold on and stay there for his sake. He had waited for me. Now it was my turn to wait and watch over him.

PART 2

Chapter 6

IN 2004, SOWETO IS A DIFFERENT place. It's a pleasure to drive over the fresh tarmac that covers many of the dusty gravel roads of my childhood. The streets are still alive with the entrepreneurial spirit that once sustained families when apartheid closed the doors of learning and employment, but now I drive past many more filling stations, corner shops, butcheries and funeral parlours, as well as a host of other small businesses, Internet cafés, museums, posh shopping centres and world-class restaurants. The tenacity of its people and their ability to make progress against all odds is evidenced by the new and bigger homes, cars and businesses. But it's still not utopia, of course. Even today, young men and women who should be actively employed are basking in the sun with little chance of finding work. And, unlike in my day, schoolchildren roam the streets in full uniform during school hours. Nobody asks them why they're not in the classroom.

My love for Soweto remains tinged with ambivalence. This township of my childhood is still a place where hearts break and dreams die, yet none who have grown up in Soweto can ever totally turn their back on it. I'm not the only professional who has migrated to the suburbs yet returns weekly to attend weddings and funerals and visit family. I get a warm reception when I visit Orlando East, and I'm amazed at how many people keep abreast of my career. Most in my old community know that I work in the media, and they insist that they listen to my programmes, read my columns and take pride in my success. Inevitably the conversation ends with 'please find me a job', or with parents lamenting that their children have no work. It's still life as I knew it back then. My old school and church are just the same. In Sofasonke Street, few houses have been renovated or extended, although many now sport satellite dishes. Despite the new faces everywhere, my childhood friends are still there, often in the same family home they grew up in. Some have jobs, while others hang out at street corners, a few have died and a few more are in jail. Yet most of them are parents now, and they express great surprise that at twenty-six I don't yet have a child.

Fifteen years have passed since these were my streets. Fifteen long years since Mabegzo was murdered. Within six weeks of his death, the school year came to an end, and I moved with my family to a new home in the East Rand and better schools awaited us in the New Year.

The last weeks at my old school were bleak. I was in mourning, but I couldn't share it with a single soul. The teachers noticed, but they had no idea what was troubling me.

'*O nagana eng okare o mosadi moholo*? Why are you always deep in thought, like an old woman?' Mistress Angela kept asking. Other teachers reprimanded me for 'thinking' too much. '*O tlo hlanya, re tla be re shebile wena o topa di pampiri le di* plastic *mo seterateng*. Next thing you'll go mad and start wandering the streets collecting papers and plastic bags for no reason.'

After school I'd walk home alone, conscious of the weight of my school bag now that he wasn't beside me to carry it. I could no longer bear to pass our corner, so I took a different route home.

The final day of the school year was a day filled with fun – for the other kids. There were no lessons. I don't know what the teachers got up to but we were left to fool around until it was time for our reports to be handed out. The girls in our class started singing a popular love song of that time, Always, by Atlantic Star. It was one of the cheesiest, but as pre-adolescent girls we loved its nasal declaration of a love that would never die, and we sang it with great soul and pathos. But when we reached the last stanza, *Ooh you're like the sun, chasing all of the rain away, when you come around you bring brighter days*, all I could see was the rain falling softly on Mabegzo's dead face.

Suddenly I found myself sobbing. I was inconsolable. The others went to call one of the wonderful nuns at our school to intervene. She held me tightly, stroking my back. '*O se ka lla*. Don't cry,' she comforted me. '*Papa o ile phomolong*. Your father has gone to rest.'

All these years have passed and yet, as ever, Mabegzo is still mauling my emotions. How is it possible? Each time I think of him my heart swells with love, longing and regret, followed immediately by self-disgust for daring to harbour such feelings. Then come the excuses: I was just a little girl; I didn't know any better; I was still in mourning for my father and warmed to the first older male who showed me kindness. Despite the intervening years, I am still unable to make my peace with him or his place in my life. He will not leave me alone. He still bangs endlessly on the doors of my heart, demanding that I be his voice, that I acknowledge his life, that I tell the world that he was so much more than just a robber, a rapist and a murderer.

But who was he? Who on earth was Mabegzo? How could anyone be so evil and yet so gentle and loving? Is it possible that he was simultaneously humane and psychopathic? Can a single human being possess a soul so worthy of admiration and condemnation in equal measures? Had he always sought to protect me, or was he merely living up to his name, Mahlomola, and doing what he did best, sowing sorrow wherever he went? What demons ran amok inside my beloved Mabegzo, and could they ever have been silenced?

The time has come for me to find out more, to try to gain the understanding that he always said I lacked. I need to know what drove him to unleash such terror on others, and to die unredeemed at just twenty-two. I want his family to account for the burdensome name they visited upon an innocent child. And I desperately hope that uncovering the conditions of his upbringing will give me the insight I need to finally forgive myself for loving Mabegzo.

Mabegzo had told me that his grandmother loved to pray, and that she was the only person who truly loved him. So I set out to find her.

I rely solely on my memory to find his house. He had pointed it out the day he brought me to Katlego, so I have a fair idea of where to look. When I arrive, I'm not certain it's the right one. In the absence of a house number the family name would help, but Mabegzo had never told me his surname, and I had never asked. I'm nervous to mention his name while asking directions; people have long memories. I doubt that they will have forgotten this notorious young man, and anyone who asks after him is likely to be met with hostility. But I walk in and ask anyway.

They look at me in surprise. 'Who are you?' the elderly woman asks.

'I'm Redi.'

'*Ufunani ku muntu o wa hamba kudala so?* Why are you looking for a person who passed away so long ago?

I tell them I was a school friend of his and need some information from his family.

They snort derisively. 'Mabegzo? School?'

Of course. I should have known better. But at least it seems they knew him. So I ask what they remember about him.

'What's there to remember?'

'As a little boy, surely he was different?'

'No, *sisi*, he was a nonsense of a child. I don't even want to talk about him. Go see the old lady, Nkgono. Maybe she can help you.'

I follow their directions, and find the old lady on the stoep, enjoying the autumn sun. In Soweto it's long been a form of entertainment to watch people pass by from the comfort of one's stoep. The house seems different. It's been nicely renovated with extra rooms added outside.

I pause before I approach, quietly remembering a different day when I stood at the corner and observed Mabegzo's sombre funeral service. The entire township had been on full alert that day. Our teachers had warned our parents to keep us off the streets. They didn't want us caught in the inevitable gunfire at a gangster's funeral. The day had dawned bright and lovely – spring in all its splendour – but the kindly sun couldn't thaw the frozen weight pressing on my heart. A friend came to play at my house, but I wasn't in the mood. And on that day of all days my mother chose to burden me with chores.

'*Why o le snaaks*? Why are you acting funny?' Cousin Thembi kept asking.

'*A se niks*. It's nothing,' I shrugged, not daring to show my grief, which was even more acute because I couldn't attend his funeral. Children only went to the funerals of relatives or classmates, and even if I sneaked in, there'd probably be so few people that I'd stand out. So after hurriedly doing my chores, I slipped out to wait for his coffin. I walked the two kilometres to the corner of his street, but strangely, there was very little activity, just a small gathering on the pavement. This was unheard of. Funerals were huge affairs attended by everybody, even those who didn't know the deceased. Even nobodies received a better send-off than this. As no one could know the final thoughts of a dead man, even a bad man received his last rites. But for Mabegzo the rules didn't seem to apply. Nobody cared what redemption the Lord had promised. He was a devil who deserved only contempt.

When the coffin was led out of the yard, I heard some gunshots and a few cars spinning nearby. But they soon took off, not wanting to draw the attention of the police. There was hardly anyone to be seen. If he had any friends, I didn't see any, not even Katlego. Nobody seemed to want to be associated with him. Some neighbours and passers-by swore as they passed, condemning him to hell. '*O sathane naye a ka mfuni*,' said one lady. 'Even the devil doesn't want him.'

As the hearse passed me I knelt down and raised my hand

to wave goodbye. According to superstition, children had to kneel when a funeral procession passed, or else our mothers would lose a breast. It was probably just a way to get children to show deference to the dead and respect for the bereaved. Even in the middle of a game, if a siren announced the approach of a funeral convoy, someone would call, '*Hey nina, guqani ngamadolo*! Kneel down, your mom's going to lose a boob.' But not this time. No one else knelt for Mabegzo, and I saw not a single tear shed.

But that was back then. I take a breath and walk over to greet Nkgono on her stoep. She's strong and pretty still; the years have marked her face kindly. We exchange greetings and immediately my nervousness is gone. How nice it will be, for once, to speak to someone who also loved him. Luckily, people in Soweto rarely make appointments before dropping in on friends and family. If you're in the area, it's quite acceptable to just arrive at the doorstep, and you're always welcomed.

'*Mahlomola? Tjo, tjo, tjo. Ngwanaka, ha ho na motho o buang ka moshemane oo.* Nobody speaks about that boy.'

'Why, granny?'

'*Mahlomola o ne a le sehloka tsebe.* He was a trouble maker.'

'I know. But why? What happened?'

She shakes her head slowly but says nothing.

'I was there moments after he was killed,' I tell her. 'I saw you standing there, looking at him. I was also looking.'

'Really? So you saw them dancing, singing and spitting at him?' I nod, and quietly she starts to weep.

'I wasn't sad that they killed him. I was relieved. I always prayed for it to happen. You're too young to understand, but sometimes the best way you can love your children is to wish them dead. It's much harder to watch them do wrong things. To live with the knowledge that others hate your children; to see the hatred and disgust in their eyes – it killed me every day. So it was best. Yes, it was for the best.'

For a little while no words are spoken between us. In the background we can hear the sounds of children playing and cars passing, each of us lost in our own thoughts. Out on the pavement, little girls and boys are touching my car, arguing about who touched it first. I smile, remembering the 'I touch' game I also played with my friends.

'Go home and be good,' Nkgono reprimands them.

'Mahlomola was a difficult child. But I accepted him and tried to raise him, because by giving him to us, God was teaching us a lesson.'

'What was the lesson?' I ask.

'To submit to his authority,' she sighs, 'and carry our crosses without abandoning our faith.'

'Did he always test your faith? Is that all you remember about him?'

'No,' she says. 'He was a normal little boy. He gave me no backchat, and always did his chores without complaining or sulking, unlike the others.'

'He was a good child, then?'

'Yes, before he became a killer, he was a good child.'

'Then how did he become a killer?'

She doesn't want to talk anymore. 'O *tsositse maqeba a ka; ke kgathetsi.* You've opened my wounds; I'm tired now.'

I try to hide my disappointment, but I know better than to ask if I can return another day. She's the only person who can give me any insight into Mabegzo's life, and I don't want to upset her. But as she bids me goodbye, she says, 'You haven't even had tea. Next time you visit, we'll have some.'

I squeeze her hand and kiss her crinkled cheek.

'What did you say your name was again?' she asks.

I wonder what Mabegzo would say about my snooping around, asking questions about him. He hated people poking their noses into other people's affairs.

On my second visit I find Nkgono sitting at the kitchen table peeling sweet potatoes. The house is very clean and a young girl is washing dishes at the sink. Nkgono introduces her as her grandchild, named after her late son, Mohau.

I exchange pleasantries and enquire about her health, and then tell her that I've come to hear more about Mabegzo.

'We can't talk about Mahlomola in front of this child,' Nkgono says, loud enough for the 'child' to hear. 'She doesn't know about him. It's better that way.'

Chuckling to myself, I help Mohau with the dishes in an effort to speed things up. Nkgono then instructs Mohau to make tea and watch the pot of sweet potatoes, while she takes care of her visitor.

We make our way to the lounge. In Soweto there is no tradition of enquiring about your visitors' preferences. You simply present them with tea and a plate of food, no questions asked. In turn, visitors eat and drink whatever they're given, regardless of allergy or appetite. As a fussy eater, I find this difficult.

'People were already pointing at Mahlomola while he was in Imelda's stomach,' Nkgono tells me. 'I took him to church in Lesotho when he was born, to remove the sin from him. But it didn't work. The sin was too much, and the devil was using him. He was the devil's child, and I had to accept that.'

'How did Mabegzo become the devil's child?'

'No, no, young lady! Don't use that name. The streets

gave him that name. He got it while doing the devil's work.'

I cannot see how the street name, Mabegzo, which has no meaning at all, can be worse than Mahlomola – sorrow. *Bitso le be ke seromo,* as the saying goes; you live up to your name. Yet his granny won't let me call him Mabegzo, and it's a sacrilege to defy an old woman. Mabegzo was right to be ashamed of his name. I try to imagine how, somewhere in a hospital ward, his mother could have looked at him as he drew his first breath and decided that this little one should be called Sorrow.

Before we can continue, Nkgono's son Tshepo arrives. Nkgono immediately reprimands him for sleeping out.

'Why don't you phone and tell us if you're not coming home? We left the gate unlocked for you.'

'*Eish*, sorry,' he says, his eyes glued to me. His body language is that of a compulsive flirt. 'Hello, my lady.' He flashes me a brilliant smile.

But Nkgono isn't done with him. 'I don't understand this life of disappearing every weekend. It's wrong.'

'Sorry, Mama, I was held up.'

'Held up for the whole night?'

'*Ja*, the whole night.' And he gives me a big wink. 'So who is our pretty visitor?'

'What's your name again?' Nkgono asks me.

'Redi. I've come to talk to Nkgono about Mab... Mahlomola.'

He looks startled. 'Why?'

'He was my friend, and I want to know more about his life.'

'Your friend? How so? Did you have a child with him? Or are you his child?'

'No, no. I was only eleven when he died, so I couldn't have been his girlfriend, or his child. We were just friends.

Maybe you can join us and help Nkgono remember some things about him.'

I discover that Tshepo is Nkgono's youngest son, and that he never married because 'women are trouble'. He's better off single, he assures me. He's the only one of his three siblings who still lives at home, and three of her grandchildren live with them. Soweto is full of children being raised by grandparents for various reasons: their parents may have died, gone off to start new families or found work far from home. Nkgono's son Mohau died in 1988, so his two children lived with her, as well as her daughter Greta's daughter Mpho.

'Mahlomola was a good boy,' says Tshepo.

'Is that so? Nkgono told me he was a trouble maker.'

'*Ja*, it was the frustration that killed him.' He pauses for a moment. 'If the adults had found a way to cure his frustration, he would have been fine.'

'Frustration?' Nkgono raises her voice. 'In a child? We didn't grow up like that. What was he frustrated about? He had food, clothes, church. What is this frustration?'

'*Eish*, Mama doesn't see it. She's old; she can't make the connection.'

'I am old, not stupid. And don't you talk about me as if I'm not here.'

I ask Nkgono if she ever spoke to Mahlomola about the events that led to his birth.

'What good would that do?'

'*Haai*, I think it would have helped him,' Tshepo interjects. 'There's no guarantee that he wouldn't have become a dangerous criminal because he came from a criminal's seed. But to live your life with people talking behind your back! These women poke their noses in other people's business too much. Even my business, they have a lot to say about it.'

111

'*Haai*, Tshepo. What business? *E ba le hlompho*. Have some respect.' She turns to me. 'I hoped that prayer and fasting would help Mahlomola. I accepted his presence as the will of God, but my husband struggled with Mahlomola's birth. He never once called him by his name, even though he was the one who gave him that horrible name.'

'*Ja*,' Tshepo says. 'If you're called Mahlomola, what hope is there for you? Of course you'll live up to it.'

'I curse my decision to send her to the shop,' Nkgono says.

'No, sending her to the shop wasn't the mistake,' Tshepo insists. 'The mistake was hiding her. That's when people started to talk. And it was a mistake not to tell Mahlomola. He heard it from others instead, and it destroyed him.'

'*Taba ena e ne e le boima. Ha o bua o wrong, ha o sa bue o wrong*. The issue was complex. You were damned if you spoke of it, and damned if you didn't.'

'How did he find out?' I ask.

Nkgono has had enough for the day. She wants to take a nap.

'May I stay and chat with Tshepo?'

'No, but come back soon.'

Tshepo walks me to the gate and recommends that I go to speak to some of Mahlomola's friends, Katlego and Koyo. I remember Katlego, and I have been planning to pay him a visit. Tshepo directs me to Koyo's house, and reveals that he changed his name and identity number several times in the late eighties and nineties to evade arrest when he was a wanted man.

'He's grown up now, but it's too late. He's not okay upstairs,' he says, pointing to his head. Then he chuckles and gives me a big hug as if we've known each other for years. 'I just love women with nice cars,' he says, and gives me a big wink.

'But I don't like men without cars,' I counter.

He takes it well and bellows with laughter.

Chapter 7

KOYO LIVES IN A SHACK IN his mother's back yard, a common feature in Soweto. Shacks are the cheapest option for large families to build extra rooms and provide some independence for family members. The shack may be just an extra bedroom, or it may include a kitchen and sitting area, often nicely furnished with a TV, fridge and smart couches. Inside I find the radio blasting out the soccer commentary while a man in a wheelchair polishes a row of shoes.

My timing is bad; Saturday soccer is a religion for many.

'*Sawubona*. I'm looking for Koyo.'

'Who's looking for him?'

'I am.'

'And who are you?' he demands. His eyes have the dead look of one who has seen too much. His hands are coarse, his face has scars and there are teeth missing. I've interviewed many ex-criminals and I've come to know this look. I extend my hand.

'I'm Redi. I'd like to discuss something with him.'

He takes my hand and studies me closely. 'I don't know your name and you don't look familiar.' Before I can say a word, he shouts, 'Nomvula! Nomvula, *woza*. Come.'

A woman in her early forties appears at the door and peers at me.

'Do you know this woman? What's your name again?'

'I'm Redi, and no, you don't know me, but I'm looking for you, Koyo. I want to talk to you about Mabegzo.'

'Mabegzo? Mabegzo? Are you his long lost child or something? Why would anyone look for Mabegzo?'

'We were friends.'

'Mabegzo didn't make friends with girls!' Koyo says.

Nomvula, who hasn't spoken until now, nods. 'We grew up here, and I'm older than them. Even I don't remember Mabegzo being friends with girls.'

'Why wouldn't he make friends with girls?' I ask.

They glance at each other. 'He was naughty,' Nomvula responds. 'The girls were scared of him, of all of them.'

'No, no. Girls weren't scared of us,' Koyo says. 'They loved us!'

Nomvula shakes her head in disgust, turns on her heel and goes back into the house.

'*Eish*, my sister has a temper. She takes life so seriously.'

'And you? How do you take life?'

'Not like her. Being in a wheelchair isn't nice so I don't make it worse by taking life seriously.'

'How did you end up in a wheelchair?'

'You said you want to ask about Mabegzo. I'm not Mabegzo.'

I tell him that I'm not only interested in Mabegzo, but in the people who shaped his life, who cared for him, who hated him; anyone who can tell me more about him.

'*Ja,* I cared for him. We had to care for each other, otherwise you died. But he was hard core, you know. If you crossed him he didn't forgive. You paid.'

'Why did you join his gang? Or did he join yours?'

'People use the word gang so loosely. Not everyone belonged to a gang. Some of us were independent. We were just a group of friends in the same business. Like colleagues. Sometimes you worked with another person, sometimes with a group, and sometimes your worked on your own.'

'And what kind of work was it?'

'Ah, the usual for boys our age. Robbery, car theft, all that stuff.'

'What stuff?'

'We beat up people sometimes, and we stole jewellery. Some of us smoked dagga – but Mabegzo didn't. He was clean.'

'Rape, murder?'

He doesn't reply, and I sense that he's being guarded.

'Mabegzo told me all that, so I already know. I just want to understand why.'

'You're not undercover or anything? It would be a joke for me to pay after all these years.'

'Pay for what?'

'For some of the stupid things we did, you know. Some of the stuff was to protect ourselves, you see, against other people, or against the police. Sometimes during a robbery people shot at us, and they left us with no choice, you know?

'But why were you robbing people anyway?'

'We all had different reasons. To put food on the table, to fit in, or because it was the only thing they knew.'

'And you? Why did you do it?'

'I don't know really. It just happened.'

'*Hawu*, Koyo, please tell me. You don't just own a gun and kill people because it just happens.'

'Seriously, it just happened. And before you know it, you've done it so many times and it's too late to back out. And you can't stop because then you'll get killed. You see, after you take one life, you're less powerful than before because the people left behind want revenge. So to show them that you're powerful you have to keep killing to discourage any thoughts of revenge.'

'But not everyone goes out to avenge the death of a loved one. So why keep up the killing spree?'

He considers this for a second, and then shakes his head. 'You don't know if someone will come after you or not, so you carry on, just in case. Today things are different. In those days criminals killed other criminals, not innocent citizens. We killed our enemies before they killed us. Not like today where these stupid *laaities* rob and kill innocent people. In our days, a robbery only turned bloody if the person retaliated or resisted. We didn't just kill for fun, so we weren't really guilty.'

Koyo sounds like he really believes they didn't kill innocent citizens, so I let it go.

'What did your family have to say about what you were doing?'

'Nothing much. My father would beat me up when people came to report me or when the police came looking for me. My mother would tell me I was breaking her heart. And my sister and late brother told me to stop. They called relatives to speak to me and try to show me the way.'

'When did you stop?'

'*Eish*, give me a cigarette. I need one.'

'I don't smoke.'

'Nozipho, Nozipho!' A teenage girl comes to the door.

'*Yebo?* Yes?'

'*Hawu*, greet the adult! Where are your manners? You can't just come out and say, "Yes".'

'*Sawubona sisi*,' Nozipho says shyly.

'Take some money from this nice lady and go buy daddy a cigarette.' I have never been asked like this before, but I reach for my purse and give her a ten rand note.

'Bring back the change. Quick. Go.'

'How old is she?'

'Fourteen this year. I had her the year before my accident, in 1990. She's a gift to me. That's why we called her Nozipho, bearer of gifts. I must have known somewhere in my heart that I would be paralysed and not have any more children after her. She lives with her mother but she comes to visit me every weekend. She loves my family.'

'What caused your accident?'

'I got injured.'

'How did it happen?'

'I got shot by the cops while working in the city centre. I was kept under police guard at Baragwanath Hospital. I prayed that I would die, but it didn't happen, so I was tried and convicted.'

'What for?'

'A lot of things.'

'How long were you in prison?'

'Seven years. It wasn't nice. By the time I came out, Nozipho was eight, and she'd never seen me walk on my own two feet. But at least she knew me because her mother brought her to visit. Mandela was president and I hadn't even voted. My parents had died and my sister never stops reminding me that they died broken-hearted and disappointed in me.'

'How do you feel about that?'

'Sore. Very sore. But they also don't understand my pain. Being in a wheelchair in prison is not nice, I'm telling you.'

His daughter returns with three cigarettes and offers me the change. 'Bring it here,' Koyo says quickly, and throws it in his pocket.

'What about the rapes? Tell me about that.'

With total conviction, he tells me that even for young girls it was a great privilege to be raped by Mabegzo. '*Be ku yiti e si phethe*. We were in charge,' he says. 'Girls always came to our hangout and walked past us on street corners, just hoping for the chance to get jackrolled and raped by us.'

'So you don't think you did anything wrong?'

'It would be wrong now. But then it was okay.'

'How can something that's wrong now have been okay then?'

'The government says it's wrong now, but then it didn't. That's because women are in the government now.'

'How many girls did you rape?'

'Oh, let me see. One, two, three... *Haai, sisi, baie, baie.* Lots, lots,' he laughs. 'Those were the days.' He's the only one laughing.

'Do you miss those days?'

'Sort of. Then we had power, you know. Now things are just shit. Children beat up adults, foreigners are everywhere, and women just want money. The world's ruined now.'

'Where did you meet Mabegzo?'

'In the streets. That's how people met, by being out there. That's how it worked in our business. You knew about someone's reputation before you met them, so when you eventually met, you knew what you were all about and formed partnerships without further discussion. Mabegzo and I took an instant liking to each other and decided to work together.'

'What did you like about Mabegzo?'

'He was a good guy. I was cut up about what happened. He kept his word and protected his friends. Until things went bad.'

'But he killed people.'

'We all did. All of us did. Mainly for protection.'

'And you raped girls and young women.'

'*Eintlik, wena*, you don't understand.'

'Don't understand what?'

'I told you. You can call it rape now, but then women were different. They wanted to be roughed up by us. Especially by Mabegzo.'

'If someone had told you what you were doing was wrong, would you have stopped?'

'*Haai, angazi*. I don't know. All I'm saying is, these women wanted it then. They wanted our seed. *Ba njalo abafazi*. Women are like that sometimes.'

'Would you tell your daughter about your past?'

'No, no, no. Never!' He says vehemently.

When I fall silent, he says, almost as an afterthought. 'Mabegzo would have lived longer if he hadn't panicked.'

'What do you mean?'

'He got paranoid, and started suspecting that everyone was after him. That made him reckless. He began making wrong judgements and endangering our lives.'

I'm not sure what he's getting at, so I ask more questions.

'Was it a wrong judgement to kill Nicchy and Hector?'

Koyo is genuinely shocked. '*Tjo, tjo, tjo!* You know about

that? You know everything! How do you know?'

'He told me. So, do you think he was wrong to kill them?'

'*Ja*, that was a big fuck-up. It was the beginning of the end for him; for us all, really. And the power of his sangoma couldn't protect him anymore. He wasn't sleeping towards the end. Sometimes he would go two nights without sleeping at all, just in case someone came for him. So he was always tired.'

He sighs. 'The police weren't the problem. Our enemies weren't either.' He shakes his head. 'It's always those closest to you that you must watch. They're the ones who kill you.'

I remember Mabegzo's restlessness in those last days. The bravado was still there, but he was full of nervous energy. The walls were closing in, and he knew it.

'So who killed him?'

'Every death had to be avenged.'

'Who killed him then?'

'Well the deaths of Nicchy and Hector didn't sit well with some of our friends. They felt Mabegzo had gone too far. And if he could kill Hector and Nicchy, he could kill any of us.'

'So you and his last friends killed him?'

'Circumstances killed him.'

'Okay. But who pulled the trigger?'

'I don't know.'

'Were you there?'

'*Ja*, but I didn't pull the trigger.'

'But you were there, and you knew Mabegzo would be killed that day?'

'Yes, we all had to be there. The decision was final. Some of us disagreed, but the majority won.'

'How many of you were there?'

'*Haai*, I don't remember. Five, or maybe six or seven?

I can't remember. We all had to be there to confuse the witnesses and to take ownership of the decision. But I didn't want him dead.'

'So why didn't you warn him or pull out?'

'Because I'd be dead, for sure.'

'I don't believe you didn't see who pulled the trigger. If you didn't do it, why won't you tell me who did?'

'We all had guns on us. One of us shot him. That's all.'

'Tell me about the moment he was killed.'

'He was standing at a corner not far from here, waiting for someone. We knew he had a gun on him, so...'

'What? You mean Mabegzo carried a gun to that street corner?'

Koyo seems genuinely surprised by my question, and looks at me strangely. '*Hawu*, he didn't just carry it that day, he carried it always, everywhere. Sometimes two. He had to.'

It's my turn to look shocked. All those times that Mabegzo waited for me, he was armed with a gun? One that he had possibly already used – and still intended to use – to kill people? I had walked the streets of Orlando East with a young man armed with the kind of deadly weapon I'd never actually seen with my own eyes except on television. This was another huge moment for me in this journey through Mabegzo's life and death. Towards the end I had come to accept that he'd done bad things, but I still never guessed that he had a gun on him at all times.

'Did he see you guys? There's no way you could have approached him from behind on that corner. You must have come from the side, from Hliso Street or straight towards him on Kuzwayo. And the shot hit him from the side, just above his right eye, and another on the right side of his chest. So it must have been from Hliso Street.'

'*Haai, wena*, tell me the truth! You're a detective, *né*?'

'No. But it was me he was waiting for at that corner. I saw him lying dead in the street.'

'Oh, it's you! You were the cheri that drove him crazy? *Haai*, you must have been very young. You were naughty.'

'Yes, I was naughty. So did he see you guys?'

'*Eish*, this is difficult. We were in a panic, remember. We had to act fast. Let me think. *Haai*, I don't really remember. One of us called his name, I think. Yes, yes, he saw us because he nodded.'

I am certain that his final nod was a sign of acceptance – not of surrender, but acceptance of his fate. Mabegzo had himself led many such missions to take out a friend, a police officer or an enemy. When he saw his friends approach, he knew he'd reached the end of the road.

Chapter 8

MY NEXT STOP IS KATLEGO'S HOUSE. He and Mabegzo may have had a fallout when Mabegzo hit his mom, but I remember the affection and camaraderie between them, and hope he can still evoke these feelings. It would also be refreshing to hear from an outsider who knew Mabegzo as a child, before the streets owned him.

It isn't difficult to find Katlego's house because it's just a few houses from Mabegzo's. Unlike many others, it's been enlarged and improved, and also has outside rooms and a pretty garden. I wonder whether Katlego's foul-mouthed mother is still alive. I'll soon find out.

At thirty-seven, Katlego looks well, despite the ravages of unemployment. His mother, Mme Shelley, was hit by a car a couple of years earlier while walking back late at night from a local shebeen. Like Koyo, she's wheelchair bound now. She tells me that she was so drunk she didn't even feel the car hit her. But the accident was a blessing in disguise, she claims, because it helped her get her life in order.

'*Le ga ke sa sebetse, ke a phela*,' she says. 'I may be unemployed, but at least I'm alive.' She receives a disability grant that she uses to buy food and help Katlego with transport money when he goes job hunting.

They flinch when I ask about Mabegzo. Time hasn't assuaged Mme Shelley's anger. 'In all my life, I had never ever been hit by a man. And to be hit by a child, a friend of my own child, and young enough to be my son – it was the ultimate insult!' I let her rattle on, but I don't believe that she'd never been hit before. Almost every woman who visited shebeens and drank heavily got into physical fights with her friends – male or female – and lovers.

'That boy was a curse!'

That word again. 'Why do you think he attacked you?'

'It was in his blood to attack people. He was just dangerous.'

'It was wrong of him to get violent. But could you have said or done anything to provoke him?'

'*Haai, wena*, nothing! He was a bad-mannered devil.' Katlego turns to me and I know that he remembers how things transpired. But his mother has convinced herself of a different version of events. There's no point in arguing. She carries right on without a pause. 'What do you expect from a rapist's son? He nearly raped me that day. If my son hadn't been there...'

She shakes her head dramatically.

'And you, Katlego? What do you remember of your childhood friend?'

He's not comfortable talking in front of his mother, and promises to call me. So I take my leave.

On a whim, I drive to Avalon cemetery to visit my father's grave. It's a risky exercise. So much has changed. Cemeteries were once the safest places to visit because of a reverence for the dead. There was an unspoken understanding that paying respect to the dead was a solemn exercise, and the graveyard was a place of solitude and prayer. Today, cemeteries live up to their names as places of death. Graves get vandalised and people get attacked and raped in cemeteries. Very recently, an acquaintance of mine lost his brother, a young medical doctor in the prime of his life, while the family was visiting the graves of loved ones. Three men approached while they were praying, and demanded car keys, cellphones and money. The family handed these over but it still wasn't enough. Blood had to be spilt, so they shot and killed his brother. The story made headlines and the culprits were eventually apprehended and sentenced, but it was little comfort to the family of this young husband and father of two.

At this moment, though, I'm not thinking straight; I can't suppress the urge to speak with my father. His tombstone is in pristine condition, and I run my hands over the letters in the marble headstone.

In loving memory of
Peter Tebonyana Direko
Born 6.03.1938 Died 26.07.1987
For it is in dying that we are born to eternal life

Born to eternal life through fatal stab wounds, leaving a wife of just thirty-five, a ten-year-old son and a nine-year-old daughter. Perpetrators never identified. Quite some price for eternal life.

'What happened to you, Papa?' Silence.

'Who stabbed you?' Silence.

'Why did they stab you?' Silence.

'Thanks for nothing.'

I walk away.

Learning the details of how Mabegzo was shot has flayed my heart raw. I keep replaying bits of the conversation with Koyo and reconstructing the final moments of Mabegzo's life. Did he wake from a restless sleep that morning and sense his demons chasing him? Or did he feel some joy, knowing that he would see me later in the day? How did he decide when to go out and when to lie low? Did he know who he was running away from? And when they revealed themselves on that street corner, what had passed through his mind? Was it relief, fear, regret, disappointment? Did he worry that I would see him vanquished? I can't suppress this flurry of questions or escape the gnawing guilt that I had helped to encourage the very routine that had provided the perfect opportunity for his friends to kill him. Although a part of me knows they would have killed him sometime, anyway, the fact is that it happened at *our* corner while he waited for *me*. This is one of the reasons I have never managed to obliterate Mabegzo from my consciousness in all these years.

My soul is in a dark place, so I decide to take a break from my mission and put some distance between his life and mine. I need some time to mend myself.

Two weeks later I feel a bit lighter, and I return to Orlando East. There is a conversation I need to have with Nkgono. I want to know how she felt about her daughter's rape and her resulting pregnancy. When I arrive, her grandchild Mpho is sitting on the stoep. Nkgono is sleeping, she tells me, and Tshepo is at a friend's place a block away.

'But wait, don't go. He'll be happy to see you. He says you're nice,' she giggles, and goes in search of her uncle.

Sure enough, Tshepo seems really happy to see me, and greets me with a hug and a kiss. He's dressed to the nines and walking with a swagger, clearly pleased with himself.

'Oh, you look nice today,' I compliment him.

'Today? I look nice all the time. I have to keep the ladies happy.'

'Well, take care they don't fight over you.'

'No, no, they must fight over me, and the winner takes all.'

'And what if the winner isn't the beautiful one?'

'Ha, to qualify for the contest, they all have to be beautiful.' We laugh together. 'So what can I do for you today?'

By now I've realised that Tshepo is just a harmless flirt, and I'm fully relaxed in his company. I tell him how surprised I was to hear from Nkgono that Mahlomola had been such a good child.

'At what age did he become troublesome?' I ask.

'By fifteen he was big already, and that's when he started to get a bit rebellious. But not enough to cause worry at first. All fifteen-year-olds get into trouble, and it was minor stuff, like smoking or stealing peaches from neighbours' trees. All the boys were doing it, so I wasn't worried.'

'Did he know who his mother was by then?'

'No, still no one in the family had told him. But by then he'd stopped asking. He'd actually met Imelda at a wedding four years earlier, but he didn't know she was his mother. And he'd stopped asking who his mother was. But he'd heard on the street that he was a rape child, and by then he knew exactly what that meant.'

'So when did his behaviour change?'

'When he returned from Lesotho, from my aunt Mme Moipone's funeral. Imelda went to live with her in Lesotho when she was pregnant, and never returned to live with us in Soweto.' Tshepo shakes his head sadly. 'The boy was so happy the day I fetched him to go to Lesotho.' He sheds a tear as he remembers, and it touches me deeply that Tshepo recognises the depth of Mabegzo's suffering. 'He was full of questions about Lesotho. He wanted to know if he would remember the first four years of his life just by being there. We caught the bus in the city that Thursday evening and arrived in Lesotho in the early hours of the morning. He couldn't believe I had come all the way back to Jo'burg to fetch him. He didn't know that it was because Imelda had asked for him.'

'Had she really?' I asked.

'Yes. And I was proud of her. She screamed and yelled and stood up for herself, demanding that Mahlomola be fetched.'

'Someone should have told him that. He needed to know that Imelda had made it happen.'

'If he'd asked me, I would have told him. But the family kept a safe distance from Imelda after that,' Tshepo said. 'They hadn't got over her outburst, and they weren't sure what she might do next. We had to return to Jo'burg the next day for work, but my mother was going to spend another two weeks in Lesotho, so there was an elder to receive the relatives. But she and Imelda had words again, so my mother didn't stay. The tension between them made everyone uncomfortable. After that trip, Mahlomola changed a lot.'

'In what way?'

'He was more confident. Cocky even. He didn't obey my mother anymore, and he answered her back. He was waiting for Imelda to come.'

Nkgono has finally risen from her afternoon nap, and she joins us on the stoep.

'You've lost weight, Nkgono,' I say. 'Are you okay?'

'Ah, my child, this old age, when it comes, it just takes over everything. Even the enjoyment of food.'

I decide to ask Nkgono what drove the family to finally banish Mabegzo from their home, something he had never been prepared to reveal to me.

'It was a Friday,' she said. 'A very angry family came to our house early that morning, threatening to burn it down. They said Mahlomola had raped their child. Then that evening the police came looking for him. It wasn't the first time. But no matter how many hidings I gave Mahlomola, he just wouldn't mend his ways.'

'He understood guns by then,' Tshepo chuckles. 'He used them all the time. Are you surprised a sjambok didn't work on him?'

'That night his grandfather had had enough. When Mahlomola arrived home, he addressed the boy directly for the first time. "*Ntswele ka ntlo*," he said. "Leave my house." I told Jakobo that Mahlomola was God's creation, and he was here for a reason. But my husband said, "Yes, the reason is to destroy our lives. The boy has been a curse."'

Pain is palpable in Nkgono's eyes now, but she continues. 'I said to my husband, "He's not just 'the boy'. He's Mahlomola. You gave him that name." And my husband slapped me.' Her tears fall softly on her tired old hands. 'In all our life together, my husband had never raised a hand to me. Never.'

Tshepo stands up awkwardly and announces that he has an errand to run. I stroke Nkgono's hand. 'Is that when Mahlomola left?'

She wipes her eye. 'When Jakobo struck me, Mahlomola hit him. That was how they parted.' She sniffs. 'Our life together was never the same after that. We never ever spoke about Mahlomola. And three months later he was in a coffin. But his grandfather wouldn't attend the funeral. He went to visit relatives in Lesotho. Even when I went to identify him in the street, I was alone. When his coffin left this house, I was alone. Jakobo wanted him buried like one who had nobody. Dead or alive, he insisted, Mahlomola must never enter this house. If it wasn't for the priest, I don't know what we would have done. He talked some sense into him, and at least he allowed me to have the funeral here.'

'Was that important to you?'

'Ha! How can you even ask? Where do you see a body leave the morgue to go straight to the cemetery? He had to pass here; it would have been inappropriate to send him straight to Avalon without passing his home.'

'You said you were relieved that he died?'

'Yes, yes,' she says without hesitation. 'I was relieved that nobody would suffer at his hand anymore. But...'

'But?'

'God says every life is precious. But the wounds from his brief moment on earth were... are... deep.'

'Why do you think Mahlomola turned into a dangerous thug?'

'He was more than a dangerous thug!' Her vehemence surprises me. 'He was a monster. Not to me, but to others.'

'Why do you think he was like that?'

'Because of his fathers. A child with many fathers cannot be right. When they raped my daughter, they all implanted their evil seed in her. That's why.'

'Do you think Mahlomola was hurt and also had wounds?'

'He was a child; I don't think he had wounds. I clothed, fed and tried to educate him. No I don't think he had wounds.

I think the evil was in his genes and I couldn't fix it.'

'So why didn't you send him to his mother when he asked you to?'

'It wouldn't have been proper.'

'But after Imelda had acknowledged him as hers, surely it would have been proper to let them develop a relationship?'

'It would have been bad for her marriage. The problems with that child started after Imelda opened her big mouth. Mahlomola was a good child before. But after Imelda spoke, it activated the evil blood he got from his fathers.'

'But Nkgono, Imelda and her husband wanted Mahlomola and he wanted them. Why did you not allow that?' I'd never argued with Nkgono, but I can hear the edge in my own voice. I know that she's a product of her time, but I'm desperate for her to at least consider that she may have made a mistake; that she missed her one opportunity to make it right and quieten the rage that demonised Mabegzo.

'Imelda taught Mahlomola the disrespect that sent him to his early grave. He had never ever disrespected us. After the trip from Lesotho, he pushed me aside when I reprimanded him. He told me he didn't need to listen to anything I said because I wasn't his mother. It was thanks to Imelda that he learnt to speak like that. After everything I'd done for them both.'

'Maybe he was just angry that his wish wouldn't be granted.'

'He was a child. And Imelda may have been married, but she was also still a child.'

This time, I'm the one who asks for a recess. I'm hurting. This lack of insight into Mabegzo's inner turmoil reminds me of my own treatment when my father died. Even as a nine-year-old, there were mornings when I felt too dispirited to get out of bed. In class, while trying to absorb what I was being taught, I'd imagine what my father had gone through as the knife sliced through his heart and gouged out his eye. At night his disfigured face would flash in front of me, and I couldn't sleep from the sorrow choking me. Nobody paused to ask what battles were raging in my soul. All I was told was, 'Don't cry'. At Papa's funeral, while I was sobbing uncontrollably, an adult relative said, 'If you go on crying, your father won't make it to heaven. He won't be able to walk through heaven's gates because your tears are going to hold him back.' So I stopped crying for him, or over him. Papa and I were done.

Mabegzo and Imelda were also done. He'd stopped waiting for her and stopped communicating with his family. He belonged to no one, and often disappeared for weeks on end like a vagabond. Sometimes he'd be gone for months as his 'operations' took him down into the bowels of the underworld. There were also regular stints in jail, but they didn't last long. He was soon back on the streets of Orlando East, where he unleashed his fiendish temper and decided who could live and who must die.

Chapter 9

WHEN I CALL KATLEGO TO ARRANGE a meeting, he agrees, but he doesn't want me to come to his house. 'If my mother's around, she'll do all the talking.' We agreed to meet at a restaurant in Orlando West, on the famous Vilakazi Street, home to Nelson Mandela and Archbishop Desmond Tutu, just a stone's throw from the Hector Pieterson Memorial. The entire precinct has become a tourist attraction these days, and hordes of tourists descend daily to visit Mandela's house, which is now a museum displaying his Nobel prize and his letters, clothes, furniture and other objects of interest.

'Did you attend Mabegzo's funeral?' I ask.

'Yes, someone had to,' he replies, 'even if it got me soaking wet.'

'Really? It wasn't raining that day.'

'No, but when my mother heard where I was going, I got a bucketful,' he jokes.

I laugh out loud at his light-hearted reference to our first meeting on his stoep in 1989, and it breaks the ice between us.

I've come to talk about Mabegzo, but Katlego wants to talk about his battle to find work. 'I know why people turn to crime – you get desperate from the indignity of being unemployed when you have a family to feed. It's been so long.'

'I'm sorry.'

'You know, if I had the heart to do it, I would.'

'Do what?'

'Apparently there's money in cash-in-transit heists.'

'There's death, also.'

He doesn't reply. 'So what was going on between you and Mabegzo? How could you be his girlfriend at such a young age?'

'I wasn't his girlfriend.'

'Oh sure, you were his "sister",' he says sarcastically.

'Yes, I was.'

'But he was in love with you, obsessed with you. Mabegzo only loved you, nobody else.'

'He loved you as well. He loved his grandmother; he loved a lot of people.'

'*Ja*, until you came along. After you, there was no one else. He lived for you.'

I swallow, unable to respond.

'He told me he'd kill for you, you know. And he did.'

The earth suddenly tilts, and my denial indicator-light starts flashing. I can feel its glow heating my face. It's one of those moments when the truth is so bitter that you try to pretend to yourself that you didn't hear what you just heard. I had always sensed that Mabegzo was involved in Siphiwe's death. I knew it. I also knew that Siphiwe's death wasn't the only issue troubling me, although for a while it weighed heavily, very heavily, on my conscience. It was the sheer force of Mabegzo's feelings for me that also left me reeling. Sometimes, when my mind flicks reluctantly back to this sorry saga, I hear that little voice that lies to me, telling me that Mabegzo reacted strongly to everything that displeased him; that he was acting in character by killing Siphiwe. But then that other little voice, the one that tells me the truth and never fails to guide me, turns up the volume and says, 'He did it for you. He could have just hit him. It was for you that he killed him.'

'You don't know for sure that he killed Siphiwe,' I say. 'And besides...'

'I was there.'

For a moment everything is surreal. Here I sit on Vilakazi Street, home to the icons of South Africa's peaceful transition, discussing my involvement in a murder.

I gather myself and change the subject. 'Tell me about you and Mabegzo. Where did you meet?'

'We were neighbours so we played together, even though many of us were told not to by our parents.'

'Why?'

'Obviously because of the rape of his mother.'

'Did your parents actually say that was why you shouldn't play with him?'

'My mother did, and many others did, long before we even knew what rape was.'

'So you played together as little boys, and you were friends right up until that day you had a fight?'

'Yes, we were at school together. But we had to meet

secretly to walk to school and back together. My mother didn't want me hanging out with Mabegzo. No parents wanted their kids to have anything to do with him. But I enjoyed his company. He was a good kid, you know. He was sweet and kind. The world turned him into something else.'

'What do you mean?'

'Adults were always pointing fingers at Mabegzo. I got so fed up with it. One day we were playing in the streets and as usual it ended in a fight. Mabegzo didn't start the fight, but the adults who came to break it up always blamed him. Ma Moloi, our neighbour, insisted it was "the rape child".'

'I got so angry, and I said, "Why are you pointing at him? So what if he's a rape?"' Katlego laughs. 'I didn't even know what it meant.

'"Shut up," she told me, "or I'll cut off your balls." That night she went to Mabegzo's home and claimed that he swore at her when she tried to stop him hitting the other children. It was a complete lie. Mabegzo hadn't said a word, but he got a hiding. You can imagine what that did to a ten-year-old child.'

I didn't need to imagine. I knew. No wonder he believed bad luck followed him everywhere.

'How was he at school?'

'Oh, he was clever, Mabegzo. If it wasn't for his temper he'd have gone far.'

'So why did he quit school?'

'The usual violence. He hit a teacher. But the teacher was harassing his cousin, Kesentseng.'

'*Kesentseng* – meaning "what have I ruined?" Geez, what's wrong with this family?' I ask. 'Giving their children such appalling names! It should be illegal.' For a moment we laugh, forgetting ourselves.

'We were all in the same class. After class, the teacher

always asked her to stay behind. Apparently he touched her and kissed her. Then he gave her money to keep her quiet.'

'Oh no.'

'*Ja*, that kind of thing was common. It was only a matter of time before he took it further. She was lucky she didn't get raped.'

There it is again, the source of my eternal rage. The gentle reminder, delivered subconsciously by decent people, that girls must be grateful if they haven't been raped. I know it wasn't really what he meant, but it's never really what anyone means. Even in this changed country and society, violence as an expression of male power hasn't changed. And it paralyses me still. I cannot countenance a society that accepts rapists in its midst and treats this horrendous crime as an inevitable part of life, while the girls are judged so harshly. It's as if being raped is like tripping over something – no big deal. Dust yourself off and move on. For a moment my rage consumes me, and I stop to breathe heavily, eyes squeezed tight.

'What's wrong?' Katlego asks, concerned.

'No, nothing. Carry on, please.'

'Anyway, Mabegzo walked in on him as he was forcing his tongue into Kesentseng's mouth. You can imagine how angry he was.'

He doesn't explain; he knows that I know. We both smile, sadly, tragically, silently admiring the love and determination to protect that lay behind Mabegzo's misguided actions.

'That was the end of his school career.'

'That's not fair.'

'Nothing that happened to Mabegzo was fair.'

'But I still can't understand how someone who hated seeing people treated with injustice and violence could do the same to others.'

Katlego goes on to tell me how Mabegzo protected him on the school grounds, and how gentle and sweet he was.

'So where did this monster come from?'

'The monster was created by the adults who made him feel useless. He figured that if they thought the worst of him when he did good things, he might as well do bad things to earn the scorn they were already heaping on him.'

'It sounds like you're making excuses for him. He still had a choice.'

'A choice? Where do you come from? For some people there are no choices. Do you think I choose to be unemployed?'

'No, but you're still not resorting to crime. That's a choice.'

For a moment he seems to contemplate my statement. 'Maybe I haven't reached the same level of desperation Mabegzo reached. And if I do, maybe I also won't have a choice.'

'So, you said you were there? When Mabegzo... when Siphiwe got killed?'

'Yes. I was there. And he killed him for you, just in case you didn't know.'

'I suspected, but I didn't know for sure.'

'But *wena*, what were you playing at? If you hadn't played them, maybe they'd both be alive.'

'I don't know what you're talking about. I was eleven...'

'And you were a naughty little girl who liked tsotsis. And one of them killed his rival to impress you.'

I'm getting annoyed with him. I count to ten to calm myself. 'Siphiwe used to bully and threaten me. And I was afraid of him, terrified. But...'

'So you got Mabegzo to sort him out. Knowing Mabegzo as you did, you must have known that telling him someone was harassing you was the same as asking him to kill that person.'

I don't attempt to argue. 'So tell me about the day Siphiwe was killed.'

'A group of us went to lift weights at the community hall on a Saturday afternoon. Mabegzo was with us. He always lifted weights so he would look strong and invincible. He worked really hard and drove himself as if a demon was chasing him. Long after everyone else had stopped exercising, he was still at it. There was no cardio equipment, but he brought a skipping rope and hopped on and on till he was really sweating. On our way home, he suddenly announced that he had a mission to accomplish, but he first had to consult his sangoma to see if this was the time. I knew then that he wanted to commit a crime. He always consulted his sangoma before and after.'

'So you went with him?'

'One boy went home, but I went out of curiosity, along with two others. I forget their names; they were more his friends than mine. I never got involved in Mabegzo's shenanigans, and every time I showed any interest in his affairs, he'd caution me and say, "This is not for you".'

I smile. Typical!

'I thank him now for looking out for me. But he never preached about the evil of crime; he didn't think he was committing crimes. He just didn't want me to get blood on my hands.'

'So he kept you away from it all?'

'*Ja*. Except for that incident with Siphiwe. I was there. I saw everything. It made me very angry because by taking us there, Mabegzo exposed all of us. We had nothing to do with it. What if Siphiwe's gang had retaliated? But if you hadn't complained to him about Siphiwe, Mabegzo would have killed one less person in his lifetime. And what if that was the murder that sent him to hell?'

'I don't believe in hell,' I answer quickly. But I know that's not the point he's making. He lets it go.

'We walked to Meadowlands to see his traditional healer, or witchdoctor, whatever.'

'That was far.'

'We were young and fit; a seven-kilometre walk was nothing. When we got there, Mabegzo told us to wait outside. He took off his shoes and left them at the gate because he wasn't allowed to bring in any darkness that could be following him.

'Mabegzo was inside for about half an hour and came out running, grabbing his shoes and running barefoot. We didn't know what was going on, but we followed him, scared that something had happened. On the way he didn't say a word. His sangoma had told him not to open his mouth until he'd finished his task.

'We ran all the way to Orlando East. Only Mabegzo knew what was about to happen; the rest of us were excited and fascinated by what the sangoma might have said to him. When we reached Siphiwe's house, Mabegzo still didn't say a word. He just signalled to us to wait outside the gate.'

'Did you know Siphiwe?'

'Yes, but not well. He was a filthy thug, always up to no good. He wasn't our friend, but we knew him. Moments later, Mabegzo walked out of the back yard with his arm around Siphiwe. Siphiwe was talking a lot and he seemed surprised and honoured to be in such proximity to Mabegzo. We walked to the corner of the street. Then just as we reached the church, Mabegzo pulled out an *oukappie* and stabbed Siphiwe deep in the neck. Siphiwe looked stunned as he fell, bleeding. But he couldn't have been more stunned than we were.'

He's lost in time as he relates this story, but there's no doubt that he's still traumatised by it. I can see Katlego hates violence.

'Siphiwe made a sound, half pleading, half enquiring. He looked really confused. I think he tried to ask what was going on. His last words were, "*Mfowethu*. My brother." Mabegzo spat at him. He said, "I'm not your brother. And if you threaten Momo again, I'll kill you again."'

Chapter 10

I'VE TAKEN TO MAKING WEEKLY visits to Nkgono's house, usually on a Sunday when people are relaxed and most likely to be at home. Saturdays are too busy with weddings, funerals and shopping. On the odd weekend that I don't arrive there, I get a call from Tshepo.

'Have you found another husband, my darling?' he'll ask. 'You didn't come today.'

'*Haai*, Tshepo. I've been too busy.'

'Busy with what? If it doesn't involve me, it's not important.'

I enjoy popping in. Even when I find Nkgono sleeping, there's always someone at her house, and because my own grandmother is in Orlando East, it's never a wasted trip;

I can always while away the time at her house. Nkgono tires easily these days, and sometimes the conversation about Mabegzo takes place only between Tshepo and me.

Today Tshepo is sitting under the fig tree, polishing his shoes. He loves to look good, even if he has nowhere to go.

'*O ya kae*? Where are you off to?' I tease him.

'A nice lady has promised me lunch.'

'Just lunch?'

'Lunch and whatever else a nice guy like me deserves,' he grins. He's middle aged but still a hottie with a smooth tongue. 'Do you know that you've never told me why you're asking so many questions about my nephew? Who was he to you?'

'Everything.'

'Huh?'

'He was everything.'

Tshepo is younger than Imelda, and I wonder how much he actually remembers and understood about what happened to his sister. So I ask.

'Well, we knew that Imelda was sent to school in Lesotho a while after the incident. Our parents never actually told us what happened to her, but everyone else was talking about it. So I was glad when she was sent away.'

This surprises me. 'You were glad? But why?'

'We were taunted every day as we walked to school and back. Everyone knew our sister had been raped and they mocked us. We didn't even know what being raped meant, but the way they said it, we knew it was something horrible.'

'Who laughed at you?'

'The stupid kids on the streets. I got into so many fights over it; it was all too much. I went home and asked my mother and father what rape was, and why someone did it to Imelda.'

'What did they say?'

'Ah, the usual,' he shrugs. 'Ntate lit his pipe and Mme said we must pray.'

'What was Imelda going through in the aftermath of this?'

He had no idea. 'Mohau and I were so busy fighting the boys who were taunting us, we didn't realise that Imelda had changed or needed help. This whole rape thing was too embarrassing. But it changed everything. Even now, Imelda isn't part of the family. She stayed in Lesotho, got married and still works there. She hardly ever comes to Soweto.'

'All the better, I say.'

'Why?'

'Because everyone here failed her.'

He pauses for a while. 'You know, *nna batho ba kgale a ke ba understandi*. I don't understand the older generation. Somehow they just treated children like things to be sent to the shops, ordered to make tea and given hidings.'

'What's your relationship like with Imelda now?'

'Nobody really speaks to her. She has her own life. She seems okay, but she doesn't have any connection with us.'

'And Nkgono? Do they speak?'

'Not that I know of.'

Tshepo has to leave for his lunch.

'Don't do anything I wouldn't do,' I tease.

'I plan to do exactly what you wouldn't do.'

'You're a dirty old man, Tshepo,' I say as we hug and promise to meet again the following week.

Although it's not easy juggling two jobs with my studies and still fitting in these visits, I'm determined to find closure.

But soon I accept a job in Cape Town and start planning the big move. I've never lived in another city before, and I find it stressful that a visit home will now require a two-hour flight. The final stages before my move keep me busy finding a tenant, arranging storage for my possessions and transferring to another university.

Telling my grandmother about my move is the hardest of all. When I arrive, she and my grandfather are sitting in the lounge watching soccer on television.

'*Haai*, man, you and this working all the time! I'm going to miss you,' she says.

'Who are you going to live with?' my grandfather wants to know.

'*Hawu*, why do you ask her such a question?' my grandmother asks. 'She's going there for work.'

'What's wrong with my question? I want to know.'

I roll my eyes, knowing that this argument will drag on. After nearly fifty years of marriage, I suppose they've earned the right to bicker like this.

My granny is the most compassionate person I know, and her empathy for others is unparalleled. She is the person you want on your side when your wounds are too deep. As I drive to Nkgono's house after this visit, I can't help wishing that Imelda and Mabegzo had had her as a granny. I know the comparison is unfair, but I find it unavoidable. Nkgono isn't a bad person, but her austere style was not what Imelda and Mabegzo were in need of.

Mpho tells me that her grandmother is sleeping. I'm running out of time to spend with her now, so I decide to wait for her to wake up. Tshepo isn't here either; he's moved in with his new lady, the one he met for lunch five weeks ago. I can easily see how a woman could let him stay in her hard-earned house without asking anything more than the charm he oozes in return. I wait under the tree, watching children run their fingers over my dirty car, writing 'please wash me' in the dust, just as I once used to. For a moment, I'm glad to see children being children. Then they turn to me, expecting a harsh reprimand. I smile and walk towards them.

'Did you write my car a letter?'

They giggle. 'No, we wrote it for you.'

'Oh I see, can I read it?'

'No, it's for your car, not for you.'

'*Haai, wena*, it's for her because it's her car.' An argument ensues among the four children, and they take it very seriously. In the end they decide I should read their letter, and it does indeed say, 'Plis washe me'.

I promise that I will, and offer them two rand each. 'But on one condition.'

'What?'

'That you put on some warm clothes,' I grin, 'because it's cold.'

'*Haai, mina angeke ngikhone, ngiyi-bourgeois*. No, I can't. I'm bourgeois,' says one girl – township lingo for fashion conscious and privileged.

'Are you really going to give us five rand each?'

'*Jo, imali engaka*. So much money.'

'No, I said two rand.'

'You said five,' the little 'bourgeois' insists. In the end I part with twenty rand for these four charmers, hoping it won't land them in trouble. We always got hidings if we had money we couldn't explain. As a girl I used to nag my favourite adults for a shilling (ten cents) and I got nicknamed Shilling by an older cousin who dreaded bumping into me in the streets. If she didn't have my ten cents I'd pester her until she found it somewhere just to get rid of me. Her friends used to laugh as I nagged her.

'*Haai*, you promised.'

'I don't have it.'

'Why not?'

'I left it at home.'

'Let's go fetch it now.'

'I'm busy.'

'You're not busy; you're standing at a street corner.'

'*Haai, uya hlupha*. You're a nuisance.'

She'd then dig in her pockets or ask a friend to lend her ten cents. One day she found twenty cents. 'Wait here while I get change at the shops.' I knew she had no intention of returning.

'I'm coming with you.'

'Don't be naughty, wait here.'

But I wouldn't let her out of my sight. 'Let me come with you, or you wait here while I get the change.'

'*Haai*, give this child the money,' her friends laughed. 'She's too clever for you.' In the end, I was twenty cents richer – enough for an ice block and *makipkip*.

I wander back to Nkgono's house, and find her lying in bed, still groggy from her afternoon nap.

'I'm sorry, have you been waiting all this time?'

'It's no problem.'

'What's your name again?'

'Redi, Redi Direko.'

'Oh, I see. And why are you always asking about Mahlomola?'

I have forgotten that she's an old lady, and although she's sharp and lucid at seventy-eight, she seems to be sleeping a lot lately, and getting more tired with each passing day. For a moment I regret badgering her so often, but I'm still hoping she'll lead me to Imelda, because even Tshepo doesn't know where in Lesotho his older sister lives; he's had no contact with her since Mme Moipone's funeral in the eighties.

In our last conversation, I asked Nkgono why she'd decided to send Imelda to Lesotho to have the baby, but she hadn't answered. This time she says, 'I had no choice. Jakobo insisted. It's not what I personally wanted.'

'Why didn't you want her to go to Lesotho?'

'Because it would look like we were ashamed of the cross God had given us to carry.'

'Do you mean the rape of your daughter and the birth of Mahlomola were crosses God had given you?'

'Yes, yes, yes, my child. They were the will of God.'

It seemed to me that God was asking a lot of a fifteen-year-old teenager to have her raped and impregnated as a lesson to her mother, but I knew better than to say so to this woman of God.

'How did you find out that she'd been raped?'

She thinks hard. For an old woman, she has an amazing ability to recall past events and tell them with accuracy and precision.

'Imelda was a bubbly child. She talked and laughed all the time. She was always happy to be sent on errands. When she didn't return on time that day, I got worried. Some neighbours saw a group of young men in their late teens playing dice at the street corner. One of them grabbed her. She struggled but soon other boys joined in. Nobody saw where she was taken because it was already dark by then. We searched for her late into the night, with some neighbours helping. The other boys had left the corner to avoid being questioned, so there was no one to show us where she was taken.'

'You couldn't have slept well that night.'

'We didn't sleep at all. I didn't know whether to go to the police or just keep on looking and asking people.'

'Did nobody hear her scream?'

'People said they didn't hear anything. Jakobo decided to keep looking for her while I went to the Orlando Police

Station, but early in the morning Imelda knocked on the door.'

'And what did you do?'

'I asked her what had happened, but she just kept quiet.'

'What did you think had happened?'

'I knew what had happened. I asked if she could identify the boys and the house where it happened. She nodded. I then boiled water and fetched soap so she could wash herself. In the meantime, Jakobo and one of our neighbours went to the Orlando Police Station to report the matter.'

'Were the culprits arrested and charged?'

'I can't remember if anyone was arrested, but there was no trial. Imelda took us to the house and three boys were found, still sleeping. They were given a hiding by the police and the community. It was a very harsh beating.'

'Did Imelda watch them being beaten?'

'Yes, we all did.'

'How did your family cope with what had happened?'

'Imelda was a different child afterwards. But my late husband didn't want to hear any discussion about the matter, and told us all never to speak of it in his house.'

'Did you want to speak about it?'

'I wanted to pray and ask for forgiveness and healing.'

'Forgiveness? For what?'

'It's when we stray from the will of the Lord that these things happen.'

'So did you pray about it?'

'Privately I did, but not openly.'

'Did your other children know that their sister had been raped?'

'I don't know. I never asked them.'

'Did Imelda speak about it?'

'Not to me.'

'Did anyone ask her how she was feeling?'

'No.'

'Why not?'

'It was forbidden to talk about it.'

'Do you have any idea how Imelda felt about the rape, and about Mahlomola?'

'I don't know what kind of life you lead where you have a name for every feeling. Or where everything you feel must be spoken about. Who are we to question God and to say, I prefer this feeling and that feeling, but not that one?'

'May I ask her how she feels?'

'She's in Lesotho; you won't find her.'

'Could I have her address or telephone number?'

She looks at me as if I've lost my mind, and maybe I have. But there's so much I'd like to ask Imelda.

'No. *Ho fedile. Tsohle di fetile.* It's done now; it's in the past.'

'Do you think Imelda is upset with you, Nkgono?'

'Why would she be upset?'

'For sending her to Lesotho, perhaps?'

'No, no. I'm her mother, so no.' She pauses a moment. 'I sent her there to protect her. If she'd stayed here, she'd have ended up like the other girls: lots of babies and no husband. Once you have one child out of wedlock, rest assured, more will follow. Lesotho was the best place for her.'

'How did you feel when your child got raped?'

She shifts uneasily on her bed, and asks for water. 'It was the work of the devil. I had to pray.'

'But how did you feel?'

'She had always been a very good child, so it wasn't good. I felt bad. And finding out that she was with child while she was still a child herself – that wasn't good.'

'And your husband? How did he feel?'

'He wouldn't say anything. Some matters are best left unspoken.'

'You said that there was no trial, even though the culprits were known. Why didn't you demand that the police follow it up?' The South African police were certainly corrupt, racist and more concerned with their political agenda than with protecting citizens, but they also had a no-nonsense approach, and relished any opportunity to punish black youths suspected of a crime.

'It didn't cross my mind.'

'Why not?' I persist.

'That's not how we did things in those days. We corrected behaviour, we didn't just run to the police.'

'Imelda doesn't visit much, does she?'

'No. She doesn't like to come here. She's busy with her family in Lesotho.'

'Does she call?'

'No, phones are expensive.'

'When last did you see her?'

'It's been many years. Too many, but maybe she'll come to bury me.'

I ask why Mahlomola was sent to Johannesburg as a four-year-old, while Imelda stayed behind in Lesotho.

'A young man was interested in Imelda. He wouldn't have married her if she came with a child.'

'Did he say so?'

'No, but in those days, it wasn't right for a woman to arrive in her new home with another man's child.'

'Did he know Imelda had a child?'

'No, we didn't tell the family when they came to negotiate *mahadi*, dowry. Are you married?'

'No.'

'Do you have a child?'

'Not yet.'

'Keep it that way,' she advises. 'It's only honourable to carry your husband's children. You'll see for yourself.' She goes on to lecture me about the honour marriage bestows on a woman. It's not nice to be a spinster, she tells me.

'How did your husband feel about Mahlomola coming to live with you?'

'He didn't want Mahlomola to come. There was a lot of arguing before the decision was made. We decided to bring the child here the day before the *mahadi* negotiations.'

I know better than to ask what Imelda thought of this. I'm almost certain nobody asked her opinion; not that it would have mattered anyway.

'The elders reminded Jakobo that Imelda had been soiled, and that it was a privilege to have another family wishing for her to be their *makoti*. "Do you want your daughter to stay unmarried?" they asked him. Eventually he saw the light. He had to agree that this was the chance of a lifetime for Imelda.'

'How easily did Mahlomola fit in with your family?'

'I raised him just like my other children. That's why I couldn't understand why he became a criminal. I fed and clothed him, I prayed for him and I treated him like all the others.'

'But he wasn't always troublesome.'

'No, he was a sweet child. He never cried, and he was always eager to be sent to the shops and help around the house. The streets of Soweto put the devil in him.' Nkgono can't seem to decide why her grandson turned out so evil. She has blamed the evil seed of 'his fathers', Imelda's behaviour and now the streets. Yet she had always still hoped that prayer would cure him.

Tshepo arrives and offers us tea. He takes a seat at the

edge of the bed and listens quietly as Nkgono and I talk.

Eventually he asks his mother, 'Why didn't the elders let Mahlomola visit his mother? Long after he knew Imelda was his mother, he asked to live with her, and she was happy with that. She said so.'

'It wouldn't have been good for her marriage. You've never been married, *wena*, Tshepo, so keep quiet. Men don't forgive women for their pasts.'

Tshepo turns to me and says, 'That boy would have been a different person if he'd been told the truth from the start. It was never too late. Even after finding out who his mother was, he was still a good boy. He was in his teens and he hadn't started these bad things. If he'd been sent to his mother then, he'd still be alive.'

Nkgono doesn't believe so. She's sold on the idea that Mabegzo's soul was tainted by a combination of forces beyond anyone's control. She is happy to explore various reasons why Mabegzo became evil, but she sees no possibility that her grandson was reacting to the taunting and the separation from his mother. It doesn't cross her mind that Mabegzo's restlessness over the identity of his mother and his perceived rejection by Imelda may have caused enough trauma to give rise to a dysfunctional human being.

I ask Nkgono if she thinks Imelda had a happy childhood before she was raped.

'Oh yes. She was a happy child. We believed in firm discipline, and our children had security and order. We weren't rich, but most families in Soweto weren't.'

'You said that your husband also came from Lesotho, is that right?'

'Yes, we were both from Teyateyaneng, and we both came to Johannesburg to find work.'

'Did you know each other from Lesotho?'

'No, not at all. But our parents knew each other. When our mothers found out that we were both in Johannesburg, they arranged for us to meet so that Jakobo could take care of me. They were worried that Johannesburg was too wild and dangerous for a woman. One Christmas holiday when both of us were home in Lesotho, our mothers tried their best to make us like each other, to make a match between us. But we were too shy. We returned to Johannesburg without exchanging addresses or planning to get together again.'

'Did your parents try again the next Christmas?'

'No. I didn't get back home to Teyateyaneng for the next two Christmas holidays because my madam needed me over the holidays.'

'Oh, so how did you finally get married?'

'My madam had a clothing factory, and she saw that I always spent my leisure time knitting and sewing my own clothes. Two and half years after I met Jakobo in Teyateyaneng, she sent me to work in her factory as a seamstress. Jakobo happened to be a messenger at the same factory.'

'And did cupid's arrow strike home this time?' I tease. Nkgono just shrugs. She won't be drawn into sharing any juicy details of their courtship. Romance is not on the menu. '*Hawu*, Nkgono, you must have felt wonderful when Ntate Jakobo started paying you attention,' I press.

'You and these feelings you like to talk about. *Haai, tjhe, ka nnete, o a makatsa*. Really, you're so strange.' All she is prepared to tell me is that they married in 1950, had their children and raised them as best they could. Their union lasted until Jakobo died in 2002 at the age of eighty-one.

I'm racing against time now and I feel that Katlego and I haven't finished our conversation. He agrees to meet me the next evening when I finish work. I find myself back in Soweto's familiar evening buzz as swarms of weary men and women pile out of trains, buses and taxis to make their way home on tired legs. Children still play in the streets until dark, as long as the shops remain open. After dark, parked cars offer unmarried couples a semblance of privacy, as boyfriends may not enter a girl's home until *mahadi* has been paid and a relationship established between the two families. The men often arrive in their cars to visit their girlfriends after dark, and if the girl's parents aren't too strict, she will go to sit in her boyfriend's car for a chat and heaven knows what else. This practice of 'go checka' your girlfriend has become dangerous, though, as hijackers and robbers sometimes pounce on unwary couples. But this is exactly how Katlego and I meet, albeit for a different reason and with the genders reversed. The risk of Katlego's mom barging in on our conversation seems infinitely worse than the risk of sitting in my car.

'I've always wondered why Mabegzo brought me to your house that day,' I tell Katlego. 'He never introduced me to anyone else – not that I introduced him to my people, either,' I add unnecessarily. He was hardly someone I could have introduced to anyone. And besides, whatever was happening between us then left no room for a third person. There could only ever be the two of us; nervous in each other's company, safe, thrilled and finally deaf to what was going on around us at that time. We lived in our own special world.

'I asked him to,' Katlego says.

I look at him in surprise.

'After he killed Siphiwe, I had a lot of questions for him. I told Mabegzo that I wanted to see you with my own eyes. I mean, it didn't make sense that anyone would just kill for a friend. And I saw the fire in his eyes when he spoke about you. He said you had no one and it was his duty to protect you. "Who is this Momo Ntwana?" I kept asking him. "Why did you kill Siphiwe for her?" He tried to avoid me, but I went to his house and followed him everywhere.'

'He was very secretive.'

'Yes, and I allowed him his dark secrets. But not this time. By taking me to the scene and doing it in front of me, he'd given me the right to ask questions.'

'And then?'

'It was only when I told him I couldn't sleep and I was haunted that he looked genuinely concerned for me, even a bit frightened. He suggested we consult his sangoma first, as only he could guide him. It seemed that the sangoma advised him to let me in on the circumstances that led to Siphiwe's murder, but only if I first went to consult him with Mabegzo.'

'Ha! But you didn't believe in this business of visiting a sangoma, did you? So it must have been quite an experience.'

'It was, but I thought Mabegzo was just stalling. It just seemed to confirm that you didn't really exist and he'd just killed Siphiwe for the sake of it.'

'So what happened at the sangoma?'

'It was scary. We took off our shoes at the gate and went into a back room full of containers and buckets of stuff that looked like grass. The sangoma lit a candle and asked us to open our eyes wide so he could "look into our souls". He came right up to my face until his nose was touching mine. He sniffed my hands and neck and told me to keep still. After a while, he threw some bones, clapped his hands and jumped around. I must have passed the test, because he turned to Mabegzo and said, "*Aba phansi ba ya mujabulela*. The ancestors are happy with him".

'Then we had to kneel, and Mabegzo explained that Siphiwe was his enemy and had threatened to rape someone

157

he cared about. I thought Mabegzo was playing games again. I didn't believe Siphiwe had started anything or that you even existed. Obviously there must have been some rivalry between them, but I wanted to see you with my own eyes first. Either he wanted Siphiwe's cheri and eliminated him for being in the way, or this Momo didn't exist and he was just trying to excuse a senseless murder.'

'But didn't he directly accuse Siphiwe of threatening me?'

'Sure, but that didn't necessarily mean anything. They could have been fighting over anything, I didn't know. I'd never seen you or heard you mentioned before, so I had to know if you were real.'

'Well, aren't you the ultimate doubting Thomas?' We laugh, which breaks the tension a bit, but I still feel judged and uncomfortable around Katlego. He's angry that he's unemployed, but I also sense his ongoing disapproval of my relationship with Mabegzo. And I can see that he still doesn't buy the story that Mabegzo and I were only friends. Who knows, maybe he shouldn't; what we had was more than friendship. Yet, what it was I cannot even explain to myself, so I leave him to his speculation. 'What happened next at the sangoma?'

'The sangoma said he had to perform a cleansing ritual for both of us because, by speaking about it again, Mabegzo had opened himself up to darkness. He would cleanse him, and that would be the end of the matter. Under no circumstances were we to talk about it again without clearing it with him first – for a fee of course – or something dreadful would happen to us and to whoever we told.'

'So have you cleared our chat with the sangoma now?' I ask mischievously. 'I don't want any bad luck, you know.' We laugh.

'He made us chew some leaves; then he poured a dark

concoction on our heads and smeared stuff on us. It was weird.'

'Did you believe you were being cleansed?'

'No, of course I didn't believe that shit; I still don't. But Mabegzo's life was so dark and sad that I suppose he needed this kind of protection. With all his horrible deeds, he felt vulnerable. He believed everything this guy told him.' He shakes his head. '*Ja*, this sangoma also made him arrogant. He knew there were people waiting for a chance to kill him, but he believed he was invincible.'

I don't agree. He might have once thought so, but the last three months of his life certainly taught him otherwise. But I don't wish to reveal Mabegzo too much to anyone else – in a way it would seem like a betrayal.

'It's true that he was arrogant,' I tell Katlego. 'On one of our walks from school, he once asked if I was curious about who killed my dad. I said no, I only wanted to know why they'd cut his eye out. He said he'd find them and ask them, and then he'd cut their eyes out, so they could also feel it. When I told him the police would catch him, he said, "The police? *A ke tshabe magata*. Ask anyone around here; they're scared of me." The contempt in his voice unnerved me so much that I started to run away. This was in the early days when he still frightened me. But he grabbed my wrist and demanded, "*O tshaba eng*? What are you scared of?" When I said, "You," he apologised and asked me not to be mad at him.'

'Oh my God, that boy was sick, sick, sick!' Katlego looks visibly shocked, but I can't imagine why. My little anecdote is no worse than many things he already knows about his late friend. I watch him struggling with himself, unable to find words.

When he speaks his voice has changed. 'While Siphiwe

was lying bleeding on the ground, Mabegzo sat on his chest.' He swallows. 'Then he stuck the knife right into Siphiwe's eye and literally dug it out.'

I feel my stomach heave. I see my father's face without the eye, and now Siphiwe's. Both caricatures dance in front of me. The nausea and revulsion take my breath away. I open the car door just in time. Katlego gets out and comes around to my side as I vomit on the pavement.

'Hey, what's wrong?' He rubs my back gently. 'What's the matter? Is there anything I can do for you?'

'It must be the sangoma,' I say, putting on a brave face. 'You didn't clear it with him.'

Katlego laughs easily and it helps cover my embarrassment.

'I have to go.'

'*Hawu*, just like that? *A re so fetsi mos.* We're not done yet.'

'I have to go. I'm really sorry about this mess.'

'It's fine. We'll pour water on it in the morning. Don't worry.'

'Please bring me a bucket of water. I'd rather do it myself right now.' We argue about it for a moment but I'm not about to let him clean up after me, so I insist and wait until he brings the water. I use the car lights so I can aim the water at the right spot.

'When will you be back? We're not done, right?' Katlego asks.

I'm too tired to answer, but I know I'm done with Mabegzo.

I drive straight home, switch off my phone, draw the curtains and lie on the floor in the darkness for what feels like an eternity. The darkness of the room is nothing compared to the darkness within. Katlego's revelation has changed everything. Spoilt everything. I never wanted Siphiwe dead.

Even in telling Mabegzo I was merely questioning how he could associate with such a person.

I know that killing a human being is the final act of hatred, the final crossing of all boundaries. But right now, for me, even that is overshadowed by this new question tormenting my mind. Not what kind of man murders another in cold blood, but what kind of human being gouges out his dead victim's eye? Having killed the person already, for goodness sake, what macabre obsession drives a man to jab a knife into a dead man's eye and yank it out of its socket? Who the hell does something that barbarous? Mabegzo has sunk to the status of my father's killers, who weren't satisfied to kill a man, but took their savagery to another level and filled my childhood with nightmares. It is this grisly act that has finally pushed me over the brink; that Mabegzo had chosen such men as his role models. I am forced at last to see Mabegzo for what and who he was: not my gentle protector, but a true psychopath.

'Say it Redi!' I shout to myself. 'Say it!'

'He was a psychopath!'

'Say his name.'

'Mabegzo.'

'Say Mabegzo was a psychopath.'

And still my heart resists, because it remembers the love, the caring.

'Stop it. Say Mabegzo was a psychopath.'

'Mabegzo was a psychopath.'

'Say Mabegzo was a rapist and a psychopath.'

'Mabegzo was a rapist and a psychopath.'

'So how could you love him?' This cruel voice will not release me from its inquisition.

But my heart has had enough. I don't have to answer this tonight. Its time will come. I have made one crucial admission today, tonight. I need to absorb its impact. All my life I have thought about Mabegzo's evil deeds but remembered how gentle, loving and protective he was; this has helped me justify my own affection towards him. I've never fully admitted that he was a thug, a sadist and a psychopath. It's a huge, taxing admission to make and I feel the mourning inside. Today, the Mabegzo I knew and cared for has finally died. He has exhausted all the sagacity my heart will allow. Now, at long last, I have to let him go, all because he wouldn't leave a dead man's eye alone.

PART 3

Chapter 11

SEVEN MONTHS AFTER LEAVING for Cape Town, I am getting ready to move back to Johannesburg. My new job hasn't worked out. But I have no regrets. When I first accepted the job offer, I couldn't have guessed what a necessity it would become for me to get away from Johannesburg. It was as if I was starting over again after a death. For me, Katlego's revelation in my car that evening had been a death of sorts.

But Cape Town has provided solace and an opportunity to quieten the noise around me. Although the Mother City is often described as cold and insular, it's the perfect place for a soul in need of solitude. The deep divide between rich and poor is more evident there than elsewhere, but it's masked by the city's breathtaking beauty. Life here is easy for those who would rather overlook the backbreaking poverty of its townships. After the first five-minute drive from the airport through a landscape of sprawling shacks, the discomfort is quickly displaced by majestic views of Table Mountain, the Waterfront and the blue expanse of the ocean.

I have begun to feel healthy and strong again, ready to take on the world once more. In these past months I have refused to think about Mabegzo, and my bewildering new working environment has kept me too busy to wallow in my feelings. But I sense that I am still wounded; otherwise there would have been no need to 'refuse' to think about him. The conscious effort involved tells me that I haven't quite worked through the damage. And the damage is great. I am profoundly disappointed that his own trauma hadn't ignited a compassion for other human beings, including Siphiwe. I am bewildered by his genuine affection for me, but horrified that he was capable of taking a life in such a cruel manner. And I am angry with myself that my turning point arose not from the knowledge that he was a murderer, but from the fact that he ripped out a man's eye. Surely the act of killing itself should matter more than the manner in which it was done? Yet the manner of this killing matters greatly to me. He murdered in the same way that my father was murdered, and this has put him in another league.

My heart is also burdened by the behaviour of the adults towards Mabegzo while he was growing up, who were unaware that every day their words, deeds and indifference towards him stung, and ultimately gave rise to a monster. I ache for all the other Mabegzos roaming the streets of my home town. As they graduate into hardened criminals, everybody claims not to know where it all started. And so, in my solitude, I have eventually dug deep to try to find forgiveness for all these things.

On my arrival in Johannesburg in January 2005, I go straight to my grandmother in Soweto to tell her that I've returned. I'm back in the arms of love again!

My next stop is Nkgono and Tshepo. I've grown very fond of them, and I'm deeply grateful for their generosity with their time, and for trusting me enough to bare their family secrets to me.

I find Mpho and her mother, Greta, who is also visiting and helping to take care of Nkgono. I introduce myself to Greta, who is pleasant and welcomes me.

'How do you know my family?' she asks.

'I'm a friend of Tshepo's,' I say without thinking.

'*Ja*, Uncle Tshepo has a lot of friends,' Mpho says mischievously.

'*Haai, wena*!' says Greta.

'How is Nkgono doing?' I enquire.

'She hardly wakes these days. That's why I'm here. There's more work to do. But I go back to work in a week so I don't know what will happen. She's not well.'

I want to see Nkgono, even if she's sleeping, just to hold her hand. But I've only just met Greta and Mpho is only a child, so I can't ask either of them.

'Do you need anything at all?' I ask instead.

'No, thanks, we're coping.'

I return to see Nkgono twice more, but I always find her sleeping. The second time, Greta has returned to Pretoria and another relative is helping out. I manage to see Nkgono, but she is not aware of my presence. I am shocked at how much she has changed in just seven months. Lying on her bed she looks as helpless as a doll. Her bones stick out through the thin sheet that covers her. Her hair has fallen out so that she is almost bald; she is truly just skin and bones. I kiss her lips and squeeze her hand, knowing I may never see her again.

She is barely alive anyway.

Four days later, on the fourth of February 2005, I receive an sms from Tshepo to say that his mother has died in her sleep in the early hours of the morning. She was reluctant to visit the doctor about her abdominal cramps, fatigue and loss of appetite, and finally died at the age of seventy-nine.

I'm under no obligation to attend her funeral, but it's the decent thing to do. Nkgono and Tshepo were always very welcoming to me, even when I dropped in unannounced and raised matters they would sooner not talk about. I phone Tshepo to offer my condolences and he tells me that the funeral will take place on Saturday the twelfth of February. I must first pay my respects to the family before the funeral, to check how they are doing. It's the right thing to do.

Tshepo looks delighted to see me when I arrive on Sunday afternoon, and gratefully accepts the groceries and scones I've brought.

'*Heyi wena*, stranger. *O re latlhile*. You abandoned us.'

'*Askies*, I've been travelling a lot and you weren't here when I came to see Nkgono.'

'Oh, you came? I'm sure you didn't recognise Mama, she got so thin. Greta's daughter had to come to wash and feed her. And my wife also helped out.'

'Your wife? *Hawu*, Tshepo! So quickly? When I last saw you, you had just met someone. You married her so quickly?'

'Oh no, not that one. She didn't work out.'

'So where did you find a wife so quickly?' I ask, genuinely surprised. Tshepo is the proverbial township uncle – happy to live at home and have children with different women, but not marry any of them. And even if he were to settle down, he isn't the type to go and find a home for his new family, so I'm impressed.

'She's a teacher,' he says proudly, 'and she owns a bonded house in Protea Gardens.' Protea Gardens is a newer part of Soweto for the 'haves'. It's nothing like the opulence of some Johannesburg suburbs, but it's a step up from the matchbox houses of most black townships.

'Wow, Tshepo, a bonded house? You've done well.'

'Thanks,' he says sincerely.

'So, you're taken now?'

'Hey, sweetheart, I'll never be taken.'

More people arrive to pay their respects to the family. I get up to help in the kitchen. Young ladies don't sit around at funerals; there's a lot of tea and coffee to make and it never stops. Every minute, more people arrive to pay their respects, and judging by the numbers here it would seem that Nkgono was welcomed back into the community and that her neighbours have forgotten about Mabegzo. They sing, pray and offer their condolences.

In the kitchen, Tshepo introduces me to some of his other relatives. 'And guess who this is?' He gestures towards the woman washing dishes, and I assume I'm about to meet his wife.

'Imelda, say hello to your daughter-in-law.'

I am completely taken aback. I wasn't expecting this encounter, and I realise that I've almost forgotten about Imelda. Although we've spoken about her several times, it was mostly in the past tense, and I've long since dismissed any hope of tracking her down in Lesotho. The chasm separating her life from theirs seemed too wide. And for some silly reason, my picture of Imelda is still of a violated teenager, a quiet young woman who had no say in the story of her life until she finally found her voice and lashed out at her mother. In my fantasy she never grew up; she was just a girl huddled in a corner, dying for a warm embrace. This grown woman, old enough to be my mother, isn't at all the picture I had in my mind.

Imelda puts her arms around me. 'I'm glad to meet you,' she says. She's very thin, with slow movements as though the world is on her shoulders.

As we continue to make and serve tea, the two of us say little to each other, but there's no feeling of awkwardness among the friendly chatter of the other ladies.

I say my goodbyes and drive home. But Mabegzo has done it again; he's unsettled me completely, stolen my peace and stability, and drawn me back into his world. This sudden encounter with his mother has been a stark reminder to me that there's still one more conversation to be had.

The funeral is held at the Lutheran Church in Tema Street, a stone's throw from the church that shaped my childhood; the church where Mabegzo bared his soul to me all those years ago and confessed to killing two friends.

During the funeral, Nkgono is described as a woman who feared God and prayed all the time, *'le ha a na welwa ke maru, o ne a rapela*; even when clouds hovered over her.' 'She was a good mother,' others say, 'who taught her children to walk in the ways of the Lord.'

Despite her flaws, Nkgono's faith was sincere and all-consuming, and I have to admire her fervent commitment to God and church, even though I no longer relate to it. Regardless of the shortcomings of the people who enter its doors, the church has been a positive force in families and communities in Soweto. But personally, I feel more challenged and liberated without the church or God to hide behind, to cushion me from the blows of life or excuse certain behaviours. I feel empowered to finally be taking full responsibility for my own behaviour and giving my own meaning to it. It feels good to love and to forgive just because I choose to, not because I am following the dictates of the church. Having now created a distance between myself and this world, the sheer force of my own values, words and emotions stir my spirit in a far more meaningful way. Yet I can still sit in church without feeling out of place. I bow my head during prayers, sing the familiar hymns and understand the universal quest to feed the soul, regardless of how we do it.

One church member asks Nkgono's children to stand up so that she can address them directly. 'Greta, Tshepo, Mohau – the daughter of Nkgono's late son Mohau – please stand up.'

She doesn't mention Imelda. I turn to look, but Imelda remains quietly in her seat. Am I the only one feeling this tension? Nobody points out that there's another daughter, Imelda. Or maybe there isn't really, not in the way that counts. With politics in a family, funerals can so easily provide a stage for these dramas to play themselves out, as at Mme Moipone's funeral. But everything remains calm, and the church elder continues to address the three adults.

'Your mother is gone now; you must continue her legacy. *O ne a se na lerata, a sa rate dintwa.* She was a quiet woman who didn't like conflict. Now that she's gone, don't bring conflict into your lives. Live as she did.'

I had thought I was through with Mabegzo. He had betrayed me, and strayed beyond the limits of my compassion. Yet here is Imelda, sitting stoically in the pew, her head held high, unflinching as the world refuses to acknowledge her existence once again. She deserves to be heard.

When we return to Nkgono's house from Avalon cemetery, I am no longer nervous about approaching Imelda. I follow her everywhere, quietly and unobtrusively, determined not to let her out of my sight. But I must wait for the right moment.

171

Soon the long queue of neighbours, church and community members is fed, but the buzz continues as always at a funeral. The yard is full of people socialising after the formalities, reuniting with extended family members and old friends. There's a white tent on the pavement where most people are sitting, hiding from the sun.

This is my moment. It's not hard to get access to Imelda; she seems always to be alone, whether standing or doing chores.

'*Dumela*, Mme Imelda,' I say.

'*Dumela, o tsohile*? Are you well today?' she asks. I don't know if it's her thin frame or the wrinkles around her eyes that make her look older than her years. But I can see where Mabegzo inherited his leanness.

'Mme Imelda, please forgive me. I need to speak to you.'

She recoils at the tone in my voice. I need to go easy. 'It's a long story,' I smile.

'What is this long story about?'

'There are just some things I'd like to ask you, but I can't do so here and now. Please give me some time.'

She nods. 'I'm returning to Lesotho on Monday; maybe you could come tomorrow?'

'Yes, thank you. I'll do that.'

I mingle with a few people, including Katlego and his mother – who asks me for ten rand.

'But you don't drink anymore,' I tease.

'*Hawu*,' she says, taking me seriously. '*Kanthe madi ke a bojwala feela*? Does money only buy alcohol?' I give it to her, knowing she won't be the only one to ask. I've already parted with a few rand to old neighbours and chancers who have asked. Such is the way of the township – if you look different, have a car and are considered well off, you'll be asked for money. If you claim you don't have any, they'll say,

'Ha, how can you not have ten rand?' or '*Wena*, you own a car.' So you pay up.

Among the funeral crowd I spot Basil, a childhood friend and neighbour who was always as gay as a fairy. He's barely changed since I last saw him as a chubby, loud-mouthed teenager, except that now he's skeletal and his hair is gingery, though clearly not deliberately coloured. Everyone in Orlando loved Basil, the most famous homosexual who was 'out' while most people were still trying to figure out what homosexuality was all about. He shaped my own thoughts on the matter, and it might be interesting to speak to him about being young and gay in Soweto where most people aren't yet out.

Basil made a huge impression on me when I was young. I loved his confidence, and I always think of him when I encounter homophobic views on the radio. Long before I covered homosexuality in my line of work, I already knew that being gay couldn't be a choice – Basil taught me that just by being himself. He was effeminate long before even he understood what the word gay meant. As children we all knew he was different; even adults knew it. His father's name was Majola, so they called him *setabane sa Majola* – Majola's homo. But those who called him *setabane* paid dearly, because he had a razor sharp tongue and he fought like a warrior. Those who were foolish enough not to retreat from his acerbic tongue soon learnt the might of his fists.

While boys played football or flew kites, the girls played house – often at my house because my brother and I had toys and Papa provided lots of food for us to 'cook'. Basil always preferred to play with us girls, and Mongezi regularly teased him about it. Basil would usually just tell him off, but the time Mongezi persisted in calling Basil 'a wife', Basil finally lunged at him. We were all happy to see him beat up Mongezi, who had a nasty streak and always spoilt our games, so there was a lot of cheering. All too soon, a passing adult separated the two boys and spoilt our fun, but not before Basil had flung a handful of soil in Mongezi's eyes and declared, 'I'm not done with you'.

Basil's confidence and charm were legendary, but he didn't suffer fools. He broke down boundaries, did Basil. And he was so well loved in the community that people generally ganged up in his defence when he was fighting off older boys.

Basil and I haven't seen each other since my family left Orlando East, and his first words to me after all these years are, 'Hey, *wena* Momo, give me a hundred rand.'

I burst out laughing. People might ask for five or ten rand, but not Basil! 'I don't have a hundred rand,' I chuckle.

'Fifty, then.'

'I don't have it,' I say again gently, still amused and glad that he's kept his devil-may-care attitude.

'*Ha o* celebrity *e jwang e senang* fifty rand? What kind of celebrity doesn't have fifty rand?'

'*Wena*, you're still full of nonsense, Basil.'

'So talk. Why are you so thin?'

Mention of my weight loss makes me prickly. 'You're a fine one to talk,' I counter. 'What's happened to your own curves that you loved so dearly?'

'I'm HIV positive. What's your excuse?'

I'm about to apologise when he says, '*Haai, haai*, I don't want your pity. *Bofebe bo bo a patalwa*. Whoring has its price.' Then he laughs. '*Haai*, I'm joking, man; loosen up. *O tla mbora*. You're too boring.'

Basil invites me to Nkgono's 'after-tears' in the next street. This unique township practice developed after I left

Soweto. Someone decided that after the tears of a funeral, a party is required to drown the morning's sorrows. So a nearby venue is chosen, and people bring their own drinks and spend the afternoon chatting and laughing. By late afternoon it becomes a full-blown party, and gatecrashers are often unaware that they're joining in the aftermath of a funeral. Yet I'm surprised to hear that these take place even after the funeral of someone elderly.

'*Ha*, it happens after all funerals. We're weary and we want to drink and laugh a little. Come, let's go.'

Although the after-tears is just metres away, Basil insists that I drive him so he can arrive 'in a celebrity's car'. In South Africa, it seems, just being on television or radio is enough to make you a celebrity. I don't bother to explain that I'm actually a journalist – a far cry from the glitz and glamour of celebrityville.

'Park closer, I need to make a grand entrance! Mrs Basil Moloi has arrived!'

This is going to be a long day.

Basil spends the entire afternoon introducing me to people and yelling at anyone who doesn't know who I am. '*Haai*, that means you're stupid and you don't read. How can you not know Redi Direko?' My discomfort doesn't concern him in the slightest. '*Haai, le wena*, what's your problem? Stop squirming, it's annoying.'

We get through copious amounts of gin and tonic, with me supplying the booze. But when I agree to share our gin with another woman, he gets upset. '*Haai*, how can you come to an after-tears without a plan?' he demands of her.

'It's fine, Basil. Let it go.'

'You shush,' he tells me. 'You don't know what's going on here. She always does this, but when she's sitting pretty she doesn't share.'

'I gave you booze at Nobuhle's after-tears, have you forgotten?'

'Don't bring up a previous decade.'

'Come, Basil. Give her some. It's no big deal.'

'*Haai wena,* don't pretend to be Desmond Tutu. You're not in line for the Nobel Peace Prize.'

The noise quietens down somewhat and we enjoy our drinks to the sounds of a popular song from the eighties lamenting the ill effects of VO brandy, popularly known as Vaya Orlando. Everyone in Orlando East loved that song, and I remember when its singers, Monwa and Son, once walked down our street while I was playing outside. We didn't care that they were too broke to own a car; there was pandemonium as we followed them along the streets of Orlando. They lapped up the attention, waving at adoring crowds who were singing the lyrics. '*He vaya Orlando, he vaya Orlando. Hangover, hangover, oh, oh, oh, ngiyekele, setlamatlama.*' I didn't know what VO brandy was, but *vaya* meant go, so I took the words to mean that they'd go along the streets of Orlando.

'So, were you fucking Mabegzo, or what?' Basil yanks me out of my reverie without warning.

The alcohol's gone to my head a bit and my guard is down. 'I wish I had.'

'You were the talk of town.'

'Perhaps. But I was a child. It wasn't about that.'

'Oh *please*, he liked pussy and he never asked; he just took it. He was always around you, so what exactly was going on, then?'

'I don't know. I honestly don't know.'

'Folks said you were his slave, and he raped you whenever he wanted to. Others saw you laughing and smiling at each other and said you were his girlfriend.'

'I know. And I don't care.'

'You were his little slut, né? Come on, admit it.'

'Whatever, Basil. Whatever you want to believe.'

'You want to know how I see it?'

'No, I don't.'

'I didn't believe what people said because your parents were so strict. But now I'm sure you were his slut. Why else would you come to his grandmother's funeral? You wouldn't have come if he'd raped you.'

'You really believe I came here because of Mabegzo's penis?'

'*Ja, vele*, nothing like it in the world.'

'Well, I never got to see it, and he never got my clothes off, either.'

Basil laughs sarcastically. 'Ha, go ask that Catholic priest if I've seen his cock. He'll also say no.'

'You're tiring me. I'm leaving.'

'*Ja*, the truth hurts. Why not go visit Miriam and compare notes about Mabegzo's cock?'

'Who's Miriam?'

'The mother of Mabegzo's baby. She was at the funeral today.'

At home that night I spend some time examining my feelings. There is so much to process. Among it all there is jealousy. Yes, I'm jealous, not because he had a child with someone else, but because he never trusted me with this secret. I hate to admit it to myself, but I felt special that he chose me as his confidante. It was to me that he confessed a litany of atrocities. He came to me with his heart on his sleeve and said, 'Here it is; take it.' And I did the same. Yet he had kept something as important as this from me. This knowledge has only added to the layers of conflict I already feel towards Mabegzo. In the end, I settle for persuading myself that he would have told me if he hadn't died.

Chapter 12

IMELDA IS WAITING FOR ME when I arrive the next day. It is Sunday, the day after the funeral. Sometimes this can be the busiest day of the entire week of mourning. The funeral service often seems to go by quickly, but the aftermath is a lot of work. Early in the morning, the deceased's clothes, blankets and other possessions are taken out to be washed and cleaned. Some families perform rituals, and then there's the family meeting to decide who will stay in the deceased's house, what will happen to the money donated by friends and the community, and how to settle the outstanding costs of the funeral. Sometimes, this is when the simmering family tensions finally boil over. Far-flung family members may not see each other again until the next funeral. And as usual, neighbours and church members who arrive to check on the family and help with the cleaning up have to be fed. So I decide to arrive in the afternoon, to give Imelda time to do whatever she needs to.

When I arrive, Imelda's two daughters and sons-in-law are just leaving to return to Lesotho, anxious to get back to their children. They eye me suspiciously.

'What do you want to talk to our mother about?'

'Don't worry. I won't do any harm,' I reassure them, but my words cut no ice. She kisses them goodbye and asks them to check on their father and their little sister. Imelda and I head back to the house where she offers me tea and scones. There are people milling around the kitchen, so I try to keep our conversation light.

'Well, it seems the bulk of the work is done here, it must be a huge relief.'

She says nothing, but busies herself washing dishes and tidying up.

'Thanks for the tea, Mme Imelda.'

She smiles. 'You didn't eat the scones.'

'I'm trying to stay nice and trim, like you. You look so lovely, Mme Imelda.'

'I eat a lot but nothing happens. It's not good; a mother shouldn't look like a little girl.'

'Nkgono was also slim, so you must take after her.'

'So what can I do for you, young lady?' she responds brusquely.

'I'd rather not chat here. Is it okay if we go and sit in my car?'

I don't know why, but I reach for her hand as we walk out. She doesn't return my grip but lets her thin hand rest loosely in mine.

'I heard you mention a sister to your daughters. Do you have another daughter who didn't come to the funeral?'

'Yes. My youngest daughter, Motlalepula – we call her Tlale. She isn't well and can't travel, so her father's at home looking after her.'

'Oh, I'm sorry. What's wrong with her?'

'She was born with cerebral palsy. She's twenty-five now, but she still needs constant attention. I had to stop teaching to stay home with her.'

Imelda a teacher? It comes as a huge surprise. Nobody has mentioned that Imelda is an educated woman. It seems remarkable that she managed to get herself a noble profession after all she's been through. I've always imagined her helpless and miserable. But I can't say so.

'I didn't know you were a teacher. That's a huge achievement.'

'You think so?'

'Yes. Teaching is such a valuable profession.'

'So what can I do for you, young lady? Tshepo said you are our daughter-in-law. I'm sorry, but I don't really know any of his children. I've been gone a long time. I wasn't even aware that he has a son.'

'No, I'm not married or engaged to his son. I've also never met any of his children.'

'Oh, okay.'

'He was speaking of Mahlomola.'

Her knees buckle and she sinks to the ground like a pack of dominos. People rush to her side to help her back onto her feet. I hold her right arm while Tshepo lifts her left arm, and another young man holds her from behind. Together we carry her to the bedroom and settle her on the bed.

'What happened?' Tshepo enquires.

But I get no chance to talk. Elders are there with an answer for everything and they don't pause to listen. '*Haai, vele*, this is supposed to happen after the death of a parent,' announces an older woman, who didn't see Imelda collapse. 'The older child feels the pain of separation the most, and suffers when her mother's journey to the other world isn't smooth. Give her water, lots of water with sugar. She'll be okay.' They're all fanning Imelda and blowing air into her face.

To me she seems fully alert, just pained and shocked. And I'm beating myself up for jeopardising any chance of speaking to her.

'I'll leave now.'

'*No!*' Imelda yells. 'Stay. I want to talk to you.'

'Should I return at a more convenient time?'

'No, stay.'

So I stay. I'm extremely nervous now. I don't know whether to hug her or leave her alone, and somewhere deep inside I'm wary of this woman whom Mabegzo said hadn't honoured her promise to fetch him and claim him publicly. His downward spiral began while waiting for her to come and claim him, and a part of me blames her for what happened to Mabegzo. If he'd been fetched, would he have left dead men's eyes alone? Yet, there it is again. This conflict. I feel a need to embrace Imelda, to hold her and stroke the pain of the rape away. Learning that she's a teacher has also humbled me.

We sit in silence, waiting for a moment alone, and I suspect she's just as desperate as I am for the others to leave us. She announces that she's feeling stronger and wants some fresh air. But it's obvious that she's still unsteady and disorientated. There are people everywhere and no place for a private moment. In the end, we make it to my car, which is parked on the pavement outside.

'So Lethabo had a woman and I didn't even know about it? Really, this family! What else don't I know about him?'

'Lethabo?'

'Yes. I called him Lethabo, Joy, not Sorrow as my mother called him.'

'He didn't tell me that his other name was Lethabo. It's a beautiful name.'

'We parted when he was just four, so he wouldn't have remembered that that's what he was called for the first years of his life. So, you were his little lady?'

'No, no, it wasn't like that. Tshepo was just joking. But it's true, I knew Lethabo well. We spoke a lot.'

'Oh, okay.'

'He used to tell me things.'

'I see.'

She bites her fingernails and massages her temple with her other hand. 'I'm surprised. Very surprised. I'm so surprised.'

'Why?'

'That there's a living person who has something to say about him. It's as if those around him want to erase him from their memories.'

'I remember him.'

'Do you know, they don't even know where his grave is? They say they forgot to take the number of the grave when they returned him to the soil. Nobody here can tell me a thing.'

'Your mother must have known, though.'

She lets out a heavy sigh and looks up to the heavens. '*E ne e le motho ya jwang*? What was he like?'

Where do I start? I wish I'd met her when I still had only tender feelings towards Mabegzo, when my deep love and compassion fiercely protected his memory. It would have been better for this heartbroken woman – and she is clearly heartbroken – to hear only extraordinary tales of a protective, loyal and gentle Lethabo. He was all those things, and I cannot deny her that. But there's another narrative, and my own sense of right and wrong has kicked in. Right now, as a woman living in a violent society where the threat of rape hovers, I've locked him away and hardly think about him at all. And when I do, it's with profound disappointment and revulsion.

In the end, I tell her everything, absolutely everything I can remember about Mabegzo. The good and the bad. Somewhere, my tale becomes no longer just for her benefit, but also an unburdening for me. For the first time ever, I feel I am being allowed to share my own experience of Mabegzo with someone else and to confront his bizarre presence in my life.

She sits quietly as I recall with precision the details of our conversations, our laughter, our tears. I recall the perplexing childhood he experienced and the taunting and neglect he suffered. She doesn't flinch when I relate tales of his macabre and repugnant actions. I try to separate the truth from the myths – and I hope she can see that even the myths reveal the full magnitude of his disposition. My narrative takes her to the street corners, the church hall, the back rooms; revisiting every corner that Mabegzo and I traversed together.

It's only when I tell her how his heart longed for her, how he waited and finally despaired, that she starts to weep.

'He was on a mission to destroy his enemies, and especially the men who wronged you. In the end he destroyed himself. That's what I remember about him.'

'I don't know how to thank you. I'm indebted to you. I'll never forget you. Thank you for this, for finding me, for helping me to find my child. For humanising him.'

'And yet, he also dug out a dead man's eye.'

'I hear you. I hear you. But he chose me. Of all the mothers in the world, he chose me. And he suckled from my breast. Maybe he suckled all my pain into him and was throwing it back at the world.'

Finally, I ask the question that I desperately need

answered. 'Why didn't you return for him, Mme Imelda? Why didn't you come to quieten the storm in his heart?'

'I did. I did. Maybe I should have tried harder, but I tried my hardest.'

In *my* mind, insisting that he attend Mme Moipone's funeral in Lesotho doesn't seem like trying all that hard, but I decide to reserve my judgement for now.

'Mme Imelda, did you love him?'

'A mother, a real mother, doesn't know anything else but to love. That's what real mothers must do. Love.'

'He thought you didn't love him because you had been violated. That must have been the most terrible experience for you. Are you able to talk about what happened?'

'It was so long ago. Rape wasn't as common then as it is today. Boys and men didn't do those things to girls and women. But they did it to me. *Ho ne ho le hotsho kellellong ya ka.* I couldn't grasp what was happening. I didn't even scream when one of the boys picked me up and carried me to a house nearby. I even remember the address. I remember. There were three of them. All familiar faces that I often saw while playing in the streets. I don't know how to describe it. But I had no tears. A lot of physical pain but no tears. They released me in the morning. I could hardly walk, and my clothes were soiled. But I made my way home. My family had spent all night looking for me. Mme was angry that I'd been out all night. I got a hiding from her.'

'She told me she was hurt about what had happened to you.'

'*Ao, ka nnete*? Really? Well she only stopped hitting me when I told her that the boys stole me. She called some elders from the community, and I had to take them to the house. They found an elderly woman and the three boys still sleeping. They woke the boys and she asked me, "Is it

184

them?" And I said, "Yes, Mme, it's them." The boys were paraded naked in the street while the elders sjamboked them. Then the police came and dragged the boys, still naked, to the police station, where they got more beatings.'

'So nobody took a statement from you, and there was no trial?'

'No. But to protect me, my parents said I mustn't go to school again. So I spent long days at home, while my younger siblings and my friends received an education. From then on I was also forbidden to play in the streets with the other children.'

Nkgono had never mentioned this, but I say nothing. I don't want to hurt Imelda more. I feel an intense rage towards those who decide that for some children there will be no childhood, that their little souls will be burdened and deprived of any exuberance and innocence. But this is not my story. It's time for someone to hear Imelda's long-suppressed voice.

'Wasn't it difficult, sitting at home like a prisoner all day?'

'I missed school, but Mme assured me that I'd return once it was safe again. That gave me hope.'

'So your mother thought she was doing the right thing, protecting you from prying eyes and potential attackers who would cause more pain?'

'No, she didn't protect me. She's never protected me. I was like a dark shame to her. She hid me because she was ashamed of me.'

'And then at some point you found out that you were pregnant.'

'I was fifteen, and I had only just started menstruating. I'd only had about three periods, which hadn't come regularly. And I had no idea then that there was a link between the monthly blood and pregnancy.'

185

'So when did you notice you were pregnant?'

She looks at me in disbelief. 'I didn't. Aren't you listening? I never knew until the adults told me I was with child.'

'Surely there were signs?'

'None that I could recognise. Now that I've given birth, I realise that a lot of what I was feeling then were signs of pregnancy. But I had become almost invisible. I spent the whole day shut away in my room sleeping, and nobody saw me throwing up. And I was very tiny so my bulge was also small. But eventually Mme suspected something. One Sunday morning, she woke me up to examine me. I was puzzled when she pressed her hand deep into my stomach and squeezed my breasts. And she asked, "*O feleditse neng ho ya ngweding*? When last did you have a menstruation period?" I said, "*Kgale*, Mme. Long ago." "How long?" she wanted to know. But I didn't know. Holed up in the house all day, I'd lost track of what day and month it was.

'She told me to wash and get ready for church. That made me so happy. It was the first time I was being allowed out of the house, to walk through the streets and share the joy of singing and praying again. But as soon as I stepped out of the gate, I realised that the world had changed. Neighbours were staring and pointing at me as I walked to church with my family. I couldn't work out the expressions on their faces. Now that I think of it, there was a lot of pity and curiosity. But some people who used to greet us just avoided us.'

'How long had you been in the house?' I ask.

'I don't remember what month it was, but it was cold and dusty, so it must have been towards the end of winter. I was so happy to be able to go back to church, but when I got there everyone was talking about me. I knew it. I just wanted the service to end. When it did, we had to wait outside for my mother, who was in a women's meeting. All the other children were questioning me. "What's it like to be raped?" "How did they rape you?" "What is rape?" That's when I learnt to keep quiet.

'My mother came out and sent my brother and sister home. Then she called me in to the meeting with the other mothers. I had to stand in front of them while my mother addressed the elders. "*Bana beso, nthapediseng*. Pray for me. *Ngwane enwa o senyehile. O mmeleng.* This child is ruined. She is pregnant. *Bashemane ba motseng ba mo lemaditse.* The boys have violated her." The mothers expressed their shock and outrage. "*Oho bathong, oho Modimo wa kgotso.* Oh people, O merciful God." Some lamented the bad place this world had become. "*Lefatshe le senyehile.* This world is ruined." Afterwards, they prayed for me. Then the reverend's wife ended the meeting by asking the mothers not to take the news "further than these walls", not even to discuss it with their husbands and children, because it was a shame that no one else should know about.

'But everyone beyond the walls of the church was talking about it, about me and the child growing inside me. I walked back home with my mother with my eyes downcast. And I remained like that for many years.'

'How did your mother treat you during your pregnancy?'

'She treated me well, like I was an invalid. She'd make me soft porridge in the mornings before going to her job at the factory. In the evenings she made sure I ate, and she told the other kids to do all the housework. I wasn't to lift a finger, just "lie down and rest" because "*mpa eo, e tlo ho imela*, my stomach would get heavier with time".'

'She showed some love, then?'

'When there's a mountain between you and another person, you don't see each other. You don't see that the other person is on the other side.'

'Did you understand that you were carrying a child, and that it was a result of your rape?'

'Yes, after the mother's meeting I understood that.'

'How did you feel about the child?'

'I had no feelings about the child. I was still fighting my nightmares about those boys. Trying to not think about it took much of my time.' She lets out a deep breath. 'What can I say? What can I honestly say? There were people who used to visit us just so they could see for themselves if I was pregnant. There were always people knocking at the door, so I was told to stay in the bedroom unless Mme called me. I was only allowed out of the room when she said I could.'

'That must have been difficult.'

'No more than anything that had already happened. I got used to Mme hiding me.'

'But how did you feel about being hidden?'

'I had no feelings. What happened was meant to happen to me. I was meant to be hidden, and it was okay.'

Imelda clearly doesn't realise how her face hardens every time she mentions being hidden. She's still biting her nails and sighing deeply, as though she's heaving under a great load. She's not what I expected, this woman who is almost the same age as my mother. I'd expected a meek and reclusive woman. I knew she was scarred, but she's certainly not impenetrable, as I'd been led to believe. She speaks, alright. But not to her family.

The moment Tshepo knocks on my car window, I watch Imelda morph from warm and chatty to detached and taciturn. The two of us have lost track of time.

Tshepo opens my door. '*Haai*, enough now. What are you two doing? You've been sitting in this car for so long.'

'Just chatting,' I say.

'Imelda, you be careful of this one. She can talk until

the sun goes down.' Only Tshepo and I laugh. Imelda sits quietly, her face inscrutable.

'Come inside, there's another family meeting.'

I'm anxious for Imelda to agree to see me again. She's due to leave for Lesotho tomorrow, and I'll have no way of getting in touch with her.

'Will you wait here for me?' she asks. 'There's so much I want to tell you.'

So I wait.

I still can't get over how easy it's been to reach Imelda's heart, when others before me have failed, or claimed to. Would her life have taken a different turn if someone had bothered to ask her how she was feeling, what she wanted and what would make her happy?

Finally she returns, and settles beside me in the car again. We pick up the story of her pregnancy.

'I used to sit on my bed when the house was quiet and stare at my growing tummy the whole day. I thought maybe I and everyone else had imagined my swollenness. That if I concentrated hard enough it would disappear. But it didn't. It grew bigger and bigger. The baby started kicking and moving inside me. At first I'd jump up, worried that it was trying to get out. I told Mme about the baby's kicks and that they had to let it out. But she just told me to go back to bed.'

'One day it got so hot in the house that I needed some fresh air. I went out onto the doorstep to breathe in some cool air. A neighbour saw me and shouted, *"Haai, wena sefebe, tloha mo, o se ka re bontsha mpa eo ya Satane.* You slut, get away, stop showing us the devil's tummy. You'll teach our children this mischief."* That evening, when Mme and Ntate were back from work, our neighbour came over and complained that I'd paraded my tummy in broad daylight, and I was a bad influence on the other children. She said my

189

presence was a blight on the community and she couldn't afford to expose her children to this.'

'Maybe this is what your mother, in her own way, was trying to protect you from.'

'No! She didn't stand up for me. She just hid me. And then she abandoned me.'

'But do you think you also abandoned Mab... Lethabo?'

'No. My conscience is clear. I never abandoned him. I'm just broken-hearted that he died thinking I had. That I was like my mother. I wasn't. I wasn't like her at all.'

She doesn't elaborate, and I leave it at that for now. It's grown dark outside already, and we still haven't walked the entire journey of her life. There's so much more that I want to ask and understand. So I ask her to come to my house and stay with me for a few days.

She's worried about her husband and her daughter, Tlale, who still needs her very much. But she calls her husband. '*Tlale o a ja?* Is Tlale eating?' I hear her ask. He says he's coping and will see her as soon as she's ready to return.

And so Mme Imelda agrees to come and stay with me. Again, I cannot believe how easy this has been. Having already observed her discomfort around her own family, I didn't think she would let me in so easily.

Chapter 13

WHEN WE ARRIVE AT MY HOUSE, I show her to the guest bedroom and invite her to make herself at home.

'Life is so different for you young ladies. I'm so glad.'

'What do you mean?'

'You have this house in the suburbs where you have all this independence to live by yourself. That didn't happen in my day. Life is better for young women today.'

I'm dying for a glass of wine, but Mme Imelda is old enough to be my mother and probably just as conservative. I recently ordered a glass of wine at a restaurant in front of my mother, but she disapproved so strongly that I had to cancel my order. We settle on the couch with a pot of tea and some fruit. Regretfully I dare not talk about anything else with her, as I am anxious to learn all I can from her while I have her all to myself. So without wasting time, I pick up where we left off.

'Did you love your parents, Mme Imelda?'

'I didn't hate them.'

'But did you love them?'

'I never thought about it that way. I didn't know them, and you can't love or hate those you don't know.'

'But surely you remember what they were like before?'

'I honestly don't.'

It's not just her parents that she's forgotten. She doesn't seem to remember what she was like 'before that day' either. It's as if, in violating her, the rapists not only imprinted themselves on her, but obliterated all memory of the life she'd had before. Even when I try to direct the conversation to her childhood, her activities, the food she ate – she automatically relates events from the time after she was raped.

'There must have been some happy times?'

'When I did well at school, as I always did, those were happy times. But Mme hid me from my school when it happened, remember.'

'Then you moved to Lesotho?'

'Yes. When Mme told me I was going to Lesotho to deliver the baby, I didn't protest. She wanted me to give birth away from the prying eyes of our neighbours, friends and church congregation. I thought I'd be gone for just a few days, and that once the baby was out, I'd come home. So I was confused when I was told to pack all my belongings. Mme carried my small suitcase on her head while I carried only my handbag and sandwiches. Nobody explained that from now on I'd be living there away from my parents and siblings. As I caught the bus from Moroka in Soweto, I was anxious about what would happen to me there. It was a bewildering time. I knew our family came from Lesotho, but only Mme used to visit, because it was expensive for the entire family to travel there. So this was my first visit to Lesotho. But in our day you didn't defy your parents, and you didn't ask too many questions, either.'

'Did the solitude there come as a shock to you?'

'No, not the solitude. My life in Johannesburg had become very quiet; there was no more laughter or activity. I missed having friends, like the other girls, but...' She lets out that familiar deep sigh and bites her nails again. '*Ke ne ke e na le ditaba for Modimo.* I wanted to share my news with God. But he wasn't ready to answer my questions.'

'What did you want to ask God?'

'Just to say something, anything, about what he wanted from me.'

'Which part of Lesotho was it?' I ask.

'Quthing. It's in the far south, known as the Place of the Wind. Today it's known for its rich rock art from the Bushmen who lived there for many centuries.' She grins ruefully. 'But when we first arrived I was surprised at how barren and desolate it was. There was poverty written all over it. It was strange coming from Soweto; I didn't see a single car. Just donkey and horse carts. Men walked behind their animals – cows, sheep, donkeys and dogs – and they carried their sticks, or *melamu*. The houses were *mekgoro*, round thatch huts made of sand, stone and soil mixed with dung, which the women painted in colourful patterns. They even made their own pots.' She laughs. 'I couldn't understand why these people were wearing blankets and hats in the blistering heat. But I soon learnt that the traditional blanket, the *seanamarena*, is a prized possession among the Basotho, and the odd ones out are those who don't have one. I also found that the air there was much fresher and we ate better.

Even the schools were better.'

'Did the people there accept you?'

'I was so anxious about how these people would react to my condition. In Soweto my mother had kept me hidden, so I wasn't used to being stared at. When we entered the yard, about thirty visitors had come to welcome us – mainly women and children, but a few men as well. They broke into song and dance to welcome my mother and me from "faraway lands". Every single person kissed and embraced us. Afterwards, the chief prayed and thanked God and our ancestors for our safe arrival. I was presented with a blanket to cover myself. At that moment I thought they wanted me to cover my shame.

'Although everyone was warm and welcoming, there was a lot of curiosity about my state, especially among the mothers and their daughters. Standing there amid the singing and jubilation, I looked around and realised how different I was from the other girls my age. They all walked bare-breasted, with the traditional skirt to cover their bottoms and privates. There was nothing to hide, and children were children. Only mothers and young brides covered themselves. But I had to be covered, again.'

'And you stayed with Mme Moipone?'

'Yes. She was my mother's younger sister. Many years earlier her husband had been swallowed by the gold mines in Johannesburg. They hadn't had any children yet. She talked about her late husband a lot. Her friends used to tell her to stop talking about him so much, or she wouldn't find another husband. But she always told them, "*Monna wa ka ke Modimo*. God is my husband."'

'Did your mother stay with you or return to Soweto?'

'She didn't return to Johannesburg immediately. She stayed and made me soft porridge every morning. I wondered why she didn't go home, but by then I'd stopped talking to her much.'

'Maybe she stayed behind to take care of you.'

'No. A week after our arrival, Mme Moipone and my mother announced that they were going to town to buy provisions for Christmas. "When is Christmas?" I asked. I'd lost track of time. I only knew the difference between night and day, nothing else. They said Christmas was in less than a week. So that's why Mme stayed. It wasn't for me; it was because it was Christmas and she would have been in Lesotho anyway.

'I was told I had to stay in bed, not lift a finger and eat all my food. Mme Moipone said it was because I was too small, and I needed to save my strength for the "big task" ahead. She said my body would have a hard time bringing this child into the world. Until then I hadn't thought about what giving birth would be like. Now I became afraid. I started crying. I hadn't cried in a long time, but I cried. Mme Moipone tried to console me. She kept saying, "*Balehela ho Modimo ngwana ka.* Run to God, my child." But my heart was too sore.'

'Were you crying because of the fear of giving birth, or because of everything that had happened?'

She shrugs. 'Mme reprimanded me for crying. She told me it was inappropriate; this was the path all women must walk.' Imelda goes quiet. She seems to be ruminating deeply so I don't interrupt. I wait until her heart is good and ready. 'She was wrong.'

'Why?'

'Because I know now what being a woman entails. *Ho ba mosadi, ha se papadi.* Being a woman is no joke. But believe me, at fifteen going on sixteen, I wasn't a woman,' she says emphatically. 'I wasn't!'

'Maybe she meant...'

'I don't care what she meant. I was a *child*!'

There it is again, that iron will that her family never knew was bubbling beneath the surface; that assertive – or maybe angry – streak that she only reserved for her late mother.

'That Christmas in Lesotho must have been a bit different from the Christmases you were used to?'

'Yes. A lot of family members returned home and the festivities continued for several days. There were big meals and traditional beer. Lambs and chickens were slaughtered to feed the family and anyone else who came through the door. I met relatives that I didn't know I had. Children got to gorge on home-baked cakes and ginger beer and Quthing came alive with merriment. What was beautiful about Quthing was that everybody was the same. There were no tycoons, and even those who had nothing were taken care of by other villagers. Life was hard for everyone. But not at Christmas; then everyone was happy. Except me. Because they were all talking about me. It wasn't meant unkindly, but to me at that age, without any notion of what life was about, it was overwhelming.

'One day all the women were sitting around in my aunt's yard with my mother and my aunt, some on the ground and others on benches. "Your stomach is hanging low. It'll be a boy," one old woman said to me. "No, no, no, *o a fosa*. You're wrong. Our girl is carrying a girl. A pretty one who will bring us lots of suitors and cows." "*Che bo*! No way. I'm telling you, it's a boy." "Come here," an elder called. Obediently, I went up to her. The plump woman stood up and put her fat hand on my bulge. She closed her eyes. "*Che, ka nnete*. No, really. She's carrying a boy. A boy to work hard and relieve our hardship." Then another woman examined my stomach and put her hand on it. Others chipped in with their opinions about the shape of my bulge, the angle, the gender, everything. "Her nose isn't swollen, so it's definitely a boy."'

Imelda's tales are making me smile. Far from what I'd imagined, she's actually very talkative, with a wicked and generous sense of humour. She tells the story without bitterness, seeing the funny side now, even though she was paralysed with fear at the time.

'Finally one mother, the raconteur among them, said, "*Bonang*. Look. All of you are right. It's either a boy or a girl!" That made them laugh and settled the debate.

'It was only Mme Moipone who sensed my fear amid all their merriment. "*Ba heso, ngwana enwa o tshohile. Nthwena e boima*. My sisters, this child is frightened. This is difficult for her. Let's ask God for strength." I had liked Mme Moipone from the moment I first met her. But now I loved her. Now all the mothers prayed, hugged and kissed me. But when it was my own mother's turn, she just held my hands and said, "*O rapele, Modimo o na le wena*. Pray, God is with you."'

'*Hao*, Mme Imelda,' I say. 'Surely that was love, reminding you that God was with you? She must have been trying to comfort you.'

'I'm glad you see that as love and comfort. But I needed to hear her say that *she* was with me, instead of always leaving that role to God. I can see now that the women of the village were showing me love and acceptance. But my feelings were so raw that I felt their curiosity as disapproval, their gaze as confirmation that I was an ogre. I was so used to being judged that I missed the kindness in all their actions. I regret that now. My child got clothes handed down by the mothers, and milk, soap, everything a child could hope for. They were good to me, and I didn't even thank them.'

She pauses a moment. '*Oa tseba ke eng*, did you know, my birthday is on the twenty-sixth of December, the day after Christmas?'

'Oh, how wonderful. So your birthday's always a time of celebration.'

She laughs, quietly at first, but then louder.

'*Ke eng?* What is it?' I ask.

'Do you know when Lethabo's birthday was?'

I realise that I never asked him. Given the circumstances of his birth, is it possible that she never memorised which day he was born? 'Sorry, Mme Imelda,' I say, 'we didn't talk about our birthdays.' It wasn't entirely true. Mabegzo had once fetched me the day after my birthday, and returned the next day with a packet of my favourite toffees. It was the only birthday we ever shared.

'Lethabo was born on December the twenty-sixth, Boxing Day 1967, the day I turned sixteen.'

Then she looks at me with consternation, because tears are suddenly pouring down my cheeks. She's as stunned by my anguish as I am. '*Hao hle*, I'm so sorry,' she says. 'I wouldn't have told you if I knew it was so hurtful.'

I just cannot believe that this wretched soul whose entire life was adrift, always longing, searching, but never finding his mother, had died without ever knowing that he actually shared his mother's birthday! This detail feels hugely significant, and there's no doubt in my mind that it would have meant the world to Mabegzo. It would have brought him some solace and, knowing him, it would have driven him to find her. I just cannot accept that the adults, those self-appointed adjudicators of who may stay and who may not, who may speak and who will be silenced, were so profoundly arrogant as to challenge the might of providence and overrule the natural kinship bond between him and his mother. But I compose myself and leave my thoughts unspoken. Imelda lets me be and doesn't pry.

'Can you see now why Christmas was always a sad time for me? I always thought of Lethabo.'

'Do you ever wish that you had rather had an abortion?'

'Abortion?' she gasps, incredulous. 'Abortion? I didn't even know there was such a thing. And God would have punished me. How do you kill a child, especially a child born at the same time as Jesus Christ?'

'Is that the reason you accepted him?'

'Heavens, no. Lethabo's birth brought me great comfort, to be born on the same day as me, to come the day after the Lord was born. He belonged to me and I belonged to him. One day when you have a child yourself, when you make that awe-inspiring connection with a life growing inside you, you'll know why it's impossible not to love and want your child, regardless of who his father is.'

'Mme Imelda, I don't understand,' I can't stop my words tumbling out. 'Why didn't you come to fetch him like you promised?'

It's her turn to weep. She rocks from side to side the way a loving parent comforts a baby. The depth of her sorrow suffocates us both.

'I did. I tried, I tried and I failed.' And she leaves it at that. For the second time she claims to have tried, but she still doesn't elaborate. I'm disappointed, but I'm still not comfortable pushing her, so I suggest a tea break. With every minute that passes, every word spoken between us, we're becoming closer; we're no longer the strangers who met a few days ago. Perhaps if I give her more time she will finally tell me what I long to understand.

'You make tea the way it's meant to be,' she says. 'Strong, with hot milk. Very nice.'

'Thank you. My mother is very fussy about her tea. And so was my father. It has to be perfect. So, Mme Imelda, that Boxing Day was your big day. How did it go?'

'When everyone was replete and asleep after the Christmas Day festivities, I woke in the early hours of Boxing Day to find that I'd wet myself. I was so embarrassed. But I had no time to worry about it, because the pains started. I remembered that Mme had told me a week earlier not to cry, so I gritted my teeth, hoping the child would stop being angry at me.' She shakes her head. 'No one had explained to me how the baby would arrive, what to expect, or what I should do when it agitated to break free. So I lay there in what I thought was my pee, hoping this great pain I'd never felt before would go away. But when it's time, it's time. Birth is like death. It happens whether you want it or not. And the world bears witness. There wasn't any privacy in that little mud hut. What I thought were soft groans were loud enough to wake my mother and Mme Moipone.

'"*Ke nako*. It's time," my mother said. "*Tsoha*. Get up." She and Mme Moipone helped me wash and prepare for the birth. I was in a lot of pain, but I don't remember which part of me hurt. Everything hurt. Besides, I was more aware of the fear that had gripped my heart. Mme Moipone and my mother started arguing. My mother wanted to pray and ask God to put his mighty hand over them and the task ahead, but Mme Moipone insisted that that wasn't the most important thing at that moment. She said, "God knows our hearts. Let's get this child the help she needs. She's small, her body is still very young and we mustn't make it too difficult for her." But my mother insisted that without God the task would be more difficult. "And if she dies while we're praying?" Mme Moipone said. "We must call the mothers of the village now." I'd never felt so much fear and apprehension in my life. The pain was everywhere, so when she said death was a possibility, I believed her. But it was my mother's response that hardened my heart forever. She said, "It's better for her to die in the Lord.""

'Why did that harden your heart?'

I see that flash of anger again. 'A good mother who prays for her children and loves them would never say that. If it were my child I would have said, "God won't forsake my child at this hour," or "My child isn't going to die." It's she who killed me, and it didn't stop there. She killed me again and again. And when I'd died a thousand painful deaths, she killed my son too.'

This is a powerful revelation, so I give her time to recover. When she's ready, she continues. 'I remember every minute of the birth of my daughters, but this one, I don't remember. I just don't remember. One minute I was screaming, Mme Moipone and Mme were arguing, and then I was bundled into a blanket.

'When I woke up it felt like I'd been sleeping for months. I was so disorientated I didn't even notice that I no longer had my huge bulge, I wasn't even aware of my surroundings. I had no strength to lift myself up. Then a mother brought a small bundle wrapped in a blanket, and put the baby gently on the bed next to me. He was sleeping. I didn't feel anything. Nothing. Over the next two days, they showed me how to change his nappy, to put him on my breast, wash and clothe him.'

'And? Did you find it difficult?'

'It's impossible to describe what I felt. Everything just felt strange. I didn't register that I was a mother; I didn't look at him and think, "This is my child". He was just there and I had to do all these things. Eventually we returned to our everyday life, but life had changed.'

Imelda can't remember much about that day, but she couldn't have given birth at a clinic because there were none in Quthing. Women gave birth in their rondavels with the help of the senior village women, and the most senior mother would cut the umbilical cord and bury the afterbirth in the soil behind the hut.

'Mme Moipone and Nkgono must have fussed over the new baby?'

'Yes, I think they did. But he was always sleeping, and so was I. They only woke me to wash and eat. It felt like I was always being woken up to eat.'

'You needed the strength.'

'Yes, and the elders told me that if I didn't eat, the baby would get no milk and starve.

'As the days went by I got stronger and managed to stay awake for longer. I was even strong enough to walk Mme to the door when she left, early in the New Year.'

'Were you getting used to the baby by then?'

'Not quite. I was still puzzled by him, and he was such a quiet baby. I just used to stare at him when he was sleeping. My day started at the crack of dawn, when he announced his thirst. Then, as the sun rose, I would milk the cow while Mme Moipone watched over him and cooked our breakfast porridge. Like my mother, Mme Moipone worked as a seamstress at a clothing factory. In the evenings after work she would make vetkoek and bread to sell to those leaving for work in the mornings. I spent the day cleaning the house, sweeping the yard, washing the baby's clothes and cooking supper. It was boring. My baby slept all the time and I often ran out of chores. I'd long forgotten about school and I tried not to think about my life before I came to Lesotho.'

'Did you miss your brothers and sister?'

'I don't know, I really don't know. I was still overwhelmed

by the baby and unsure of myself, but I found great comfort in Mme Moipone's affection and compassion. When I had a nightmare or a flashback from... from...' she avoids the word rape, 'she soothed me and assured me that God would take pity on me. "This child is a sign of his mysterious ways," she told me. "Try to accept this and you will find joy. But if it's too difficult for you, I'm here, I'll help you."'

'Did you love your baby?'

'At first I was hesitant to show him my feelings. I wanted him to first show that he wanted me.'

'And did he show you?'

'When he was a few months old, yes, he did. He was a good baby, he hardly cried. And when his eyes could see, they followed me everywhere. The villagers were also thrilled to have him, and provided clothes and food for us. There was no judgement then. I didn't feel watched anymore because it seems all eyes had turned to my baby, my baby with the bad name, Mahlomola. One day I asked Mme Moipone if I had to call my baby Mahlomola.'

'And?'

'Mme Moipone pulled me into the bedroom we shared. I worried that we might wake him. But she just pulled me over to my sleeping baby. "Look at him," she said. "What do you see?" "A baby," I said. "No, look at him with your heart; open the eyes of your heart," she said. I was confused; I didn't know that my heart also had eyes. "How do I look at him with the eyes of my heart?" I asked. "When you look at him, do you feel *mahlomola*?" "No," I said. "When you hold him and feel him, is it anger and sorrow you feel? Do you feel pain?" "No, no, no, Mme," I said. "I feel *lethabo*, joy." "Then that is what you call him," she told me. "Lethabo." I loved the name, but I worried that my mother wouldn't be pleased if she found out. "*Re tla bona.* We'll see," she said.'

'Do you think you were happier in Lesotho then than you would have been in Soweto?'

'I felt loved and nurtured by Mme Moipone, but I still had no friends. I had nothing in common with other girls my age – they gossiped and giggled about boys, but I'd been denied all that and forced into a precarious adulthood. Yet I didn't belong with the adults, either. To them I was still a child. I was something in between, something odd. But it didn't hurt as much as when I was in Johannesburg.'

'So your mother had made the right decision, then?'

'Yes, in spite of herself. She did it for herself, not for me, but it worked better for me, initially.'

'When did you next see your family in Soweto?'

'Near the end of that year. When my baby was nearly one, Mme told me to bring him to Soweto, so his rituals could be performed. I couldn't quite understand why the rituals couldn't be performed in Quthing. But I'd learnt not to express any opinions to my mother, so I asked Mme Moipone. "*Haai, ngwana ka, ha ke tsebe.* I don't know," she said. "But remember, a married woman no longer belongs to her own clan, but to that of her husband. Your mother is most likely fulfilling the wishes of the Bakwena clan." I still didn't want to go, but I couldn't defy my parents.'

'It must have been difficult returning to where the sun had set on your innocence and childhood.'

'No one even came to meet us at the bus station. Mme Moipone and I got lost trying to find my old home. I'd never travelled alone before and it was frightening. I kept expecting bad men to appear and harm us. It was a great relief when I found the gate and knocked on the door. But my father barely greeted us. And my brothers and sister didn't know whether or not to approach me.'

Privately, I wonder whether their own suffering and

constant teasing as a result of her tribulation were part of the reason. 'They were sad for you,' I say. 'And Tshepo wasn't happy with the way your parents managed this affair. He believes you and your son were wronged.'

She shrugs. 'Perhaps. But between us there's a barbed-wire fence now that can never be removed. It's not their fault; they were children. Mme put that fence between us.' There's a long pause. 'I'll never forgive her.'

'How long did you stay?'

'Mme decided that Lethabo and I should stay for the festive season, during which time the ritual could be performed. I had no clue what this ritual was all about. But I wanted it over and done with because the eyes of the township folk were on me again. I was back in this dreadful place where hearts don't connect; where eyes stare, not with love and forgiveness, but for gossip and injury. It was the longest December of my life. Old friends, relatives and neighbours found silly reasons to pop in. They claimed to be visiting my mother and Mme Moipone, yet they stared at me and my child. Even my mother noticed what these visits were about.

'"They haven't been here in ages, some not at all, yet here they are today to see God knows what," she moaned. But she still told me not to be seen. She still hid me.'

'Did you want to be seen?'

'Not really. But I didn't want my own mother to be so ashamed of me. When would she stop putting her reputation ahead of me? I didn't care anymore.'

Imelda may not care now, but what she says next reveals that she still cared back then.

'One day while I was polishing the stoep early in the morning, a married man from our street asked me, "*Ke wena Imelda wa* rape? Are you Imelda, the rape child?" I carried on polishing the stoep. Then he said, "*Nna* why o *ntima* rape? *O tlo mpha neng?* Why deny me the 'rape'? When will you give me some?" I threw the tin of polish at him and screamed, "*O ntja, o ntja!* You dog, you dog!" I didn't even see my mother and my aunt coming out to see what the noise was about. My mother actually gave me a hiding for being rude to an adult! Mme Moipone tried to intervene but my mother reminded her that this wasn't her place. So I, a mother myself, got a hiding! She didn't even ask what had happened. She just silenced me, as always. I decided then never to speak to my mother again unless I was spoken to. That was what she wanted, anyway.'

'How did the rituals go?'

'They didn't happen in the end. Early one Sunday morning Mme woke me and told me to get ready. I didn't resist. Some male relatives had arrived to accompany us to "the homes". Whose homes, I didn't know. So I put my baby on my back and went with them. Only as we were entering the first yard did it dawn on me whose home we were visiting. No one asked me if my heart could deal with this. Ntate wouldn't even come, because it "disturbed him too much". So he asked other men from the Bakwena clan to represent him.'

'If your father said nothing and was too disturbed to go, could he have been affected and hurt by what had happened to you?' I desperately want Imelda to see her parents in a different light, to see that they hadn't known any better than this austere style of parenting. I hope it will bring her comfort to consider that their actions weren't driven by malice and rancour; that they hurt her unintentionally because they too felt hurt and helpless; that their way of expressing love wasn't the love language she understood. By not wanting to set his foot in the homes of her rapists, could her father have been saying, 'I'm too hurt to face my child's tormentors,' or 'I don't trust myself when faced with those who harmed my child'? In not going along that Sunday, could he have been saying 'I love you too much'? But this is Imelda's story, filled with a sorrow none had understood, and to her love is never aloof, regardless of circumstances.

She starts giggling, and it quickly turns to uncontrollable laughter. I'm growing used to this laughter before she expresses cynicism or sarcasm. She throws her head backward, laughing even louder. 'So I, the victim, must go and seek out the rapist and beg him for acknowledgement? He invaded me and it is I who must go and find him?' She roars with laughter. 'And they talk about the wisdom of the previous generation! What wisdom?' She laughs again, but only to block the tears.

I let her give vent to her poignant observation, and give her the space to recover from this rant – it is clearly a spiritual necessity. She has earned it. She was just sixteen at the time, and has still never had a chance to speak and be heard.

'I had to walk with the elders through the same door I'd been forced through. My memories of that terrible day came flooding back. I nearly gave in to my trauma, but I remembered the child on my back. He helped me avoid a breakdown. I had to protect him. It was a typical Orlando East house, but it was a mess. Soweto mothers who cared about their reputations taught their daughters to wash the dishes, keep the yard clean, and wash the windows. My own mother had taught me these things. But no one had taught the children of that family. I tried not to focus on my surroundings; I just shut my eyes and rocked my baby. I truly don't recall what was said or how we were received. I was only aware of my baby.'

'What else was going through your mind?'

'I thought they were going to make me leave the child there. I don't know why, but people are obsessed with fathers. Even when the father wants to remain absent, the girl's family will still go and seek him out. Why, when he's made his intentions clear?'

'So what happened at the house?'

'I kept my eyes closed, but I heard them say, "*Haai, o montsho haholo o*. He's too dark." "*Mahlo a hae a honyetse*. His eyes are sunken." Only then did I realise that the purpose of this "ritual" was to determine the father of my child. There was a family debate going on. Some said that all three were the fathers, but one elder insisted there must only be one, and we must find him. He thought that if they could identify the dominant male, then Lethabo would belong to that clan. But they agreed that if all three were the fathers this had to be established. But now they decided that this one couldn't be the father, because Lethabo bore no resemblance to him.'

'What did you believe?'

'Well, I thought all three could have provided the seed that impregnated me. Only when my daughter became a nurse did I learn that a child only grows from the seed of one father. Until then I thought they'd each contributed to different parts of him. But I preferred to think that he had no father.'

'What do you remember about that particular guy?'

'Nothing. But the adults asked him to point out the homes of the other two culprits.'

So there was Imelda, walking with her family and relatives, her baby on her back, while her rapist, the tour guide, walked alongside to point out the homes of the other boys who'd stolen her childhood and turned her life upside down forever.

'At the next home I just held Lethabo even tighter and breathed in and out, drawing in his warmth and filling my heart with this comfort. Suddenly there were shouts and screams. A woman in her nightdress hurled a flower pot at us, which smashed against the wall. "*Voetsek*, don't talk shit!" she screamed. "My child wasn't involved in this nonsense. These girls are too free with their bodies." His grandmother tried to calm her. "No, no, let's talk peacefully. No shouting." But his mother yelled, "Shut up, Mme! This has nothing to do with you. They're trying to dump this bastard on us. Just shut up!"

'Nobody in my family liked noise. Swearing was taboo and our elders didn't know how to respond. The boy didn't even come out so they could "assess" him. The adults were deeply disappointed, but they didn't learn their lesson. They just set off for the next house. On our way to the third house, the first boy decided that his friend in the second house must be the one. "We can't all be responsible," he said. "*Ufihlani yena*? Why's he hiding?" Mme slapped him across the face. "Shut up, you rubbish!" she said. "Speak when you're spoken to."'

I'm surprised to hear of such an outburst from Nkgono. But I know better by now than to suggest to Imelda that her mother was being protective of her.

'What happened at the next house?' I ask instead.

Imelda laughs with genuine amusement this time. 'My child, this is why education is so important. Once you have that, you could never do such stupid things.'

'Why, what happened?'

'We arrived at this household of Zulu Zionist worshippers. There was a group of them in blue, white and green uniforms, singing, beating their drums and shouting and wailing. My elders started arguing about the wisdom of entering the yard. But in the end they decided to go in. We were greeted politely but with reserve. After all, we weren't in uniform and we spoke Sesotho instead of isiZulu. Mme asked to see the mother of the house. But a burly man asked, "Who is she, this mother of the house that you're looking for?" "We haven't met her," my mother said, "but we wish to meet her today." "No one enters my house and doesn't ask for me," the man said. The drumming and singing stopped and all eyes were on us. "*Ningobani*? Who are you?" he asked. "*Re ba ha Mofokeng*. We are the Mofokeng family," Mme said. "*Haai, abe Sotho*? You're Sotho?" He turned to his kin, and said, "*Bafunani abeSotho lapha*? What are Basotho doing here?"

'We were asked to return to the gate, so the congregation could consult the ancestors before deciding whether to let us in or not. After what seemed like an eternity, we were invited back in, but not into the house, only into the yard where a tent had been erected for the service. This meant it would be a long, uncomfortable meeting. One by one, we took up six chairs, and then they began to address our male elders.

'"*Nithi ni ngo bani*? Who do you say you are again?"

'"*Ba ha Mofokeng.*"

'"*Nilethwa yini la*?" What brings you here?"' They spoke only in isiZulu, making it difficult for my elders, who were struggling to communicate. But they explained as best they could that they'd come to search for their grandchild's father, whom they believed lived there. There was no mention of the rape. "It's not important what happened," an elder said, "but we wish for the child to be acknowledged by his family." The boy was called and asked, "Do you know these people?" And he said no.'

'How did that make you feel?'

'Relieved. I just wanted this to end. I couldn't look at him or anyone else. I kept my eyes down and my arms firmly around my child. It was better not knowing who the father was. I didn't want him to have a face or name.'

'Then a woman spoke. "*Hambani.* Go. You heard him. He didn't lie with her. Our blood doesn't mix with that of the Basotho."

'My people weren't combative, and they quietly got up to leave. But before they could go, an elderly man said, "*Cha, cha, cha,* this isn't how we do things. Even if they're Basotho, *thina, kwamele sifeze izidingo za baphansi.* We must fulfil the desires of the ancestors. Girl, bring the child. Is it a girl or a boy?" I didn't answer. "Can't you talk?" he said. "It's a boy," Mme Moipone answered.

'The man took Lethabo from me. Instinctively, I looked up to be certain he wouldn't harm my baby. He was such a good baby. He didn't cry. One by one, they examined my child, shaking their heads and murmuring. Finally, the old man announced that he would perform a test to see if Lethabo was one of them. My family seemed confused, but since we were guests, we couldn't do or say anything.

'"This is the only way to see if the child is of this family," he said. With my baby in his arms, he instructed the males in the family to form a straight line. They put my baby on the ground, but still he didn't cry. Then the man said, "Every member shall put his right foot, for *umzuzwana* – a short moment – on the child's chest. If he cries, he's definitely not one of us, but if he accepts our footprints and doesn't make a sound, we will open our home to him. The ancestors will speak."

'I was afraid and looked at Mme Moipone, hoping she'd put a stop to this. But she gave me a reassuring smile. Lethabo lay peacefully on the ground, not making a sound. Then my rapist put his foot on my baby. Oh, I've had so many moments where I was powerless in my life, but that was the worst. I put my hand to my eyes. I couldn't bear to look. Then Lethabo let out a loud cry. "He's crying," the man declared. "He's not one of us." I marched straight up to my baby and snatched him away.'

'Well done! You were so brave!' I say, so pleased at what she'd done.

'You'll see when you have your own child. He'll bring out your strength and your weaknesses. The cry of your child will bring out the warrior in you. The pain is unbearable. It was the first time in my life that I was defiant. I picked up my baby and stormed off, ignoring my mother's reprimand. And I heard the man who'd initiated this stupid paternity test shouting after me, "*Abaphansi abazizo izilima*. The ancestors aren't fooled."

'So no one claimed Lethabo, and there was no ritual for him. And perhaps that's why his soul was restless. Even though the exercise was stupid, I know why my family searched for his father. A child belongs to his father's clan.'

'So you thought it was right that they exposed you to these men that you would rather forget?'

'No, not at all. They could have made an exception in this case. I'm sure the ancestors would have understood. But I do realise the importance of always knowing who you are.'

She falls silent. I've learnt to read her, to know when her silence means I must talk and when it means she's preparing to give her final thoughts on an issue, or reveal a deeper part of her soul.

'If it had been my daughter, I would never have made her face her tormentors again. A good mother wouldn't allow that.' She pauses again. 'I also wouldn't have been able to restrain myself if I'd come face to face with the men who raped my child. But my mother could.'

I can feel Imelda's total sincerity, but I long to ask again why she didn't fulfil her promise to her son, who had made desperate appeals to Nkgono to send him to Imelda when he realised she wasn't coming. But I know I must wait. I wonder if her love has become more determined since his passing, when she realised that she had in fact been an absent mother. To love him now may ameliorate her pain.

'Did you go back to Lesotho after that?'

'Even before the New Year, Mme Moipone announced that it was time to go back to Lesotho. We had spent a "strange" Christmas at her sister's house, she said, and it was time to get back to our lives again. I couldn't wait to pack. But Mme announced that I wouldn't be returning to Lesotho, because it didn't matter anymore. People already knew that I was a mother.'

'Mme Moipone pleaded with her, knowing that I preferred the solitude and simplicity of village life where people cared for each other, and put the importance of other human beings above their own selfishness. But Mme would have none of it. I was to stay and find a job in the city. Mme Moipone fought ferociously for me. "A job?" she said. "She's still a child. She must go back to school." And that's when I accepted her as my mother. I'd long regarded her as my mother, but that moment settled it. I pleaded my case to Ntate, but as always, he said little. When Mme Moipone ran out of arguments to persuade Mme, she said, "What does Imelda want? Where does she want to go?" I had turned seventeen a few days earlier, but even if I'd been an adult, because I was unmarried I was still regarded as a child. And even then, a woman's voice is still barely heard. My voice wasn't even considered.

'Mme insisted that I was going nowhere. "She's a child. If you had your own children," she told Mme Moipone, "you'd know that you don't raise them according to what they want. The Bible doesn't teach that." Mme Moipone was deeply hurt. Despite her vivacity, her biggest regret was that she had no children of her own, and these words opened a deep wound. It was the first time I saw Mme Moipone cry. She was always so strong and positive, but Mme managed to make her cry.' She pauses. 'Only Mme could manage that.'

'So what was it like saying goodbye to the person you loved?'

'*Oa hlanya na*? Are you crazy? You think I stayed in this cursed place? No, I left with her.'

'How did you manage that?' I ask, incredulous. Imelda may have developed an iron will, but back then she was still a frightened young mother, shell-shocked and unsure of herself.

'I'd learnt never to open my mouth to Mme. So I kept quiet, knowing what I would do in the morning. I was still breastfeeding then, so I knew my baby would be fine on the journey. I could have cooked some pumpkin or sweet potato for the journey – those were his favourites – but I didn't want anything at all that belonged to my mother. There hadn't been space for me to unpack my suitcase when I arrived, so quietly, without Mme noticing, I put my belongings together to return to Lesotho. I was done with Soweto. I resolved never to return here again, to where the devil lives.

'The next morning, Mme called the family together to pray for Mme Moipone's safe departure. "Open the way for her, so she can travel in your light." After they said amen, Mme Moipone kissed each of them goodbye. When she reached Mme, she wept and said, "You're a good person, but you're making a mistake." Mme didn't respond. When Mme Moipone kissed me she was so overcome with emotion that she couldn't stop crying. She held me and said, "*O motle, o motle haholo*. You're beautiful, you're truly beautiful." And I said, "You'll still be seeing me. Lethabo and I are coming with you." I fetched my suitcase from under the bed and turned to my family. "*Ke tseleng, le sale hantle*. I'm off; stay well."'

'Your mother must have been very surprised.'

'Hmm. Those who described Mme as a woman of prayer at her funeral a few days ago would have been even more surprised to hear her then.'

'What did she say?'

'No, my child, I'm old enough to be your mother. I can't possibly repeat such bad language. But she left us in no doubt that she despised us both. She reminded me that I was a child and must do as I'm told.' She pauses again. 'But I was beyond hearing. I didn't care what she said anymore. And it made me fearless. Mme was so wild with anger that she was like a different person, admonishing, threatening and lashing out at Mme Moipone for being immoral and a bad influence on me. "*O nahana ho ba le bana, le ho ba hodisa ke papadi?* You think giving birth and raising children is a game?" She even said that Mme Moipone wanted to poison me because she herself was barren.

'Mme Moipone was weeping as we left that house, and when Mme said to us, "I never want to see you again," Mme Moipone began to sob. Ntate had stood by quietly all this time, watching the whole drama unfold, but he fetched us both some water to drink. All this time, Mme was throwing insults at us. She even said to me, "If you behave like this, you'll be raped again!" That was too much even for Ntate. He told her to stop, and we walked out.'

For a while we are both quiet. With Nkgono I had also had moments when I felt exasperated and angry. But I understood that her generation was stoic, stern and austere. And I understood that for her, feeding, clothing and praying for your children was the ultimate expression of love. Yet

I am saddened that this was the only way she knew how to love. Nonetheless, I still believe that she was a decent person, despite her sometimes acidulous behaviour. But this is Imelda's story, I keep reminding myself.

'So you went back to Lesotho?'

'I did, and Mme Moipone sent me back to school there.'

'Was that easy?'

'I hated it. I'd already missed two years of schooling, so I was much older than my classmates. My life had changed so much, and no matter how hard I tried, I wasn't a child anymore. The other students worried about homework, boys and the "in crowd", but all I was thinking about was my baby that I had to leave with my neighbour. By two months into the new year, Lethabo was sleeping through the night. But Mme Moipone and I still woke at the crack of dawn every morning to milk the cows, clean the house and bake bread and vetkoek. We didn't have watches, but we woke at least two hours before sunrise every day.

'I didn't mind any of that, but I hated the walk to the river to fetch water. We took turns. When I fetched the water, Mme Moipone made the coal fire, and the next day we'd swap roles. My favourite time was the morning, when I washed my baby and suckled him at my breast before dashing off to school. I also loved fetching him from his minder after school and spending the entire afternoon with him.

'But I still didn't like being outdoors. I felt as if I was being watched. Nobody spoke badly to me, but being outside and facing people reminded me that I was different. They meant no harm. They just couldn't help staring and being wary. I don't think they meant to be cruel. The kids my age were just lost for words, and neither they nor I had the guts to make the first move. I was still happy to be in Lesotho, though, because here it was the child that made me the centre of attention, not the rape. It was never possible to forget the rape, but Mme Moipone helped me by keeping it a secret and making me believe I wasn't cursed.

'Unfortunately, though, the migrant labourers who worked in Soweto came home sometimes, and they told people what had happened. But the villagers were by nature more timid and respectful than the horrible Soweto people. They weren't rude at all, and anyone who was rude was quickly chastised. Once when I was walking home from school, some schoolmates heard a young man say to me, "*Le nna mphe ngwana; akere o rata ho fa banna bana?* Give me a child too; you like giving men babies, don't you?" They reported him to the elders, who told the chief. A "trial" was held and his family was ordered to pay a sheep. But Mme Moipone and I donated the sheep; we didn't want any bad energy in our stomachs.'

Chapter 14

IMELDA AND I HAVE NOW SPENT several days together talking, sharing and travelling back in time, and by now we have shared so much. Yet I still don't know why she's talking to me.

'Do you want to use what I'm telling you for good or bad?' she asks.

'I just want to understand Lethabo. And maybe you,' I respond.

'That's good. That's why I'm talking to you. My spirit says you're a good person.'

'And mine says you are, too. Yet you left him, or that's what he believed. And I know how excited he was when you acknowledged that you were his mother. He felt it would be a new beginning.'

'It would have been, if my will had been done. In January 1970, when I had just turned eighteen, I met a young man on my way home from school. By that age most girls had left school to find jobs in Maseru or to marry and raise children. There was never enough money to educate girls, but Mme Moipone was firm and loving, and she insisted I stay at school. I was probably the oldest pupil in the whole school by then, but I wasn't self-conscious about it anymore. I'd grown so used to people staring and talking about me that eventually I stopped noticing. It also helped that Lethabo was an adorable baby. That's what happens with a child. You forget everything. Even enemies agree on their love for children. When a child is present, it's impossible not to feel love. The villagers soon got used to me and had kind words for my child. It also helped that I was a quiet person and didn't have many friends; there was little chance of conflict with other people.'

'Did the attentions of this man make you happy?'

'I wasn't swayed at first. He had two jobs: at a farm and a general dealership, both owned by the same white man. In the early evening he would conveniently wait around at my home, hoping to catch a glimpse of me. When that didn't work, he became bolder, bringing sweets and braaied corn to our home. I didn't even want to eat these treats, but Lethabo had just turned two, and he enjoyed them. And it didn't help that Mme Moipone was encouraging this courtship. "*O a o rata*. He loves you," she would say to me. "Talk to him, just talk. Nothing more." But I was too shy. I was embarrassed by his attention and would run off every time he called my name.

'But eventually I fell in love with him.' She blushes. It's only at these moments that I remember that she's old enough to be my mother. She's a traditional woman in many ways, and she'd rather die than reveal any details of her romance, so I let it be.

'A few months later he asked for my hand in marriage. I accepted. I was so excited. But we still had to follow the traditional customs before we could be officially engaged. A messenger was sent to inform Mme Moipone that the Teane family wished to start discussions about the marriage of "the children". They were so eager that they wanted to visit the very next week. Mme Moipone was beside herself.

'But one matter dampened her joy. It was more than a year since we'd had any contact with Mme and Ntate. It wouldn't be appropriate to go ahead with the *mahadi* negotiations without them. But I didn't want them to know. I'd written them off; they were dead to me. Mme Moipone had reached out and tried to make peace since that day when we'd left Soweto. But there was no response from Mme, and so she eventually stopped trying. And for the first time ever, Mme hadn't come home for Christmas in 1969. It was a clear snub; a message that she would never accept my decision to leave and that she blamed Mme Moipone for it. We prayed a lot, asking God and the ancestors to guide us about what to do now.

'In the end, Mme Moipone decided to inform Mme and Ntate. Surprisingly, they arrived promptly on the Friday before the Teane family was to visit to start the negotiations. But my parents hadn't softened; they were still strained.'

'And you? How were you to them?'

'I didn't know how to be happy around them; their presence weighed too heavily on me. Mme went out of her way to make me miserable, and I was tired of it.' She doesn't seem prepared to consider that she may have been too bitter to be receptive to their presence, and that time had also failed to thaw her own heart. There was just too much hurt and anger. But she rejects this outright.

'Before my future husband's family arrived, Mme proposed that we pray. She asked for wisdom and appealed to God to keep the devil away from the proceedings. But they were just words. Her prayers were always just words; she never practised what she preached. As soon as I was asked if I knew the man who was proposing to me, I had to leave the room. But the talks broke down and they left.'

'*What?* Why?'

'I wasn't there, obviously, because these talks only take place between adults. But Mme Moipone asked if the family wished to take my child as well. If not, she said she'd understand, and would be happy to raise him herself. But they were horrified. "*E se e le mosadi? Tjhe, ha ra tlela ntho tseno rona.* She's been a wife already? We didn't come here for that." They cursed us for wasting their time. They'd come to acquire a good bride, they said, not a grown woman with a child. So they left, and that was the end of it.'

'That must have hurt a lot.'

'It did, very much.'

'But didn't he know you had a child?'

'He knew. I'd never actually said, "This is my child," but he saw me taking care of him, and in all our conversations I spoke about my child. I don't know what he did or didn't tell his family. I assumed that when he asked for my hand in marriage, knowing I was a mother already, he accepted Lethabo. Maybe it was his family that rejected the little one. But a man who can't stand up to his family is no man. I wasn't going to hide my child.'

She pauses. 'Mme reprimanded Mme Moipone severely for mentioning Lethabo without consulting her. She said she'd always known it would cause a problem, and it should have been kept away from my suitor.' She sighs deeply. 'She was determined to hide my child now. But I wasn't going to allow it.'

'But in the end you did marry.'

'Yes. Motsie came along two years later. It was a typical meeting for that time; he was on his horse and saw me on my way home with a bucket of water on my head. We exchanged a few words. From that day on, he returned to that area every day, hoping for another meeting when I came to fetch water. I had to resist the temptation to visit the stream every day, in case I came across as desperate or eager. But we met again and struck up a longer conversation. We began to walk together, laugh and even tease each other.

'Then the message came from his family that he'd found the one he wanted to marry. I was about to turn twenty, but I tried not to get my hopes up, knowing it was only a matter of time before he, too, left me. Mme Moipone said I was lucky to be asked again so soon after my first proposal. She was also excited because he came from a family of chiefs, and marrying him would improve our family's stature in the community. She suggested that we shouldn't tell him about the child at first, and that once we were married, I could find an opportunity. I trusted Mme Moipone's judgement, but something was wrong about her proposal. I told her I wasn't happy to hide my child.

'When my parents arrived to start the negotiations this time, Mme sat me and Mme Moipone down and laid down the law. She said I was blessed to be asked to be a wife again, and that in my situation marriage would be hard to come by. "You saw for yourself," she told me, "men don't want to raise other men's children."'

'And what did you say?'

'Nothing. I'd resolved never to say a word to her.'

'Do you feel that you did hide him?'

'Yes, in the end I did. I hid him just like my mother hid me.'
She starts to cry as she remembers. 'Mme Moipone consoled
me, saying "*Ho tla loka*. All will be well. Remember, he's
the son of a chief. We must be careful how we inform them
about the child." But it was a terrible mistake. The price
you pay for lies and deceit is too high. You don't sleep when
you don't know where your child is. I never slept a wink
for the eighteen years that Lethabo wasn't with me. And I
always feared what would happen if Motsie found out later
in our marriage, once the adults who had forced me to lie
had gone to their place of rest. I'd be the one left trying to
make everything right. I was happy to be getting married but
extremely anxious about the burden of this lie. And I was
tortured about abandoning my child.'

'Had Motsie not seen Lethabo at all? I mean, while you
were courting, did the two of them not meet?'

'We didn't do things the way you modern people do,
visiting each other's homes and being alone behind closed
doors before marriage. When we started our courtship, Mme
Moipone advised me not to mention my child at first, but to
wait until the right time came. So I didn't mention him.'

'But he must have seen him?'

'I'm sure he did, but he wouldn't have known that he was
mine. He could have been Mme Moipone's child. And we
never set foot in each other's homes until we were married.
Our courtship took place in the open fields of the village
under shady trees. So I wasn't sure what Motsie did or didn't
know.'

It seems hard to believe that someone from the same
village wouldn't know something of Imelda's background,
but I let it go.

'Where did you celebrate your wedding?'

'During the negotiations they set the dates for the two

223

wedding feasts, the one at my family home and the other at Motsie's family home. But Mme wanted my family celebration to take place in Soweto. For me that was a problem, but she was determined, and reminded Mme Moipone that *she* was my mother, and that her husband's ancestors had to welcome their son-in-law.

'Parents are usually proud when their daughters marry,' I remind Imelda. 'A man can always get a wife, but for a woman it's regarded as an achievement. Maybe your mother wanted to shine and show the people of Soweto your success and good fortune, despite what had befallen you.'

'Her demands were impossible,' Imelda says. 'Most people in the village had never been to Soweto and couldn't afford to travel to the wedding.'

'But surely the people of Quthing could still attend the ceremony at your husband's home?'

'That's what both Mme and Ntate said. But it never once crossed their minds that I didn't want to get married among the people who had hurt and ridiculed me. As soon as my parents left, ready to start preparations for the feast to welcome Motsie to the family, I told Mme Moipone that I'd rather not get married if I had to do it in Soweto. All the talk at my wedding would be about the rape. No! In the end I got my way, and the celebrations all happened in Quthing. But Mme never smiled once the entire weekend.'

'Where was Lethabo during the celebrations?'

'Mme Moipone told me not to worry about him. She'd take care of it all. And she did, because I didn't see him once that weekend. But I missed him terribly. He was on my mind the entire time, and I knew he was missing me too. But I was now with my husband's family, being trained into the ways of my new family and taught how to be a good wife.'

'It must have been a big adjustment living with your in-laws.'

'The wives of Motsie's two married brothers helped to orientate me, and I knew the unspoken rule that I had to work harder than everyone else to prove that they hadn't wasted the cows they paid as *mahadi*. As a new bride I had to focus on his family and spend time cooking, cleaning and washing clothes for my parents-in-law and my husband. But the homestead of my in-laws was opulent compared to the modest houses of their neighbours. Their land was much bigger, with chickens, cows, sheep, goats, horses and an assortment of vegetables and fruit to feed the family. They shared their surplus with fellow villagers and also sold some produce in Maseru, the capital of this small kingdom. Even when the crops failed and the animals died, it didn't bring them anywhere close to a life of poverty.'

'When did you get a chance to see Lethabo again?'

I hear the deep sadness in her voice as she speaks. 'I had no way of knowing that while I was being inducted into the world of my in-laws, the fight to end all fights was taking place at Mme Moipone's house. On the second Monday afternoon I got a message that Mme Moipone wanted to see me. I knew it was urgent, because a week after my wedding, it wasn't appropriate for me to visit my own family. It was also too soon for her to visit me at my in-laws. I couldn't just sneak over to Mme Moipone's house because it was ten kilometres away. And if I asked Motsie to accompany me, he was likely to see Lethabo. At that moment, I wished I'd told the truth.'

'Why didn't you tell him then?'

'No, no, I had to at least consult Mme Moipone first. But I came up with an idea. I said I wanted to go to church on Sunday, knowing that Mme Moipone would be there with

Lethabo. Motsie said he'd tell his mother of my wish, and he didn't foresee any problem. But the church was still a long walk from my new home, and my mother-in-law wouldn't let me go alone. So I decided not to go. It was pure agony. Then around lunchtime that Sunday, Mme Moipone arrived bearing gifts. It was like a ray of sunshine. I was thrilled to see her, but still sad because she couldn't bring my child. I'd much rather have visited her.'

'How did Mme Moipone manage to justify visiting you so soon?'

'She was very cunning. She claimed that some relatives who couldn't attend the wedding had brought me a gift, and she thought it urgent to bring it to me. She brought one of her beautiful blankets and pretended it was the gift. My mother-in-law came to greet her, and soon more family members gathered and we didn't get a moment alone. Then Motsie, his brothers and their father arrived from a community meeting, and they also spent time with Mme Moipone. A big lunch was served and she was treated like royalty. It was a pleasant afternoon. My new family was very welcoming and generous to her. But my mind was far away. All I could hear was the laughter of my child who I was so desperate to see and hold. After what seemed like an eternity, my mother-in-law suddenly said, "*Haai, ha re e itlheke. Re fe ngwetsi ya rona sebaka le mmae. Ke a kgolwa o mo hlolohetsoe.* Let's go and give our daughter-in-law some time with her mother. I'm sure she's missing her." I was so relieved and grateful. My mother-in-law was always so kind and warm, as if she knew I'd been an abandoned child.'

'What did Mme Moipone have to say?'

'"*Mme wa hao o nkile ngwana rona!* Your mother has taken our child!"' As she describes this moment she rocks back on the couch, one gnarled hand on her stomach and the other clutching her heart while she groans, softly at first, then louder and louder, rocking to the rhythm of her tortured cries.

Finally she becomes still again. 'It was like being told of the death of a loved one. Fortunately, on that vast property we were too far for my in-laws to hear my howls.'

I think of the blue and yellow police van driving off with my father's body, and my frantic and futile pursuit of it. It *was* a death, I think quietly to myself, the death of the sacred bond between mother and child, the beginning of the social isolation that was to lead her child to a lonely, bloody death alone on a street corner. How is it that a single decision taken in a brief moment can set the trajectory for the rest of one's life? The decision to separate Mabegzo from his mother, it seems, ostensibly to secure and protect her marriage, had cost him his life.

'When Mme Moipone left, her shoulders were drooping. She had also helped to raise Lethabo, and he had often asked her if she was his father. "No, I'm your grandmother. A woman can't be your father." "*Ntate ke mang*? Who is my father?" he would ask her.'

I feel pain as I think back to the day Mabegzo wept and told me how he'd asked the same questions of Nkgono. But I keep my thoughts to myself. In Quthing at least, the identity of his father wasn't an obsession yet because he was still too young to make friends, and many other local boys were also raised in the absence of their fathers, who were working on white men's farms and mines.

'When I recovered from the shock I felt helpless and full of regret. If only I had told my husband about my child, it would have been easy to make a plan to travel to Soweto to fetch him. But I had lied. And my loss and pain were the price for lying. Mme Moipone advised me not to rock the boat for now, but to continue being a good wife until we could devise a plan. She felt that my marriage was too new to withstand any turbulence. Time would strengthen it and I had to be patient, she said. I trusted her wisdom and I was sure she was right, so I followed her advice.'

'And now? Do you still think so?'

'The initial decision to hide my child was wrong. This decision to keep up the lie was to put a lid on that first bad decision. That's the trouble with lies. You have to keep lying to protect yourself. Human beings never learn, even the wisest among us.'

'But you're not angry with Mme Moipone, who persuaded you to go along with the lie?'

'Mme Moipone had a good heart. She wasn't motivated by malice, shame or the desire to control me. With her it was always about love and wanting my happiness. Remember that with my first marriage proposal, it was she who had revealed the existence of my boy. So this time her advice was motivated by love. And I guess she also didn't want to clash with Mme. And on her deathbed in 1982, she apologised again. My own mother never, ever apologised to me, even when it was clear that she was in the wrong.'

'Did it get any easier with time?'

'No. The burden in my heart didn't abate. I continued to keep the biggest story of my life from my husband. But my in-laws were loving to me. They liked my gentle ways, and often said that I was easy to get along with and *"Ha se motho wa ditaba*. She doesn't like to chatter and gossip". There was no contact from our family in Soweto. Even when Mme Moipone asked for Lethabo to visit, it fell on deaf ears. Mme neither acknowledged nor responded to her letters.'

'Meanwhile, I was expecting my first child with my husband, which made travelling to Johannesburg impossible.

I hoped that the new life would create such joy in the family that my husband would be receptive to the news I had to share with him. I knew he would be angry, but I hoped he'd forgive me in time. In February 1973, ten months after my wedding, I gave birth to Mamello. I hadn't seen Lethabo since the previous April, when I got married. But my husband was too happy at the birth, and somehow it didn't seem right to raise the subject then. I didn't want the birth of our child to be tainted by a possible fight, perhaps a final one, between us.'

'So you kept up the lie?'

'Yes, I did. I was still waiting for the right time.'

'Mme Moipone wrote to Mme, again, telling her about the birth. This time, Mme responded, expressing happiness and wishing me and my baby well. She also told us not to worry about Lethabo, that he was thriving and had stopped asking about me. How do you tell a mother that her child has stopped asking for her? I knew it was a lie. I was all he knew; there was no way he would forget me just like that. Maybe he did later in life, but not a mere year since we were separated. I knew he was crying for me.'

Yes, I think silently, right up to his death he was crying for you.

'I heard Lethabo's cries, you know; they woke me up at night.' She can see I don't totally buy this. 'It wasn't just my imagination. I really heard him cry, night and day. One day, my child, you'll know. You'll know that a child chooses its mother, not the other way round. And because it's the child who chooses you among all other women, it's the child who decides to stop loving you. And all a child knows and can do is love. So your child never stops loving you.'

'But you stopped loving your mother?'

'Yes, and perhaps my son stopped loving me too, but he

229

was no longer a child then. I wasn't a child when I stopped loving my mother. I'm talking about a child's love. It's clean, uncomplicated and sincere. And then we raise them and teach them to stop loving.'

'Did you find any other opportunity to talk to Motsie?'

'At the end of that year, 1973, Motsie announced that he was going to study in Maseru. This meant that I was separated from my husband, and again, I lost the opportunity to reveal my secret to him.'

'What led to this decision?'

'He and his brothers used to speak about the kingdom's politics all the time. Although they'd grown up comfortable and lacking for nothing, the world was changing. They knew that to survive and make something of their lives, they'd have to further their education. The economy was shifting and the land alone could no longer support them. Agriculture was still important, but the kingdom needed an educated citizenry. So my in-laws decided that their sons would move to Maseru to train as teachers. My mother-in-law didn't approve of me leaving my child to travel to Maseru, so it was left to Motsie to visit us. And although we had our own rondavel on the property, it wasn't private enough. I needed to be truly alone with him to tell him.

'Then I fell pregnant again during the Easter holidays in 1975, and I gave birth to my second daughter, Mpho, in December. But every time my girls laughed or cried, I thought about my son whose laughter and cries I still heard in my sleep and as I cared for my family or visited friends. He was everywhere. But there never seemed to be the right time to tell Motsie. He was away, and then there was the birth, but I was going to do it someday soon.'

'You must also have continued your education, because you became a teacher too.'

'Yes, on one of his visits, Motsie suggested that I should also study. I hadn't finished high school, but I'd gone far enough to resume my studies and at least get my Senior Certificate. My in-laws objected that it wasn't necessary for me now, and I should perhaps wait until the children were a little older. But Motsie insisted that the children and I should come with him to Maseru. His parents were always so supportive. They loved me and the children and I understood why they resisted. But I was also proud of how Motsie asserted his authority as a father and a husband, and made his own decisions. It gave me hope that when I broke the news to him, he wouldn't reject me because of his parents, but only if he found the situation intolerable himself.

'We moved to Maseru when Mpho was one and Mamello nearly four years old. It was January 1977, and Motsie was starting the final year of his teacher's diploma while I started an adult high-school programme. I'd done well at the mission school in Quthing before my marriage, and I needed only one more year to complete my high-school education. Finding accommodation for our whole family wasn't easy. It had been much easier for Motsie to live as a student at the teacher's college, but we survived on the stipend he received as a student teacher. Mme Moipone came to take care of the children while we both studied. She sometimes returned to Quthing on weekends to ensure that her home, vegetable garden and cows were taken care of, but she had good neighbours and relatives to take care of things in her absence. My husband encouraged me not to stop after my Senior Certificate, so at age twenty-five, I started a teaching diploma.'

Impulsively I reach out and give her a big hug and a kiss. 'Oh, Mme Imelda! Your family should have been so proud of you!'

'They didn't know. We didn't communicate at all by then. Mme Moipone still wrote tirelessly to Mme asking her to visit with Lethabo, and even suggested visiting Soweto, but nobody bothered to write back. Then, in November 1977, Greta got married.'

'How did you learn about her wedding?'

'Greta was an adult by then. She was only two years younger than me. She took the trouble to find Mme Moipone's address and write to her, inviting both me and my aunt. All the other relatives in Lesotho were invited by Mme, but not Mme Moipone. Mme knew that her sister would take the snub to heart. Mme had never forgiven me for leaving her house with my baby in 1968 and choosing to live with Mme Moipone instead.'

'It seems rather extreme for something that happened so long ago.'

'When someone has an evil heart, they turn everything into an irreconcilable battle.'

'Did you have any doubts about going to the wedding?'

'I hadn't been to Soweto in nine years and I wasn't sure I was ready for it. But it was a great opportunity to see my baby. I hadn't seen him in four and a half years, and with Motsie staying behind to mark exam papers, there was no risk of him finding out. It was the perfect opportunity.'

'How did you feel about seeing him?'

'Not a day had passed when I hadn't thought about him. At night he was a source of my nightmares. I had no peace.'

'Was it guilt that kept you awake?'

'Guilt, yes. A lot of guilt.'

'How was your arrival in Soweto?'

'We arrived to a house full of people who were strangers to me. I kept to myself, but I felt people's eyes on me. It was a Friday afternoon and my mother's house was abuzz with preparations for the wedding the next day. My eyes were searching for my child, but I couldn't see him among all the people there. Conversations were brief and superficial, but some relatives were surprised to see me. "Oh, you've grown." "Oh, you're a wife now." "Oh, your children are beautiful." They hadn't expected me to amount to much, and they were surprised I'd made something of my life. Maybe they thought I didn't deserve success and a good life. The rape was supposed to destroy me. Well, it didn't, it really didn't. Some of those who had pointed fingers at me had made bad decisions in the meantime: some were unmarried or hadn't completed their schooling; others had children out of wedlock or were ravaged by alcohol, and yet...' She searches for the right words.

'Yet you'd been judged for something you hadn't brought on yourself?'

'Yes, yes, that's it.'

'It was pelting with rain on Greta's wedding morning, which people take to mean that the bride has eaten out of a pot because she was too lazy to dish up properly. Then the tent collapsed in the downpour and the fires under the pots of wedding food went out. For a while it looked like Greta's day would be a disaster, but suddenly the heavens stopped weeping and all became calm. The sun shone and created the perfect setting for a wedding. Although I was happy for Greta, I was watching from the side-lines all the time, feeling that these weren't my people.'

'Yet your siblings didn't like what happened to you,' I tell her, hoping it might melt some ice.

'I'm sure they didn't. I feel sorry for them, living with her all their lives.' She pauses a while, and then adds, 'They knew where I was. They could have tried to reach out to me.'

'And I suppose you could also have tried to reach them.'

'When something horrible happens to a person, it's not that person who must say, hey I'm here, come and see me.'

'But they were children.'

'They didn't stay children forever. Once they understood, and were adults, they could have come. Greta found me for her wedding.' And then she declares, emphatically, 'We'll only meet at funerals now.'

'What made you return for your mother's funeral?'

'I only came because of Mme Moipone.'

'Mme Moipone? But she's been gone well over twenty years.'

'Not in my heart. She's always there. She would have advised me to go. She would have come, even though her sister treated her so badly. I came for her.'

'How did it feel to see your little boy again at Greta's wedding?

'I found him playing and singing in the streets as throngs of people gathered around the newlyweds. Except he wasn't little anymore, he was nearly ten. My heart exploded with love and longing. But it didn't last long. He didn't know who I was. He looked straight past me with no recognition at all, and, and...' She starts to cry again. 'While I was sitting agonising in Quthing, wondering how to explain my absence to my child, Mme hadn't even told him he had a mother. Nothing.'

Imelda relates the events at the wedding exactly as Mabegzo had described them to me fifteen-and-a-half years ago.

'When we saw each other again, the elders were talking and made some reference to his mother, but when he asked who his mother was, Mme reprimanded him for asking too many questions. I could forgive her somehow for hiding me when I was a child, for hiding Lethabo and then suddenly wanting him with her, for whatever reason. I could still live with that. But in all this time she had obviously never spoken of me! She didn't try to keep my memory alive in my child's life. For that I can never forgive her. Never.'

'Yet he knew the two of you were somehow connected.'

'He thought I was his sister. Have you any idea how that felt? Mme allowed him to forget me, his own mother. There's no excuse for that. To deny my existence to my child when he asked about me was unforgivable. Mme Moipone again advised me to maintain my composure and try to handle it in a dignified manner. But I was at the end of my tether. Watching the adults laugh every time my son asked who his mother was – it was unbearable. I had to walk away.'

'He thought he'd upset you.'

'I know, and he came to say sorry. I told him to ask Nkgono who his mother was. And to tell her that Imelda wanted to know.'

'He didn't tell me that.'

'I was hoping it would make her tell him the truth, and open the way for me to explain everything. But she gave him stupid answers. God is your mother, I am your mother... It was unforgivable.'

'He suspected you were his mother. People were saying so, and he just needed confirmation. You could have confirmed it right there and then.'

She doesn't respond directly. 'A child shouldn't wonder about this kind of thing. He should know with certainty.'

'He was so happy when you kissed him on the lips that day.'

'I couldn't stop myself.'

'Someone had told him he was the product of rape.'

I hear her sharp intake of breath. She struggles to speak. 'I owe him everything. I hope heaven gives me a chance to heal him when we meet there again.'

While many in Soweto condemned her son to hell when he died, perhaps it's good for her peace of mind that she's a Christian, and that she believes there's a chance of redemption in purgatory in preparation for an afterlife in heaven.

'When I returned to Lesotho with my daughters and Mme Moipone, I was still traumatised by the encounter with my son, but I believed it wasn't too late to make it right again. I decided to tell my husband everything. Mme Moipone didn't think it was a good idea yet, and advised me to first get my education finished and my career off the ground, just in case my husband got too angry. But I'd had enough of the deceit. I couldn't live with myself knowing that my child was paying such a price for something he didn't bring on himself. It was already November, and I decided to tell Motsie early in the New Year. I was in the middle of my end-of-year exams, and Motsie was busy with final year marks for his students. December also meant a visit to Quthing with the family until the New Year. I didn't want any tension that my in-laws could notice, and I didn't want everybody's holiday celebrations spoilt by my news.

'But I didn't enjoy that festive season. There was a cloud hanging over me, and even my husband noticed that my smile wasn't reaching my eyes. On the fourth of January we returned to Maseru, leaving the children behind to spend more time with my in-laws. This was the perfect time. Mme Moipone started the conversation with Motsie. "Let's pray," she said. Then she related to Motsie how the elders had let me down with bad advice every step of the way, and that I was an honest child who always wanted to obey. She asked for forgiveness for her own role in what I was about to reveal. Motsie sat listening, not showing any reaction to her vague introduction.

'Then I told him. "*Ke na le ngwana.* I have a child," I said, "a son who now lives in Soweto with my parents. Mme Moipone and I raised him for the first four years and four months of his life. But when we married, the elders said it wouldn't be appropriate for you and your family to know or for me to bring a child into our marriage." I was crying as I told him this. But he didn't say a word, so I got desperate, trying to explain every angle and apologising for deceiving him.'

'That must have been so difficult. What did he say?'

'He cleared his throat and said this was indeed a big thing. And then he stunned me. He said, "*Kgale ke tseba ka taba ena, ebile ke dutse ho dima yona.* I've known about this for a very long time. Like you, I've been sitting on it. It feels good to have it out of the way." I was so shocked, I couldn't believe my ears. It turned out that Motsie had known about the child all along. But he'd decided to take his cue from me, and when I didn't say anything, he decided not to press me.'

I am so elated at this that I get up and jump up and down. 'Yes, yes, yes, Mme Imelda! So you had the unconditional love you deserved. But how did he know?'

'That's exactly what I asked him. "Can anyone keep a secret in Quthing?" he said. "When we met you were alone. But like any self-respecting man, I asked questions about you to weigh my chances of winning you." People had cautioned him, warning that I had arrived pregnant from Johannesburg and that my first engagement broke down because of this. They warned him not to get involved. But Motsie said I was the one, and he wanted to be with me, with or without the child. "I saw you with the child," he told me. "You were on your way back from church. But you didn't see me, because I was hiding!" We laughed a little together over that. But I kept asking him questions. "Why didn't you say anything?"

And he said, "Why didn't *you* say anything?" "It was our fault," Mme Moipone insisted. "Your wife didn't make any decisions. She wanted this out in the open before you got married."

'Motsie said he'd also hoped that when the marriage negotiations started, my family would reveal the existence of the child to his family. If they had objected, he would have insisted that the marriage go ahead, but the child would have had to stay with Mme Moipone where I could visit him.'

My tears flow now as I think of Mabegzo and what his life might have been. As disappointed as I am in him, right now, my compassion wells up. 'Oh Mabegzo,' I cry out in front of his mother, 'I'm so sorry you carried such a heavy cross.'

Imelda reaches for my hand and places it between her tiny wrinkled fingers. '*O motho, o motho*. You're so humane,' she says.

'Motsie assured us that he wasn't angry and didn't see why we couldn't carry on with our lives. But he had one question. "Who is his father, and where is he?" Before I could answer, Mme Moipone said, "This child was raped by the child's father, who was a stranger to her. He was beaten by the police. We don't know where he is." I was happy not to reveal any more than that. The most important issue had been dealt with, and I agreed with Mme Moipone that it's one thing for a man to accept that his wife has been with another man, albeit violently, but there was no need to add further injury by telling him that there had been more than one.

'Motsie seemed hurt by this and comforted me, saying, "*Ho lokile, Modimo o moholo*. All is well. God is great." We never, ever spoke of the rape again. Motsie asked us to keep this to ourselves while he decided how best to handle it with his parents. He felt it was one thing for them to find out at the beginning of our relationship, but to learn that we had conspired to keep them in the dark for six years was a bit much.

'I wasn't happy with that. I just wanted my child back, and to prolong our separation was too much. But Motsie had been kind to me and I needed to support him and wait until he was ready to face his parents. And at least I could now visit my child openly without worrying about covering up the visits to my husband.'

Chapter 15

It's Wednesday, the third day of Imelda's stay at my house. Soon our week will be over. She plans to leave on Saturday morning, and I don't know when I may next see her. I would also dearly like to give her a gift before she leaves. So I lie to her. I tell her that I'll be late coming home this evening because of a story I'm working on. In a way it is the truth.

I drive to Orlando East through grid-locked traffic on the M1 South. I'm on a mission to find Basil because I need his help. I arrive at his home, just a few houses from the home of my childhood where my father had grown up, married and raised us. Despite the passing of time, I still cannot drive past that house, which is almost unchanged, without picturing his gold and brown casket being moved from his bedroom into the tent for prayers and then into the hearse.

I find the incorrigible Basil drinking tea in the back room at his home.

'*Haai, wena*, why are you visiting when I'm watching Isidingo? You must come during the news.'

'Hello Basil. So you do drink tea!'

'Just because you saw me tipsy once, you think that's how I live? No way! The ARVs don't work without a healthy lifestyle.'

'Good, Bas, I'm proud of you.'

'Oh please! Stop this "a friend with Aids is still my friend" drivel.'

'So what do…'

'Shhhh! I'm watching!'

I sit in silence while he watches his soapie, and when it ends, I ask permission to speak, lest he silence me again.

I get straight to the point. 'Tell me about Miriam and her child.'

'Aha! You see, you did have a thing for Mabegzo.'

'Basil!'

'Yes, *wena*, you devil! Admit it. You had a thing for him.'

'Okay, I had a thing for him. Now listen. I need you to take me to Miriam.'

Basil admits that he doesn't really know her well.

'How can this be a problem for someone who just barges in and commands attention wherever he goes? I'm sure she knows you. Everyone knows you. You're like the mayor of Orlando East.'

This pleases him, and he agrees to avail himself over the weekend. But I'm in a race against time.

'Now? *Haai*, it'll cost you! *Phela*, this is my "me" time, and I'll never get it back.'

We arrive at a house not far from Mabegzo's. Many

homes in Orlando East have been extended, altered and repainted, but this one shows no signs of progress, which tells its own story.

I thank Basil for bringing me here and say goodbye.

'*Haai, wena*, you think I'm going to walk home? Forget it, *sisi*, you're taking me home. I'll wait for you.'

Miriam must be in her mid- or late-thirties, but in some ways she looks much older. She's a big girl, but I remind myself that I'm here to meet the young woman who had a child with Mabegzo, not the grown-up standing in front of me. She's not unfriendly as she opens the door to me, just surprised about who would visit at this hour. Still, she lets me in and I sit on a small chair next to the coal stove.

'My name is Redi and I was Mabegzo's friend.' She doesn't react.

'I cared about him very much and I'm trying to speak to anyone who has memories of him.'

She nods.

'May I talk with you?' I imagine that in her world, too, people have been keen to erase all record of his existence, and I hope that she's at least willing to affirm this chapter of her life.

'*Haai*, there's nothing to say really. It's so long ago. I don't think it's good to talk.'

'Please. I have come quite far to be here. It will be so good to talk to you.'

'Are you a journalist?' she finally asks.

'I am, but I'm not here in that role. I'm here as a friend.'

'Whose friend?'

'Mabegzo's, and his mother's.'

'His mother? Nobody knows his mother.'

'I do, and she's a lovely woman. I love her very much. You would too if you met her.'

She doesn't answer.

'You had a child with him?' Silence.

'I won't use this information to harm you or his child.'

'Why are you here? You know how many years have passed?'

'Fifteen years and three months.'

'So if you know everything about him, why are you here?' Her manner is now aggressive and sarcastic. I don't expect her to pour her heart out to me, but I'm finding her completely impenetrable.

'Miriam...'

'And how do you know my name, anyway?'

'I was at Nkgono's funeral, and someone mentioned that...'

'Someone has a big mouth.'

I could leave and return another day, but Mme Imelda is leaving soon, and I really want to do this for her.

'I'm sorry if I upset you. Please forgive me. I just wanted to speak to you and maybe meet your son.'

'Which one? I have two.'

'Oh, you had two children with Mabegzo. That's lovely.'

'Are you asking me or telling me?' she hits back, annoyed at my assumption.

'I'm asking, Miriam. Only asking.'

I manage to extract from her that only her first son is from Mabegzo, and that his name is Potlako. Black names tell a story, and Potlako means hurried, so it could mean that he was premature, or that she fell pregnant young.

'How old is he?'

'Sixteen later this year.'

'Oh,' I say, 'he must have been a baby when Mabegzo died. You must have been very young when you had him. It would have been hard. You're very strong.'

Again she says nothing. 'I'm asking you to help me, Miriam,' I tell her. 'I loved Mabegzo. He was a good friend of mine. I love his mother and she's in a lot of pain, so I…'

'She's not the only one. Does she want my son now, after all these years? Has she sent you to take him away from me? Forget it. It won't happen.'

'She doesn't know about Potlako. No one has told her anything. I also only found out recently. Mabegzo's mother has had a tough life. Very tough.'

'All of us have, but we don't leave our children behind for their grandmothers to raise.'

'She was very young when…'

'So? I was also young. I was eighteen when I had my child and nineteen when his father died. But I didn't just pack up and go.'

'That's not what happened. She was the age of your son now when she fell pregnant. I bet you still see Potlako as your baby.' I pause to let that sink in. 'Imelda was also a baby, and the adults made all her decisions for her. She didn't just leave.' I'm desperate for Miriam to believe me, but I can't in all fairness reveal the intimate details of Imelda's life. Imelda will have to do it when they meet. And I'm determined that they will.

'Potlako's grandmother is a decent human being. You will be very glad to meet her. She lost out on the chance to know her son and she will tell you all about that one day. But since you knew Mabegzo and had a child with him, I thought it could be good for the two of you to meet.'

'I'll think about it.'

'Do you want to take my number? You can call me when you're ready. Or may I have your number?'

'I don't have a phone,' she says, holding it in her hand as she speaks.

'Okay, no problem. Thank you, Miriam, thank you so much for speaking to me. I'll come and visit again soon.' I search in my handbag for a piece of paper and a pen, and leave her with my contact number, even though I doubt that she'll ever call. But at least I now know where she lives.

It's nine pm when I arrive home and Mme Imelda has cooked us a meal. I'm pleased that she's feeling comfortable in my home.

'You work too late, my baby. How will you ever find a husband?' I smile, having heard this many times from the elders in my family.

'*Eish*, Mme Imelda, there are no good men left.'

'You're a baby, there's plenty of time, and these days a woman must work harder than a man. You must use the good brain God gave you, so that when the man and the children come, you have fulfilled your dreams.'

'Oh, I love the way you think Mme Imelda!' I hug her as we sit down for supper.

'So,' I say. 'Life must have been easier once your husband knew everything.'

'Yes, it was. I was a bit worried about his parents, but so relieved that the person who had brought me into this family was on my side. But Motsie was still mulling over how to break the news to his parents when I fell pregnant again in April 1978. I was in the second year of my teaching diploma, and Motsie had also decided to study part time to further his teaching qualification. My mother-in-law hinted that she'd like to take care of our children while we studied, but I wouldn't have it. My children belonged with me.

'Motsie suggested we wait until the birth of our third child before telling his parents about Lethabo. Again I wasn't happy, but I went along with the plan. But I asked to visit Soweto, along with Mme Moipone. I didn't want to wait until my pregnancy was advanced. It would make it too difficult to travel.'

'Oh, so you visited Soweto? I don't remember Mabegzo sharing this with me.'

'Yes, I travelled to Soweto. Mme Moipone was still respectful of her older sister and thought it would be inappropriate to just arrive unannounced. So she wrote to Mme, announcing the date of our arrival and why we were coming. All I wanted was to introduce myself to my son, and tell him that soon I'd come to fetch him. When we arrived on the set day, about three weeks later, he wasn't there. Mme claimed he was on a church camp and wouldn't be back for another week.'

'It sounds as if you didn't believe her.'

'I didn't. I believe Mme deliberately sent my son away so that he wouldn't be back before I was gone.'

'Really Mme Imelda? It's hard to believe that Nkgono would be that vindictive.'

'It's good that you don't believe bad things about people. I hope you never lose that. I'm just telling you what happened. But I was done talking to that woman. I didn't even want to be in her presence. In fact, it was a mistake to go there while I was pregnant. It was her spirit that caused me to give birth to a sick child.'

I know better than to go down this route. Where there is faith and deep conviction, it's usually best to let people be. 'Did you look for him at his school?'

'It was a Saturday, so there was no point. And we had to return on Sunday because I had lectures and Motsie had to be at work on Monday. He couldn't miss work to care for the children, so we had to return. The trip was also costly. We had very little money for our growing family, and it would take us a while to save enough money for another trip to Soweto.'

'So what did you do?'

'Mme Moipone took a conciliatory approach, and wrote to invite Mme to Maseru so that Lethabo could meet his stepfather and sisters. She repeated that Motsie knew about Lethabo and was very happy to meet him. And he was, although he wasn't yet ready to tell his family. But as usual, her letters went unanswered.

'I became depressed. Motsie promised to help me to get my child back, but for now he asked me to focus on my pregnancy and my studies. I wrote my exams in November 1978, and gave birth to Motlalepula during torrential rain in January 1979. The heavens were in revolt, as though they were sending an angry message to the world.'

After a long pause she sighs. 'She was born with cerebral palsy. But she's my child.' Another long pause. 'Life was very difficult. I was stressed and I felt guilty that I wasn't celebrating the birth of my child. We were all worried and tense. Afterwards, it wasn't easy for me to travel anymore. Juggling my studies and taking care of a sick child while my husband earned a living and pursued his studies was taxing. But between Mme Moipone and my mother-in-law we managed, and they made sure the children were clothed, fed and taken care of. They were champions.'

Unexpectedly, she starts to sob bitterly. 'That was when I betrayed my son!'

'What do you mean?'

She takes a deep breath and then throws her head back and looks to heaven. 'My fight to have him return to us took a back seat. I'm ashamed of that. Raising Tlale was very difficult. Even though others helped, I was her mother, and I couldn't leave it to them to do all the work. I didn't forget my son, but for the first year of Tlale's life, I was utterly preoccupied with meeting her demanding presence without letting the other children suffer. Mamello had also started school and needed support. Motsie was churning out diplomas, determined to be successful so that our family could survive. And I was also in my final year of studies, still breastfeeding, and...' She sighs again. 'I felt so exhausted and so helpless with three small children, and one very sick.

'But I managed to pass my teacher's diploma. In 1980 I was posted to Mate Primary School, where I taught practically everything: English, Maths, Geography, History and Sewing. Motsie was the Maths and Science teacher at Moshoeshoe High School in Maseru. He also took an active interest in local politics and was a Political Science student at Roma University. He was rising through the ranks, and he became heavily involved with his political activities. He had very little to say about informing his parents of the existence of another child. He even suggested that as so much time had passed we should abandon the idea. But when I objected he promised we would deal with it after his exams.

'Motsie was also becoming more politically active. He was a member of the leftist Basotho Congress Party, which had won a big victory in the post-independence elections of 1970. In response to that victory, the leader of the ruling BNP and Prime Minister of the kingdom, Leabua Jonathan, had nullified the elections, declared a state of emergency, suspended the constitution and arrested the BCP leaders. This alienated the local population. The late 1970s also saw exiled members of Nelson Mandela's party, the African National Congress, arriving in Lesotho to escape South Africa's apartheid regime and set up underground operations. South Africa was threatening direct action against the Lesotho government. There was violence and internal disorder in

Lesotho as many agitated for change. Unbeknown to me at that time, Motsie had befriended the exiled South Africans opposing the apartheid government. This piqued his interest in politics and he became a fully-fledged member of the BCP, which aimed to remove Jonathan's government and also help the exiled community. In the early 1980s, Motsie brought his South African friends home and provided a safe place for them while the South African government was staging cross-border attacks. It was a dangerous time, because Motsie was fully immersed in these affairs. But my husband had been very good to me. I was caught in the middle. I wanted my child, but I wanted my family to stay together. And he kept reassuring me that we would solve the problem; I just had to be patient.

'1981 was a difficult year. Mme Moipone suffered a mild stroke and remained in Maseru for medical care. She was no longer strong and self-sufficient after that, so she couldn't take care of our children anymore while Motsie and I went to work. But a kind, hardworking neighbour came to work for us.

'There were regular police raids on our home, and with Mme Moipone weak and Tlale incapable, Motsie suggested I take the children back to Quthing, while he stayed on in Maseru to pursue his studies and his political activities. This was a very dark time in our lives. I was always afraid. I didn't want to break up our family, but I couldn't abandon Mme Moipone in her hour of need. I had to be with her. So I left my job, hoping to find a teaching post in the village.

'I wrote to my mother, telling her that her sister was ill and that a visit with Lethabo might lift her spirits. She wrote back to say that she was sorry she couldn't afford the cost of the trip. We were pulling hard then, and I couldn't afford to send the money, but we agreed that she would visit with my child in December. I believed her. But December came and went with no word. I had really believed that with her sister dying she would at last come.'

'But surely you couldn't have known Mme Moipone was dying, so you wouldn't have told that to your mother. She probably didn't realise the seriousness of her illness.'

She thinks for a moment. 'I knew her illness was very serious. Mme Moipone was always up and about, so when she became unable to do anything for herself, I knew she was gravely ill. I told Mme. Mme Moipone had taken me in when Mme didn't want to take care of me, so surely she could find it in her heart to come to Quthing?'

'Then early in the New Year, Motsie was arrested. He didn't say much about the politics, but I was terribly worried about him. I still hadn't found work, so I spent my days taking care of Mme Moipone and Tlale. Even after Motsie was released a few months later, he wasn't sending money as regularly as he used to, but his parents were very kind to us. We had food, milk and fresh water all the time. And my mother-in-law helped a great deal with the children.

'In the winter of 1982, Mme Moipone died. She was only fifty-four.' Pain is written across Imelda's face as she remembers the woman she felt had loved her like a true mother. 'I felt it terribly. To lose a mother, especially a good mother who still has so much to give, is a bitter loss.

'Mme Moipone died on a Monday morning, and the Soweto people dared to arrive late the very next day, expecting us to host them for an entire week when they had never bothered to visit in our hour of need. I was so quarrelsome that week,' she laughs. 'My husband often had to calm me down. It started when they arrived without Lethabo. I was so angry that I think Motsie feared I would lose my temper in front of his parents, who had never seen me angry. I was seething, and he was afraid I would say things I could never take back.'

'But Lethabo hadn't been a part of your life for so long. Why was it so important to you that he should attend the funeral?'

'Do you think it's right for a child not to be allowed to throw soil into his grandmother's grave?'

'Of course not. But weren't you worried that having Lethabo there would blow your cover?'

'No. As a teacher, I knew how children behaved. He wouldn't run to me and call me Mme. And even if he had, in Sesotho every mother is your mother. My in-laws wouldn't have just assumed that he was my son.'

'And the villagers?'

'They hadn't seen him in many years; I didn't think they'd remember him. I just wanted him with me. I was adamant that he should be there. After all, Mme Moipone had raised and cared for him when the Soweto people thought he was a curse.'

'Yet they still raised him, and he loved Nkgono.'

'Yes, but only because he didn't know how hard she'd worked to keep him away from me. And when he became rebellious, she threw him out.'

'Who told you that, Mme Imelda? It isn't true you know. Nkgono didn't throw him out.'

She doesn't respond.

'There was a lot of tension in the days leading up to the funeral, but then Lethabo arrived with Tshepo, and seeing my boy brought me a lot of comfort.' She sheds more tears. 'I welcomed him with a kiss and a hug, and I told him how glad I was to see him. But he'd changed. He wasn't a happy and welcoming child any more. He seemed like he didn't trust anyone, and he kept to himself.

'Motsie and I quarrelled badly soon after Lethabo arrived, because I insisted I couldn't carry on like this anymore. He could see I'd lost my head and he calmed me down, asking if I planned to give Mme Moipone a noisy send off. This was the afternoon before the funeral, and the coffin had arrived. Noisy behaviour is sacrilege at this time, so I had to bite my tongue as always. The villagers were arriving for the evening prayer service while the men cut up the meat and the women cooked. So there was no chance to interact with the Soweto people.' Referring to her parents and siblings as 'the Soweto people' reveals the depth of her alienation and anger as she remembers their indifference towards her.

'The day after the funeral, I blew up again over the cleansing ritual. I may not have been Mme Moipone's biological daughter, but in every way that counted, she was a mother to me. I insisted on having my hair and eyebrows shaved as a sign of mourning, and I wore the black scarf until the second cleansing ritual. Mme felt strongly that I shouldn't do this since it wasn't my mother who had died.' She closes her eyes. 'I wasn't trying to spite her. I honestly didn't care what she thought.'

'She thought you'd chosen Mme Moipone over her.'

'And I had, for obvious reasons. But it had nothing to do with Mme. It was a tribute to the woman who had shaped my life. An hour or two after that incident, Motsie called me aside to say that he had told his mother about my son.'

'What was her reaction?'

'She told him that she'd always known, but had worried that he didn't know.'

'Oh, Mme Imelda! Now it makes sense why he asked Lethabo to come and stay with you, while the two of them were chopping wood.'

'Oh! You know everything!'

'Lethabo was so happy when he asked.'

'But Motsie's father didn't know, and his mother felt it prudent that he be informed at a family meeting. He was a very strict, proud and traditional man who tolerated no nonsense. I didn't expect him to just accept this. But I was comforted and relieved that my mother-in-law and my husband were now on my side. And so I decided to follow my mother-in-law's advice. Lethabo would return to Johannesburg, a family meeting would be held, and once everything was out in the open, there would be a ritual to ask the Mohale ancestors to accept a child that wasn't theirs. This was more than I'd hoped for, and I prayed that my father-in-law would agree.'

'But how did your mother-in-law know?'

Imelda laughs. 'We asked her, and she answered that we too would become detectives when our own children grew up and had suitors. And in this village there are always many witnesses willing to share what they know or think they know.'

'Didn't it bother her, knowing that you had a child and had kept this from them – and from your husband?'

'She said that at first she was worried that Motsie didn't know, but then she convinced herself that he must know but was keeping it away from them in case they rejected me.'

I am so relieved to hear that Imelda's life story is not just one of betrayals and irreparable family relations. It's good to know that at last she could breathe a little, knowing that the most important people knew who she truly was. This secret had clearly been eating away at her, and the longer it was kept, the further her son had drifted. For a while at least, she'd had great hopes that he would become a part of her life and her family. Yet I'm still not convinced that she tried absolutely everything to get him back, but I withhold my judgement and listen.

'Once he was returned to us, the first thing I was going to do was change his name to Lethabo and close this painful chapter. So when it was time to say goodbye to my child, my heart wasn't too sore because I knew it was only a matter of time before we saw each other again. When I said goodbye I was actually in great spirits.'

'He told me that you kissed him. He remembered that kiss vividly.'

Imelda is silent again. 'You tell me that they loved him, that they truly loved my child. But if he'd had love, why then did a simple kiss mean so much to him?'

For Mabegzo it wasn't just a kiss. It was a new lease of life, a taste of true love and acceptance and the promise of a better tomorrow. In the world he occupied, a single kiss, a gesture that should be an everyday part of a child's life, had meant that he actually had a life. In kissing him, Imelda had reminded Mabegzo of the aching void that was a permanent part of his life. There she was, promising to fill it with all that was good and wholesome, promising him that she would come to fetch him.

'I didn't plan to blurt out that I was his mother. But when my child said, "my grandmother won't be happy," I lost it.'

'Were you jealous that she was the authority in his life?'

'It wasn't jealousy. Not at all. This child was mine; nothing could change that. What tied us together couldn't be replaced. I had no reason to be jealous.'

'Then why did you hit the roof when he said Nkgono wouldn't be pleased for him to live with you?'

'Because she had already directed the course of my life, Mme Moipone's life and my son's life. And now once again she should have the final say? No!'

I tell Imelda how much it meant to him for her to acknowledge him; that in saying 'I am your mother' so ferociously, she had given him the sweet taste of belonging. But it also made his fall greater, and the bitterness of his dashed dream harder to endure.

With renewed optimism, Imelda picked up the pieces of her life. Mme Moipone's death had hit her hard, but the knowledge that she'd soon be reunited with her son cheered her up. Her heart was lighter because of Motsie's support and the anticipated reunion with her son.

'The main reason I had moved back to Quthing was to care for Mme Moipone. So early in 1983 we moved back to Maseru. With the help of my father-in-law's small-scale commercial farming, we were able to move to a better middle-class suburb in Maseru. Motsie got back his post at Moshoeshoe High School that he'd lost after his arrest, and I was now employed at St Francis Primary, where Mamello and Mpho also went to school and thrived.'

'Your mother-in-law must have been sad to see you and the children leave Quthing again.'

'She did protest, but with Mme Moipone gone, I was determined that our family should stay together. Even though Motsie's political activities were now becoming legendary, I decided to weather whatever storms might arise. Those in the know had a lot to say about his activism and leadership. But with me he was reticent. He believed that the more I knew, the riskier it would be for me and the children, so I didn't ask too many questions.

'In Maseru it was also easier to get work, as well as expert help for three-year-old Tlale. The doctors in Quthing had always said that there was nothing more they could do for her and that she wouldn't live long. I didn't believe them. I was convinced that with better care she'd be okay. I used to pray day and night, asking God to consider that in many ways I had already lost a child, and I couldn't go through that again.' She pauses. 'And he heard me. He listened. She's still with us. She's twenty-five years old, and she may not have had the kind of life my other children have, but it's still a life – just a different one. She attended a remedial school in Maseru for the mentally handicapped, which focused on speech and language therapy, physical therapy and recreation. And you know, the loving way Motsie treated our youngest child is the main reason I supported his political activity and tolerated his delay in helping to bring Lethabo into the family. He used to push her wheelchair, brush her hair and feed and wash her, even in her teens. *E ne e le mohlolo*; it was a miracle. I had never seen or heard of any man who did that. But it made it even harder for me to press my own wishes.'

This brings tears to my eyes, as I remember another man who did the same for his daughter. And I have no doubt that he would still have treated me like a princess if I'd been born with a disability.

'I could also see that my husband was troubled by something, but I assumed it was the politics. Sometimes, when he thought no one was watching, he used to pour his heart out to our daughter.'

'What did he say?'

'No, no, if he'd wanted me or the world to know, he'd have told me. But he didn't. He chose his youngest daughter as his confidante.'

'So did your father-in-law ever learn about Lethabo?'

'*Feela, Mme o tshwara thipa ka bohaleng*. Sometimes a mother has to take the knife by the sharp end. My mother-in-law warned me that she and her husband were coming to visit us at our home, but asked me not to tell my husband. After months of trying to initiate a family meeting where her husband would be told about Lethabo, she concluded that if it were left to Motsie, the meeting would never happen. She couldn't bear sitting on this secret any longer. Her husband was ageing, and she wanted to know his wishes so that she wouldn't be left after he'd passed having to make a decision that might displease the ancestors.

'We asked the children to go outside and play while we sat down to talk. My father-in-law was an imposing man and his presence intimidated me. At seventy-three he was very much the patriarch, regal, stoic and serious about matters of lineage and tradition. He was also very strict. But I never saw him being unkind to anyone. When his wife told him that I had another child, he didn't say a word or react in any way. Finally she asked him, "*So Ntate, re ne re kopa ho wena, hore o re bontshe tsela ya ho rarabolla taba ena.* So father, we are asking you to show us the way to resolve this matter."

'He cleared his throat for what seemed like an eternity. "So why am I being told about this matter?" he asked. My mother-in-law began, "Our daughter…" "No, no, hold on, let her speak," he said. "Can our daughter not speak for herself?" Looking pointedly at me, he asked, "Can you not speak for yourself?"

'"I can, Ntate," I said. "Then speak, while our ears can still hear." So I said, "I have a child." "We have heard that already," he said. "Go on." So I said, "For the reasons Mme has already mentioned, I was separated from him. I wish to be reunited with him. With your blessing, of course."

'My father-in-law turned to Motsie. "Son, are you privy to this information?" Motsie nodded. "And so is your mother. It seems all of you have been keeping secrets from me." Nobody said a word. Then he stroked his long beard and said, "Daughter, I fail to see why we have travelled all the way for this. To whom are you married?"

'"To him," I said, pointing at my husband. "Him? Who is him?" "Motsie. Motsie Mohale." "And you have been married to him for how long now?" "Eleven years, Ntate." "Eleven years. And you have called me here to do what exactly?" "To, to guide me, us…" "You say you have a husband of eleven years, yet you seek guidance from me?" I dropped my eyes, not knowing if this was going well or horribly wrong. "No. If he is truly your husband, then it is to him, and only him, that you must account. He is the head of your family. I am the head of mine. I would like to believe that I have raised a man who can take responsibility for himself, his actions and his family. What does he say?"

'For the first time Motsie spoke. "I say, I accept the wishes of God and our ancestors." "And what are these wishes, may I ask?" "They wish for me to comfort and guide my wife. And accept the road that she has travelled." "And do you accept the road that she has travelled?" "I have," he said. "And I do still."

'"*O monna. O buile. Ha ho be jwao.* You are a man. You have spoken. Let it be so." The two men shook hands and the meeting was over. The family spent the afternoon enjoying a meal, laughter and conversation.'

'Oh, Mme Imelda, I love your husband's family!'

'They were very good to me. That day was very special. But afterwards there were hushed conversations between father and son. I knew Motsie well. Something was brewing, but he would only tell me when he was ready.

'The next step was to make plans to get Lethabo back with us in Maseru. I hadn't seen my mother since the day after Mme Moipone's funeral when she sulked. But I was ready and finally able to fetch my child. So in December 1983, I took the seven-hour bus ride to South Africa, determined to return with my son. I was hoping to be back in Quthing by Christmas. Although my husband's brothers and their wives had long since left the village to study and take jobs in the city, we all still returned every Christmas to their original family home to spend the festive season with their parents. We had already set the date for the ritual to introduce Lethabo to the Mohale ancestors and welcome him into the family.'

'Were you nervous?'

'No, not at all. Just excited.'

'After that last botched attempt to fetch my son, I decided it was better not to announce my arrival in Soweto. I deliberately chose to travel during the festive season, knowing that my parents, who still worked at the Faraday factory, would be at home for the December holidays. They had long since stopped travelling to Lesotho for the Christmas break and had no relatives anywhere else. Or so I thought. It was the longest trip of my life. I was excited and nervous, and I imagined the trip back when I would be travelling with my son. I was happy, I was truly happy.

'I arrived in Soweto on the nineteenth of December. But when I got to the house in Orlando East, I found my father at home alone. He told me that my mother had gone to visit Greta in the former homeland of Bophuthatswana, where she now lived with her husband and children. She had taken my son with her. It was soul destroying. I couldn't believe that this was actually happening. I felt like screaming and shouting.'

After a long moment while this terrible turn of events sinks in, I begin to chuckle in spite of myself.

'What's funny?' Imelda asks, looking disconcerted.

'Your son would have said, "*Eish, Lala, ke dibad.* This is bad luck. I was born with it."' I've managed to make her smile a little, and I'm glad of it.

'Ntate told me that Mme would only return early in the New Year. How I regret now that I didn't stay on until then. But Ntate had nothing more to say, and the house felt so oppressive and claustrophobic. And it wasn't only the house. Soweto just made me sick – the smell, the people, the houses... I hated that place. It crushed my spirit and I couldn't breathe. I left the same day I arrived. Perhaps I should have travelled to Mafikeng and tried to find Greta's home. But it didn't occur to me at the time. Instead, I hoped the New Year would bring better luck.'

'And did it?'

'Quite the opposite. On the sixth of January 1984, just as we returned to Maseru from Quthing, Motsie got arrested again. The government suspected him and others of plotting an uprising. We also got wind that he was on South Africa's wanted list for aiding exiles intent on overthrowing the apartheid government. A guerrilla war against Lesotho's government had started in 1979. It wasn't safe for him or his family to travel to South Africa. I was shattered. This meant a further delay of my longed-for reunion with my child. But the apartheid agents were brutal and corrupt, and they were known to do untold harm to unarmed enemies and anyone close to them. So I had to stay put to protect my husband. Once someone was marked, their mail was intercepted, so I couldn't even write to my son. But I sent messages via friends who worked in Johannesburg, hoping they would reach him. But they didn't.

'Despite it all, Motsie completed his degree and travelled within the SADC region on business I knew little about. The tentacles of the apartheid government were everywhere, and I was positively cowed and stayed put. I continued to send handwritten notes via friends asking my mother to bring

Lethabo to Maseru, as I couldn't get to him. But I heard nothing back.

'In desperation, I suggested to my husband that if I could find a way to slip into South Africa, I could ask the police there to help me get my child. Motsie was livid. "The police? You want help from the South African police? And what if this leads them straight to me or to our ANC friends? What then?"

'Then in 1985, Ntate Jakobo's mother died in an area fifty-six kilometres from Maseru. I was excited, hoping that this funeral would give me an opportunity to take my child back. But Mme and Jakobo arrived without him. I marched right up to Mme, and without a greeting, asked her, "Where is my child? I want my child." She told me that if I wanted him, I must fetch him from jail. So I called the local police and asked them to arrest my mother for stealing my son. It was chaotic. A big scandal. The police arrested her at the funeral, and there was condemnation from everyone. Even Jakobo, who hardly ever opened his mouth, found the words to deplore my actions. "Your own mother? You do this to your own mother? If it weren't for her, that dog that you call a child would be dead." Not a single relative was on my side. "Your mother gathered your shame and took it upon herself, and this is how you thank her?" they said.

'I started to doubt myself when Mme Moipone crossed my mind. She wouldn't have approved of this. She would have asked me to be conciliatory, but I couldn't find it in myself. I looked to the heavens and asked her to forgive me. But I was determined. And I went ahead with the charges against my mother. The police had a lot of questions, wanting to know how old the child was and where he was.'

'Eventually the senior officer asked, "Does this young man know where you are?" I said yes. "Then why doesn't he come to you?" "Mme is preventing it," I explained. "But he's practically a man," he insisted. "Surely he can make his way here?" He then told me that my mother claimed she had brought up Mahlomola because I couldn't, and that I was now trying to destroy her. "You had the child when you were fifteen," the officer continued. "How could you possibly have raised him without her?" I tried to explain, but in the end the case was dismissed. The officers informed me that it was a matter for the South African police and that they could do nothing about it. But they advised me not to be so bitter towards my loving mother and to show her some gratitude for raising the child I'd "abandoned".'

'Oh, Mme Imelda! That was messy. It must have destroyed your relationship with your mother.'

'What relationship? It had long died. And I didn't care to revive it. I just wanted my son. I had lost my last chance to be with my child. In 1986, a military coup by the head of the Lesotho army, General Lekhanya, ousted Jonathan and returned all powers to King Moshoeshoe II. There was widespread suspicion that the South African government had backed this coup, and soon South Africa lifted the border blockade. The consequences for Motsie's ANC comrades were dire: the military administration rounded them up and deported them to Zambia. Under the new government the BCP members remained under siege. Some paid dearly for their support of the exiled South Africans, and Motsie and his brothers were high up in the ranks and caught the attention of the authorities.

'Fetching Lethabo just seemed impossible now. And there was too much pain. I gave up after that. I gave up. And that's where I went wrong. I just gave up.'

Imelda is wailing now, and I hold her. I know that this was the exact time when Mabegzo himself stopped waiting for his mother and gave up himself. At this point he was no longer a petty criminal but had tasted jail. He'd lost everything; there was nothing more to lose except his life, and even that he didn't value at all. The streets owned him now and gave him the validation he sought. There he was king of the jungle, and the weak succumbed to his power and authority. In the streets he was the final arbiter of who would live or die. In his kingdom he didn't have to seek anyone's acceptance; it was his verdict that determined who was accepted and who wasn't. He was all-powerful and supreme.

'The wall between me and my mother never came down. All my transgressions – leaving for Lesotho with Mme Moipone all those years ago, mourning Mme Moipone as if she were my mother, exploding and telling my son that Nkgono wasn't his mother – they all paled in comparison to having the police arrest my mother. Mme would never forgive me now. And fortunately for her, but unfortunately for me, she had the bait. She had my child. So she won.'

'No one won, Mme Imelda. You all lost.'

'Lethabo most of all.'

'Yes, Lethabo most of all.'

Chapter 16

Since my return from Cape Town a month ago, I'm back in the broadcasting world, and as a new beginning I've also decided to pursue post-graduate English literature – the joy of learning from the country's most respected professors is unparalleled. But I've become so immersed in my discussions with Mme Imelda that I've been missing my lectures as I try to juggle my work commitments and my trips to Orlando. I'm still on my quest to introduce Imelda to her grandson, in the hopes that this will palliate some of her pain.

We've spent close to a week talking late into the night, and each morning I have woken to the sounds of Mme Imelda making me coffee and breakfast and packing me lunch, taking care to ensure that the sandwiches are nicely wrapped with the fruit in a separate bag. I'm not into eggs in the morning or sandwiches for work, but I eat it all and take the lunch pack as a gift. I have loved having her around, and tomorrow she will be gone.

I get through my work as quickly as possible, and then rush off to try to reach Soweto before the peak-hour traffic, skipping my Friday afternoon lecture once again. I find Miriam on her stoep, plaiting a little girl's hair while the child cries from the pulling and twisting.

Miriam is still not in a charitable mood.

'Are you well today?'

'*Ja*, I'm well.'

'And you, little one, you're going to look so pretty when Aunty Miriam is finished. You look pretty already.'

The little girl is not appeased, and I squeeze her hand to comfort her as she cries. I know exactly how she feels. Even for an adult, having your hair plaited is painful.

'Have you thought about my request, Miriam?' I ask. She carries on as if I haven't spoken, but I let the silence stretch between us, knowing that she's heard me.

'My son has been told that he doesn't have family on his father's side. Now you want me to start with a new story? *Haai*, no.'

'I understand, Miriam. You don't have to decide now, but think of what could come of this. She's a good woman.'

'It's not that.'

'What is it?'

'My mother won't like it. And my father will turn in his grave. My parents were shocked when they heard I was pregnant.'

'Did you tell them that Mabegzo was his father?'

'They found out. I didn't even tell them I was pregnant.

265

My mother heard it from my friend's mother. She kept asking me about the father, but I didn't know his family name, only where he lived. My mother was still furious when she woke me that Sunday morning to visit his family and tell them about my pregnancy. I knew my parents would be horrified when they realised who he was. But when they knocked on his door they still had no idea. His grandmother was getting ready for church, and they exchanged awkward greetings. But when my family learnt that it was Mabegzo, they made a big scene.'

'What did they do?'

'*Ag*, just shouted at them.'

'Did Mabegzo at least acknowledge you?' I ask, knowing that denying her would probably have been better for her family.

'They didn't give him the chance. They just got up to leave, shouting at Mabegzo and his grandmother. They said Mabegzo had raped me, because that's the only way I could be pregnant with his child.'

'Oh, Miriam, I'm so sorry,' I try to console her, feeling suddenly terrible for badgering her to introduce Potlako to Mme Imelda. Just as Imelda hadn't wanted to see the father of her child, it's reasonable for Miriam not to want to start a relationship now with the family of the one who stole her innocence.

'Sorry for what?'

'I didn't realise you'd been so hurt. I thought you were his girlfriend.'

'That's what I'm trying to tell you. He didn't rape me. We were lovers. I just didn't think I'd fall pregnant.'

'Oh, okay,' I say, greatly relieved that Potlako isn't another 'rape child'. Although we'll never know if Mabegzo fathered other children, perhaps through rape, I'm very glad for now not to have to tell Mme Imelda of another victim who was forced, like her, but this time by her beloved son.

'Did you try to explain that to your parents?'

'Explain? Children were never allowed to explain anything. I just kept quiet.'

'How much does Potlako know about who his father is?'

'My parents helped me raise him, and they told everyone that his father was a comrade who died in the struggle. But those who'd seen me with Mabegzo spread the rumour that he was the father. My parents must have heard it, but they wouldn't allow any discussion. They warned me that I'd be in big trouble if I ever went near that "evil dog" again.'

'So he didn't ever know about his child?'

'Oh, he knew. And he wanted to be a part of Potlako's life. But it was impossible. He disappeared so often that there was no chance for me to sneak around while I was pregnant, and as I got closer and closer to my time, I was too conspicuous. Afterwards, when I took my baby to the local clinic for check-ups, I sometimes thought of dropping in at Mabegzo's grandmother's house so he could meet his son. Fortunately our homes were close, and I saw Mabegzo on my way to the clinic one day. He came along with me and gave me money for the baby. He was so happy, and he kissed Potlako over and over again. But he didn't see his son more than six times in the first few months of his life. He often disappeared for a while, but always reappeared with loads of cash that he'd send via a friend. So that's why I can't meet her, can you see? My mother would be very angry, and my child would find out that his father was a bad man.'

'Did you know he was a bad man when you dated him?'

'Everyone knew. But he was... I don't know how to say it. He was...'

'Yes, I know. I know.'

Before I leave, I ask her to think again about my request. I promise her that it'll be worth her while, and that I'll happily facilitate the meeting. 'But only when your heart is okay with it.'

'No, no, I'll never do it.'

'Just think about it, that's all. She's had a hard life, Miriam, and meeting your son will heal her. I know it.'

Then, just as I leave, a thought comes to me. 'Why were you at his grandmother's funeral a few days ago?'

'Because she always gave me money for my son. Every month after Mabegzo died until a few months before she died, she sent me money to buy food for Potlako. And when she retired in 1992, she gave me a lot of money. A lot.'

Nkgono, the provider. Her love was imperfect, but she did love, and maybe one day, when Mme Imelda learns that Nkgono used her meagre income to feed her flesh and blood, her heart will warm towards her. Maybe.

Mme Imelda has made fish and chips for our last supper. I smile, knowing that elsewhere my own grandmother and mother are also eating fish tonight. It's our usual Friday meal, and I'm pleased as I sit down with this woman who I admire and respect. I am astonished at her wisdom and capacity to love and empathise with others. She has a natural instinct to nurture and support. But not with her own mother. There her resentment runs too deep, and I doubt that she remembers a time when she didn't resent Nkgono.

We pick up where we left off, talking about Motsie's growing political activism. 'Were you happy with Motsie's new interest, or was life easier when he was a teacher?'

'Of course it was easier being a teacher's wife. But I was now used to Motsie's quiet ways and I trusted that he knew what he was doing and wouldn't put our family at risk. I knew he'd lost some comrades and had escaped attacks himself, but he didn't speak much about it, so I just loved him and prayed. He knew that I lived with constant pain in my heart about my son, and he tried to console me, apologising that the crisis caused by his politics was prolonging my anguish. But he could sense my restlessness. I couldn't sleep while I was out of touch with my child. I never had any peace in the eighteen years Lethabo wasn't with me. That's what my mother bequeathed me.

'In 1988, a letter arrived at Mme Moipone's house while a neighbour was taking care of it. It was Tshepo, telling me that our brother Mohau had died, and that Lethabo was no longer living with them.'

'Did he explain why he wasn't living with them anymore?'

'No.'

'Would you like to know?'

'Yes. I knew he'd lost his way, but I didn't know what had happened.'

'Your father threw him out.'

'But why? After all these years? It doesn't make sense to take the child from his mother and then throw him out.'

'Nkgono told me that Ntate Jakobo had had enough of him. He was tired of being the pariah of society when he hadn't committed a crime against anyone. Lethabo's criminal activities were dragging the family name through the mud.'

'Your children are your children. You can't throw them out, because then they're lost forever.'

'It was worse than that. Lethabo hit him.'

'Children who are raised well don't raise their hands to adults. It's because he wasn't raised well. The people who raised him caused this.'

'So do you think he was blameless?'

'Yes and no.' She doesn't elaborate.

269

'Can you accept that he committed against others the same crime that was committed against you?'

'Yes. I accept it. And if those who committed this crime against me were treated like him when they were children, then I forgive and accept them too.'

'Why didn't you go to your son's funeral?'

'Oh, if only I could have! I would have gone to Soweto to bury him. But no one told me he'd died. No one!'

'Tshepo told me that he'd taken for granted that someone would inform you. He never thought there was so much damage that your mother wouldn't tell you about the death of your own son. But I saw your mother at that street corner, crying and stroking his forehead. And Mabegzo always spoke fondly of her. Even when he had strayed from her, he missed her and always smiled when he thought of her.'

'I wonder how he would have felt if he'd known that she actively kept him away from me and frustrated all my efforts to reach him, even while he was longing to come and live with me. When my son died in 1989, I hadn't seen him since Mme Moipone's funeral in 1982.'

'Yet I believe she loved and defended her grandchild in her own way until she couldn't anymore.'

'Do you know how I found out that Lethabo had died? Some relatives dropped by to ask me why I hadn't gone to the funeral. "Whose funeral?" I asked them. "The funeral of your son, Mahlomola."' Imelda crouches on the floor like a woman being beaten, and begins to hit her knuckles against the wall. Over and over she murmurs, 'How could she do that? My own mother? My own brother, my own sister, my own father; how could they do that?'

'I wonder if you would have been able to endure his funeral,' I say gently. 'There weren't many mourners.'

'If I'd been the only person in the world, I would have

buried him! I believe my mother was also punishing me for not attending my brother's funeral the previous year. But there was no way I could have gone without endangering my life and that of my family.

'It was only then that I went crying to my mother-in-law. As a mother herself she would at least understand my anguish. Motsie didn't know Lethabo. He had nothing to say to me except, "Be strong". But there's nothing like the loss of a child to take all strength from you.'

'What about Mamello, Mpho and Tlale? Did you tell them they'd lost a brother?'

'No, not then. Children are innocent and they would have welcomed him. They would have been excited to have a big brother, but Motsie and I had both agreed that it was best not to tell them until he was actually with us because if we got them all excited, they would have asked every day when their brother was coming. And we didn't yet have an answer.'

'So did your in-laws offer comfort after you heard about Lethabo's death?'

'My in-laws were old. Ntate was seventy-nine and Mme was seventy-five, but I didn't know who else to turn to. They had never questioned the circumstances of my pregnancy. They had been prepared to welcome him into their family, but they hadn't asked many questions. I got to Quthing by the grace of God. I remember nothing of that trip. And I just told her everything, everything that was in my heart. I'd even forgotten that Mme Moipone had lied to Motsie and told him that I'd been raped by just one man. I just told Mme the whole truth.'

'What did she say?'

'She said and did what a mother should at a time like that. She first prayed, and asked God to heal my wounds.

And then she told me that what had happened to me was a horrible thing that I didn't deserve. But what soothed me most was her assurance that she loved me. "*Ke o rata ka lerato le makatsang. Ke a leboha hore kotsi e na e mpe ha ka na, ha ea senya botle ba pelo ya hao.* I love you with a love that has no bounds. And I'm so grateful that this dreadful episode didn't destroy the beauty of your heart."'

She laughs. 'My mother-in-law used to threaten her son that she'd wake from the dead and haunt him if he ever left me! She and her husband died on the same day, you know. My mother-in-law died in the morning at the age of eighty-eight, and her husband died the same afternoon, at ninety-two.'

All too soon it's Saturday morning and our time has come to an end. I'm dreading Mme Imelda's departure. This week has been like a lifetime. I've tried to persuade her to stay longer, but she's anxious to return to her husband and daughter.

Through telling her story, she has once again made Mabegzo human for me. I am deeply grateful. Were it not for her, I may never have forgiven myself for loving him. In loving him so violently herself, she has at last made it alright for me to love him. I can face myself in the mirror again. I can accept that part of me that loved him, despite all that I know about him. Gouging out a dead man's eye has challenged my love for him and pushed it to its furthest boundaries; but it hasn't ended our relationship. My love for him has survived, and imperfect though it is, it is pure and heartfelt all the same.

'Thank you,' Mme Imelda says to me.

'For what?'

'For the gift of my child. You radiate love.'

'It's you who understands love, Mme Imelda, to have

loved your child even after what they did to you. That is a miracle.'

She wipes the tears from her eyes. 'One day, when you have a child,' she repeats, 'you'll understand. That's why my mother's actions were such sacrilege.'

'Forgive her, Mme Imelda,' I beg. 'Forgive her, please. Even if she never said sorry, forgive her. She continues to rule your life, and your soul is too beautiful for that. Let her go. It's the only way you can win. Let her go.'

She throws her arms wide for a final hug. 'Whose child are you?'

'Yours!'

We cling to each other, tears rolling down both our faces. And all too soon she climbs into a metered taxi that will take her to the bus station.

'Will I see you again?' she asks.

'Definitely.'

It's a promise I plan to keep, just as soon as I've convinced Miriam to share her child with her. Everyone deserves a mother and grandmother like Imelda.

Chapter 17

After Imelda's departure, my life is even busier than usual. I am also in the early stages of a love relationship with a man, and I don't have as much time as I would like to pursue Miriam. But on the odd weekend when I visit Orlando East, I make a point of popping in to see her. When she isn't home, I chat with her mother instead. Mme Tshidi is a big, strong woman with a booming voice which she loves to use without pausing for breath. I'm grateful that in her company I don't have to say much, but can sit on a small kitchen chair and listen to her chatting away about her *malwetse* – hypertension, diabetes and fatigue. I always arrive with a bagful of groceries: rice, peanut butter, jam, cheese, chicken, milk and some treats for Potlako. She laughs when I suggest that shedding some weight and eating more healthily can help control her *malwetse*.

'*Nna? Ke slime?* Me? Lose weight?' she laughs. 'You're joking. I'm too old for that. I've been eating all my life; I'm not stopping now.' She clearly doesn't take me seriously. I don't know her age but I imagine she's close to seventy.

Mme Tshidi hasn't once asked who I am, and seems content when I claim to be Miriam's friend. She thinks I'm just a caring angel, and doesn't guess that I'm hoping to wear down her daughter and persuade her to introduce her beloved son to his other grandmother. She doesn't even find it odd that her daughter often has little to say to me while she does all the talking. Miriam isn't particularly friendly, but always accepts the groceries with gratitude.

'Thanks. *Eish*, it's tough not having work.'

'I know Miriam. I hope everything will be okay.' She shrugs, resigned to her fate. Gradually she's warming to me, but she remains adamant that Potlako should not meet Mme Imelda.

After a three-month gap I return for another visit. I find Miriam on the stoep listening to the radio.

'*Haai, wena*, you're so stubborn!' she exclaims in surprise. It's October 2005 and I'm keen for Imelda to meet her grandson before the year is out. I follow her into the kitchen where she makes us some tea.

'Miriam, do you realise it will soon be the festive season?' Then I drop my voice to a whisper, not sure who might be in the house. 'Wouldn't it be nice to give Potlako and Mme Imelda a gift?'

'I don't have any money.'

'No man, not that kind of gift,' I chuckle. 'I'm talking about the gift of love. Let them meet.'

'*Haai*, I'm not sure about that.'

'Do it, Miriam. Do it for your child. He deserves to meet his granny and his cousins.'

'And what am I supposed to say to my mother? I live in her house, you know. She won't like it.'

'I'll speak to her.'

'*Uyahlanya manje!* Now you're crazy!'

'Is she here now?'

'No. Not now.'

'And Potlako?'

'He's here. Potlako! Potlako!'

A slender, awkward boy appears from the bedroom. He doesn't bear a strong resemblance to either his mother or his father, but he has Mabegzo's fair complexion and height. He's not very friendly, although he's quiet and polite.

I assume that Miriam has merely called him to introduce him to me, so I'm taken aback when she says, 'This nice lady wants to talk to you.'

'To me?'

'*Wena, vele.* Yes, you.'

I'm completely unprepared for this, but words have always come easily to me, so I start slowly.

'My name is Redi. Your late father was a very good friend of mine. I'd like to talk to you about your father and your grandmother in Lesotho. Is that okay? May I carry on?'

He nods, but doesn't show any emotion.

'I think you should sit down,' I suggest, and he reaches for the remaining chair in the kitchen.

'Your grandmother, your father's mother, is a lovely woman who lives in Lesotho. But she doesn't know about you, because if she did, she would never have let you out of her sight. As you know, your father died when you were a baby, and because she was so far away, he didn't get a chance to tell her about you. Nobody told her. And your mother didn't know where your father's family was, so she couldn't tell you anything about them, either. She really didn't know. Do you understand what I'm saying to you?'

Again he nods.

'Someone recently told me about you, and because I know your granny, I came to find you. Your granny is such a wonderful woman, I know she would be so glad to meet you.'

He nods.

'But you don't have to meet her if you don't want to. It's up to you. I know this is a big surprise for you, but I had to tell you. Do you have any questions you'd like to ask?'

'*Eish.*' He puts his hand on his head and shakes it from side to side. '*Ja, imibuzo ngi nayo.* I have questions.'

'You can ask me anything you want.'

'How do you know she'll want to see me?'

'She would. Because I know her.'

'Okay, when will she come here?'

'We can arrange that. But first I want to know if you would be happy to meet her.'

'Yes, I'd be happy.'

I can't hold back my tears of relief and joy as I hug Potlako and Miriam. It feels like a huge weight has been lifted off my shoulders. But I sense Potlako's discomfort with my display of emotion, so I release him from my tight embrace.

'You'd better be prepared,' I laugh, 'because your wonderful granny just loves to hug and kiss!'

We agree to arrange a meeting once I've spoken to Mme Imelda. I leave in high spirits, impatient to reach the privacy of my home and call her. I'm delighted to be the bearer of good news for Mme Imelda, with whom I haven't spoken in a while.

A male voice answers the phone.

'Hello. It's Redi from Johannesburg. I'd very much like to speak to Mme Imelda.'

'Redi? So you're for real? I thought my wife had lost her mind.'

'Oh, Ntate Motsie, it's nice to speak to you! It will be lovely to meet you one day.'

'Yes, yes, it will be good. It will be very good. You must come and visit us. Mme would like that a lot.'

I really like this man, even though I haven't met him. My respect for him increased tenfold after each conversation with Mme Imelda. In a world that had completely dishonoured her, her husband has continued to love her unconditionally and without judgement for over three decades.

Mme Imelda comes to the phone. 'Oh, my child, how I've missed you!'

'I've missed you too, Mme Imelda. Grab a chair. You're going to need one for this.'

'O, *ke eng jwale*? What is it now?' she asks, a little apprehensive.

'Mme Imelda, you have another grandson!'

Silence.

'Hello? Mme Imelda, are you there?'

'Yes, yes. I'm just surprised! I didn't know you were pregnant when I saw you last. Are you happy? If you are, it's all good. Congratulations.'

'No Mme. I am talking about Lethabo's son. Your grandson. He was born in 1988, and his name is Potlako. I've found him and he's a handsome boy. I've told him about you. And his mother has agreed that the two of you can meet.'

'Oh, God of peace! Oh my God. My God.'

'I'll tell you everything. But first tell me, do you want to meet him?' I know what her answer will be, but all she can say at the moment is, 'Oh my God.' Now I can hear that she's crying.

'I'm so happy,' she sniffles. 'Oh, you wonderful child. I'm so happy.'

'You deserve to be happy, Mme Imelda.' I explain that Miriam and I have agreed that the festive season will be ideal for her to meet up with Potlako.

But Mme Imelda can't wait. 'No, no, no,' she says. 'That's too far away. I must meet him now. I will come to Johannesburg right away.'

I promise to speak to Miriam and get back to her. 'But if she agrees, we must wait until the weekend when I'm off work.'

'Oh, the weekend is so far away. But okay, I'll wait. You're going to call me back straight away to tell me, right?'

'Yes, I promise.'

I call Miriam to tell her about Mme Imelda's response, and that she wants to meet Potlako this coming weekend. I'm sure her mother's at home now, and I'm anxious to know how their conversation has gone.

'*Wena*, my mother's going to hit you. She's not very happy. But anyway, she's still prepared to meet Mme Imelda.'

To be quite honest, I'm not all that concerned about Mme Tshidi right now. With Miriam and Potlako on board, I'm confident that the biggest hurdle has been overcome. I'm too driven by the need to bring some joy into Mme Imelda's life, and I have no doubt that Potlako will benefit from her loving kindness and nurturing. His new grandmother will be a positive influence. Just like his late father, this young man must have a litany of questions about his identity. But the world shut its ears to Mabegzo's questions and he raged against it; Potlako mustn't suffer the same fate.

'And Potlako? Is your mother okay for him to meet Mme Imelda?'

'Ah, I don't know. I'm sure she'll be fine. But we can't travel to Lesotho.'

'No need for that. Mme Imelda wants to come to Soweto this Saturday.'

'Ha! *Haai*, it's too soon! Why is she in such a hurry? I don't...'

I know how stubborn Miriam can get and I don't want to antagonise her, but gently I say, 'Miriam, I can imagine just how overwhelming this is for you all. But when you meet Mme Imelda, you'll wish you'd met her sooner. She has so much love in her heart and she's just dying to pour it all out on your son. Please say yes.'

For the second time that day, Miriam gives in to me.

Mamello and her husband John agree to drive Imelda to Soweto that Saturday, the fifteenth of October. I certainly don't want them to have to go to her mother's house, but John is confident that he can find his way to Baragwanath Hospital without getting lost, so I arrange to meet him there. I will lead him the last three kilometres through Orlando East to Potlako's home.

When Saturday comes, I pull over to park in front of them, and before I can open my door, Mme Imelda jumps out of John's car and walks straight towards me with her arms wide. She squeezes the breath out of me and I return her embrace with gusto, tears flowing down both our cheeks. While cars, buses and pedestrians go about their business along this busy road, time stands still for the two of us.

'How are you feeling, Mme Imelda,' I enquire.

'Too happy!'

'But you haven't met him yet.'

'It doesn't matter. When we meet, I'll make everything right.'

They must have left Maseru around five am, but Mme Imelda doesn't seem tired at all, she just wants to go straight to Potlako's home. 'There's no time to waste,' she insists. I greet John and Mamello, and then we set off.

Our cars draw attention as we park on Mme Tshidi's pavement – clearly this is not an everyday occurrence. Curious onlookers mill about, and the children playing in the streets stop their game, fascinated by this entourage.

Mme Imelda wants both Mamello and John to be a part of the introduction so that 'our hosts know that we're a family'. Watching her chatting away as we walk into the yard, I smile, proud that this moment has arrived, but also keen that she won't be disappointed. It's a warm spring afternoon and the kitchen door is wide open.

'Knock, knock,' I call out.

'Come in.' It's Miriam's voice. As we enter, the aroma of cooked food greets us. A good sign, I think. They've cooked, and food means fellowship and a warm welcome. We step from the kitchen into the living room.

Sitting on the couch is Miriam's mother and an elderly gentleman I haven't met, while Miriam is on the big chair nearest the front door. There's no sign of Potlako. The kitchen chairs have been moved into the living room in preparation for the visitors. Everyone seems nervous, and Mme Imelda has clearly toned down her excitement lest she overwhelm her grandson and his family.

I greet everyone individually and introduce myself to the elderly gentleman, who turns out to be Miriam's uncle, Mme Tshidi's younger brother.

Miriam is fidgeting and doesn't return my smile. But I remain unfazed; I'm used to her by now.

'Mme Tshidi, I've brought you some visitors.' It's her home, so I address her.

'Thank you, we're glad that you've arrived safely,' she responds. This pleases me; she's not angry or cold.

I introduce everyone in the room, and once all the names and handshakes have been exchanged, Mme Tshidi invites us to sit down.

The elders engage in some small talk about the weather, road accidents and the cost of living. I know Potlako is probably in the bedroom, waiting to be invited to join the adults in the living room. But this can only happen once the visitors have formally stated the purpose of their visit. Once the small talk has been exhausted, I decide that it's time for me to leave, to allow them all some space.

'Mme Tshidi, thank you so much for welcoming us into your home today. I will leave you all now and come back later to...'

'*Hawu*, you're not staying? Not even to have a meal?' Mme Tshidi asks.

'No, no, I have to visit my grandmother, and I'm sure she'd like me to share a meal with her.'

'Good girl,' Mme Tshidi says. 'Never forget the old people. You'll be blessed.'

I am confident now that their meeting will go well. Mme Tshidi seems happy and her brother is also quite chatty. Only Mamello and Miriam have had little to say, but I'm no longer worried. It's now after half past twelve and I promise to return in two hours. I don't want to leave them for so long that they run out of things to talk about – not that it's ever likely with Mme Tshidi in the room!

As I drive away I think of Mabegzo. Wherever he is, I know that this meeting today will bring him a lot of '*lethabo*'. If he were alive, I know he would have loved and protected

Potlako fiercely. Mme Imelda will always be heartbroken about her son's demise, but perhaps meeting Potlako will assuage some of that pain.

I return to Miriam's house at the appointed time. I can hear laughter and Mme Tshidi's incessant chatter before I even step inside. When I do, I'm taken aback by the scene that meets me. Potlako and Mme Imelda are alone at the kitchen table, washing up in the big enamel bowl. This is an old house that still doesn't have a kitchen sink or a tap, so boiled water has to be poured into a large bowl in which the plates, cups and glasses are then washed. I was sure the meeting would go well, but I wasn't expecting to see Potlako and his new granny engaged in an activity together.

'Oh, this is nice, Potlako! Are you teaching your granny to wash dishes?'

He laughs loudly, and Mme Imelda beams at him. Her eyes are swollen; she's obviously been crying. I'm pleased to think that for once these were tears of joy.

The others are all in the living room, and I decide to join them, leaving Potlako and Mme Imelda on their own a little longer to continue bonding. I'm dying to hear how everything went, but no one is giving anything away. It's clear, though, that there's been a lot of crying in this room; even Miriam looks like she's shed some tears.

Eventually, Mme Imelda and Potlako are done with the dishes, and Potlako wants to join his mates. The two of them hug and Mme Imelda says, 'Are you sure you've given me the right number? I'm going to call you tomorrow.'

Potlako laughs at his grandmother and takes her cellphone to check that she has indeed saved the number correctly.

'*Ee, e* right. Yes, it's right.'

Before we all part, Mme Tshidi starts a popular hymn,

Re a o boka Morena. We praise you Lord. There is silent weeping as she prays. 'Oh God, keep this wonderful family, and protect them on their journey back to Maseru.' Everyone exchanges hugs and promises to stay in touch.

'And you, my girl,' Mme Tshidi says to me. 'Thank you for everything.'

'No, no. I have to thank you and Miriam; you've made so many people happy today.'

Mme Tshidi decides that the walk to the gate is too far, and leaves it to Miriam and Potlako to walk us out. Mme Imelda puts one arm around Miriam and the other around her grandson. Her happiness is palpable.

I've invited John, Mamello and Mme Imelda to spend the night at my home and get a good night's sleep before their long drive back tomorrow. When we reach my home, Mme Imelda hugs me and says, 'Oh, it feels so good to be here. You're an angel. I can never thank you enough.'

'So, it went well, then?'

'Very well.'

'Oh, Mme Imelda, I'm so pleased.' I give her another big hug and Mamello joins us, while John takes a seat on the couch. The three of us stand there holding each other for a long time.

That entire evening, Mme Imelda doesn't stop talking about how happy she is and how decent Miriam's family was. Mamello and I can't get a word in as she rattles on about her grandson's visit to Lesotho in December, and how she plans to have a big feast to welcome him when he arrives.

'So will he spend Christmas with you?'

'Yes! His grandmother has agreed and my family back home will be ready for him.'

'I'm so happy for you, Mme Imelda. How did you get through to them, especially Miriam's mother?'

'It was easy, my child, very easy. If you remember to speak to people's hearts, they will always let you in. She too is a mother and a grandmother. She knows how important this bond is with our children and our grandchildren.'

'So what did you say?'

'*Jo*, Mme did so well,' Mamello answers. 'She told them that she and Miriam are just the same. They were both just children when they had their children, but in Miriam's case she was lucky to have a mother like hers, who not only accepted her daughter, but her child as well.'

'Yes, I thanked her for raising my grandson and apologised for not being there. I told her that the adults had separated me and Lethabo and that I hadn't been allowed to raise him. I asked them to imagine what it would have been like to grow up without parents and without love, and that that's why Lethabo turned out the way he did.'

'Did they understand?'

'Yes, they did, after I told them about my efforts to get my child back, and how I long to make amends by connecting with my grandson. I assured them that I would never ever take him away from them. That I only want to know him.'

'And?'

'And Miriam's mother responded the way a mother should. She said it doesn't matter now. It's all in the past, and we must fix what's been broken.'

'And Potlako? How did he react when he saw you?'

'After I'd explained my long absence and my wish to meet him, they called him in and introduced us. I told him that I loved him and I was sorry I hadn't been there for him, but that now that I know about him, I want to be a part of his life.'

'And?'

'And he said thank you.'

John speaks for the first time. 'He also said he was happy to see us.'

'Oh yes, and he has a cellphone, you know. So we took each other's numbers and he says he would love to visit Maseru. He smiled a lot, you know!'

'Oh, Mme Imelda, that's wonderful.'

'He is still shy, but all boys his age are like that. With love and patience, I'll break down that wall, you'll see. Every child can be healed.'

Epilogue

I HAVE NO GRAVE TO GO TO, so I address Mabegzo the only way I know how. I don't believe in ancestor worship, and I don't believe that the corner where he was killed is anything more than just the place where he took his last breath. But that's where I go to speak to him. I park my car close to my old school and walk slowly towards our old corner. Memories of laughter and joy, tears and tragedy flood my mind and heart, despite the voices calling my name: 'Redi, can I take a picture?' 'Hey, find me a job!' 'Redi, I want to be on TV.'

I walk up to the corner for my final confrontation, and Mabegzo turns and walks towards me. A winsome smile breaks across his face. 'Hello, Lala,' he says gently, 'I've been waiting so long.'

This time I'm not falling for his seductive charm. I'm a grown woman now and I've experienced these powerful feelings many times. He was just my first. I walk resolutely towards him and face him; not Mabegzo my charmer, my protector, my confidante, my obsession, but Mabegzo, the murderer, the rapist, the gouger of dead men's eyes.

'You raped women, didn't you?'

'I'm sorry.'

'You killed people didn't you?'

'I'm sorry.'

'And you dug out Siphiwe's eye, didn't you?'

'I'm sorry.'

'You hurt a lot of people, Mabegzo.'

'I'm sorry.'

'You hurt me.'

'I'm sorry.'

And I believe him.

I give him his gifts: 'I found your mother for you, Mabegzo. And she has loved you always.'

'Thank you. And you?'

'I also love you.'

'Thank you.'

'I found your son, Mabegzo. And now your mother also loves him.'

'Thank you.'

'Now you must leave me alone.'